COMBINATIONS

The Heart of Chess

IRVING CHERNEV

DOVER PUBLICATIONS, INC.
NEW YORK

Published in Canada by General Publishing Company, Ltd., 30 Lesmill Road, Don Mills, Toronto, Ontario.
Published in the United Kingdom by Constable and Company, Ltd., 10 Orange Street, London WC 2.

This Dover edition, first published in 1967, is an unabridged republication with minor corrections of the work originally published by the Thomas Y. Crowell Company in 1960. This edition is published by special arrangement with the Thomas Y. Crowell Company.

Standard Book Number: 486-21744-2
Library of Congress Catalog Card Number: 66-29186

Manufactured in the United States of America
Dover Publications, Inc.
180 Varick Street
New York, N. Y. 10014

TO KARL AND ROBERT MARQUARDT

With esteem and admiration

WHAT IS A COMBINATION?

*A combination is a blend of ideas—pins, forks, discovered
checks, double attacks—which endow the pieces with magical
powers.*

It is a series of staggering blows before the knockout.

It is the climactic scene in the play appearing on the board.

*It is the touch of enchantment that gives life to inanimate
pieces.*

It is all this, and more—

A combination is the very heart of chess.

CONTENTS

1. Easy Combinations   1
2. Simple and Pleasing   19
3. Blending of Themes   29
4. A Mixed Bouquet   36
5. Combinations in the Notes   59
6. Convincing the Kibitzers   77
7. Boomerang Combinations   86
8. The Old Master: Adolf Anderssen   97
9. King of Chess: Paul Morphy   105
10. Tactician by Instinct: William Steinitz   117
11. Large-Scale Operator: Harry N. Pillsbury   124
12. Man of Method: Siegbert Tarrasch   136
13. Great Fighter: Emanuel Lasker   143
14. Deadly Attacker: Frank J. Marshall   152
15. Sacrifice Specialist: Rudolf Spielmann   160
16. Artist of the Chessboard: Akiba Rubinstein   169
17. The Fabulous Original: Aron Nimzovich   178
18. Modern Morphy: Paul Keres   186
19. Superb Strategist: Mikhail Botvinnik   194
20. Chessboard Magician: Alexander Alekhine   208
21. Master of Masters: José R. Capablanca   227
     Index   241

1

EASY COMBINATIONS

Chess has this in common with making poetry, that the desire for it comes upon the amateur in gusts.

—A. A. Milne

White to play

1

TAL-KLAMAN
U.S.S.R. 1957

In this position, the brilliant young player Michael Tal demonstrates in two moves the most devastating Knight fork you ever saw on a chessboard!

      1   **Q–B4 ch**

Attacks the Rook, and forces Black's reply.

      1 ...   **K–Q2**
      2   **Kt–B5 ch!**

A terrific family check! The Knight attacks King, Queen, Rook and Bishop. Black may not capture the Knight, as his Pawn is pinned.

      2 ...   Resigns

Playing on is useless, since White wins the Queen.

White to play

2

TAIMANOV-KUSMINICH
U.S.S.R. 1950

It is remarkable how much brilliance, wealth of ideas, color and

1

variety can be packed into a combination only a few moves deep. Take this elegant specimen for example, where White offers Knight, Rook and Queen in rapid succession to his opponent:

1   Kt–Kt6

Threatens 2 Q–R8–mate on the move.

1   ...   Kt–R2

If 1 ... PxKt instead, 2 BxB ch in reply wins the Queen.

2   RxB!   PxR

And here, if 2 ... PxKt; 3 R–K8 ch wins the Queen by discovered attack.

3   QxR ch!

Surprise! Surprise!

3   ...   QxQ

Refusing to take the Queen leaves Black a piece behind with a lost position. So he dies gloriously!

4   BxP mate!

White to play

3

SELESNIEV

How does White win this? If 1 P–Q7, K–B2; 2 R–Q1, K–Q1, and Black draws by later capturing the Pawn. Or if 1 R–Q1, R–KR7; 2 P–Q7, R–R8 ch; 3 K–K2, RxR; 4 KxR, K–B2, and again Black draws.

Here is the way it's done:

1 P–Q7	K–B2
2 P–Q8(Q) ch	KxQ
3 0-0-0 ch!	K–B2
4 KxR	

White wins.

White to play

4

AUGUSTIN-BONGRANTZ

A Pawn reaching the last square of the board does not automatically become a Queen. It may be promoted to any piece the player desires. The possibilities can be interesting, as this ending shows.

1   P–B6

Threatening to follow with 2 K–Kt6 and then force mate.

1   ...   K–R2

Keeps White's King from approaching nearer. There was no hope in 1 ... PxP; 2 K–Kt6, nor in 1 ... QxBP; 2 QxQ, PxQ; 3 K–Kt6.

2 P–B7

Intending 3 Q–B5 ch, QxQ; 4 PxQ, winning easily.

Black has a pretty defense.

2 ...   Q–K4 ch!

To this White dares not play 3 QxQ, as the response is 3 ... P–Kt3 mate.

3 P–Kt5   QxQ

Now if White makes a new Queen, he gets mated on the move by 4 ... P–Kt3.

4 P–B8(Kt) ch!

But White makes a Knight instead, attacks King and Queen simultaneously, and wins.

White to play

5

RICHTER

Winning by zugzwang is always

interesting. Zugzwang is the compulsion to move, but having to move can be embarrassing.

1 K–Kt7 ch   K–R2

Black's King must stay near his Queen.

2 Q–R2 ch   K–Kt1
3 Q–R2 ch   K–R2

On 3 ... K–B1 4 Q–R8 ch wins the Queen.

4 Q–B7!

Zugzwang! Black must move, by the rules of the game (if he could only pass he would be safe).

Black's King has no legal move, the Pawn is pinned, and his Queen has only one square open.

4 ...   Q–KKt1
5 Q–R5 mate!

Black to play

6

BATUYEV-SIMAGIN
Riga, 1954

There are subtleties in the simplest positions. The move that seems ob-

vious can expose you to mortal
danger.

1 . . .   P–K7

Convinced that almost any move
wins, Black moves his Pawn up to
make a new Queen.
This is what struck him:

2   Q–Kt1 ch   K–Q7
3   Q–QB1 ch   K–Q6
4   Q–B3 mate!

Black wins, but White could have
won had he played (instead of 1
R–Kt8):

1   P–Kt3 ch   RxP

If 1 . . . K–R6; 2 KxKt wins a
piece and the game.

2   Kt–B5 ch   PxKt

Moving the King instead costs a
Rook.

3   R–R6 mate!

White to play

7

NEDELKOVIC-UDOVCIC

The player who fails to see a
mating combination often himself
becomes the victim of a mating combination.

1   R–Kt8

Threatens a deadly check. White
visualized this continuation: 1 . . .
Kt–B2; 2 R–QB8, R–B2; 3 KtxP,
winning an important Pawn.

1 . . .   Kt–R6 ch
2   PxKt   R–B6 mate!

White to play

8

KRETSCHMAR-VASICA
Olmütz, 1938

The pin is simple and deadly. It
paralyzes an enemy piece, holds it
tight so that it cannot or dares not
move.

1   QxKt

Exploiting the circumstance that
Black's Bishop Pawn is pinned,
White captures a Knight and threat-
ens mate.

1 . . .   PxKt

Regains the piece and prevents the mate.

2 Kt–B6 ch

Another attack by a piece which is immune to capture!

| 2 | ... | K–R1 |
| 3 | Q–R7 mate | |

White to play

9

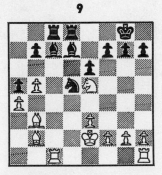

LASKER-STEINITZ
Match 1894 (Variation)

Simplifying a position by exchanges before clamping on a pin accentuates the power of the pin. With little material on the board, the opponent finds it difficult to complicate matters.

1 KtxB

Reduces the number of pieces on the board, and also draws the Rook at Q1 away from protecting its fellow Rook.

| 1 | ... | RxKt |

Black's remaining Bishop is now pinned. It cannot move away without exposing the Rook to capture.

2 BxKt

A further reduction of material to simplify the position.

| 2 | ... | RxB |
| 3 | P–Kt6 | |

Again attacking the pinned Bishop. White wins a piece and the game.

Black to play

10

ERNST-LOOSE
Hamburg, 1946

A pin may sometimes be broken. One of the cleverest ways is by applying a counter-pin.

| 1 | ... | RxP |

This looks good, as it removes a powerful support from White's Knight. The threat is now 2 ... BxKt pinning the Queen.

| 2 | QxR | BxKt ch |

Double attack on King and Queen!

3 B–Q2!

Interposes with a pin! If Black plays 3 ... BxQ, the reply 4 BxQ leaves him a Rook behind.

Black resigns.

White to play

11

OLSEN-JACOBSEN
Aarhus, 1953

Black breaks out of a pin by brilliant means. He sacrifices his Queen to secure a counter-pin.

1 R(K5)xQP

With a triple attack on the Bishop, which is pinned. The Bishop must stay put, for if 1 ... BxQ 2 RxR mate is the drastic penalty.

How does Black free his Bishop from the pin?

1 ...   QxKtP ch!

By giving up his Queen!

2 KxQ   BxQ

Removes the pinning piece, and

in turn restrains the Rook from mating. Black regains his Queen and wins a whole Rook by the counter-pin.

White to play

12

CHATARD-AMATEUR
Paris, 1906

An off-hand game of Chatard's provides us with a classic example of pin and counter-pin.

1 R–Kt1

Anticipating Black's threat, White prepares a refutation.

1 ...   BxKt
2 QxB

White's King and Queen are in line, apparently vulnerable to a pinning attack.

2 ...   R–B7
3 R–QB1!

Beautiful! White rescues his Queen by a double pin. Black may not play 3 ... RxQ ch, exposing his own

King to check, nor can he break the pin by 3 ... RxR, as the recapture by 4 QxQ costs his Queen.

White wins a Rook and the game.

Black to play

13

HALOSAR-POSCHAUKO
Graz, 1941

The Cross-pin is a pretty device. Black demonstrates it here neatly and effectively.

1 ...   **B–KB4 ch**

The opening up of the King file for Black's Queen adds strength to this check.

2 **B–Q3**

The alternative 2 K–R1 loses by 2 ... BxP ch; 3 BxB, Q–K8 ch; 4 B–B1, QxB mate.

2 ...   **Q–K7!**

The Cross-pin! White may not play 3 BxQ exposing his King to check, nor does he dare take the Bishop, uncovering an attack on his Queen.

Black wins, as there is no defense.

White to play

14

TROITZKY

A quiet setting for as brilliant a Cross-pin as you are likely to see.

| 1 | **P–B6** | **P–Kt7** |

If 1 ... B–K5 instead (to give up the Bishop for the invaluable Pawn) 2 P–B7, B–Kt2; 3 B–Kt2, K–R2; 4 BxB, KxB; 5 K–Q8 wins

| 2 | **P–B7** | **P–Kt8(Q)** |

Or 2 ... B–Kt3 ch; 3 K–Q8, P–Kt8(Q); 4 P–B8(Q) ch, K–R2; 5 Q–B7 ch, K–R1 (5 ... K–R3, 6 B–B8 mate); 6 B–Kt2 ch, B–K5; 7 K–B8, and White mates at Kt8.

3	**P–B8(Q) ch**	**K–R2**
4	**Q–B7 ch**	**K–R1**
5	**B–Kt2 ch**	**B–K5**
6	**Q–KR7!**	

A startling move! Black's Bishop, now twice-attacked, may not capture the Queen, and does not dare take the Bishop.

6 ...   K–Kt1
7 BxB

White wins. He attacks the Queen and threatens 8 Q–Kt7 mate at the same time.

White to play

15

KUBBEL

White gives up his Queen to get in two checks by his Knight. He gets good value, as the Knight skips over to pick up the Queen, and then the Rook.

1   Q–R2 ch   K–Kt5

Moving to Kt4 or Q6 instead allows a Knight check and a discovered attack on the Queen.

2   Q–Kt2 ch   K–B5

Of course not 2 ... K–R5, when 3 Kt–B3 checkmates.

3   Q–B2 ch   K–Kt5

Here too the replies 3 ... K–Kt4 or 3 ... K–Q4 succumb to 4 Kt–B3 ch, winning the Queen.

4   K–Kt2

A quiet move, but it faces Black with two threats: immediate mate by 5 Q–Kt3, and in two moves by 5 Q–B5 ch, K–R5; 6 Q–B4 mate.

4 ...   Q–Q4

The only way to guard the two squares involved. Black could not defend by 4 ... K–Kt4 as 5 Kt–B3 ch uncovers an attack on his Queen.

5   Q–R4 ch!   KxQ
6   Kt–B3 ch   K–Kt5

Forced.

7   KtxQ ch   K–Kt4

If instead 7 ... K–R5 or 7 ... K–B5; 8 Kt–Kt6 ch wins the Rook.

8   Kt–B7 ch

Wins the Rook and the game.

Black to play

16

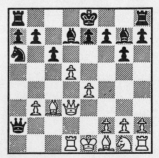

PLAYERS UNKNOWN

Counter-attack is often the best defense to a threat. Black's Knight does a fine job here.

Black's King Bishop is attacked. How does he defend? If 1 ... BxB; 2 QxB in reply attacks the Rook and also threatens to win the Queen by 3 R–R1. Or if 1 ... 0–0, then 2 BxB, KxB; 3 Q–B3 ch, P–B3; 4 R–R1 again catches the Queen.

So Black counter-attacks!

1	...	Kt–B4
2	Q–B4	

The Queen must protect the Bishop.

2	...	BxB ch
3	QxB	QxBP ch!
4	KxQ	KtxKP ch
5	K–K3	KtxQ

Black's extra Pawns insure the win.

White to play

17

ZNOSKO-BOROVSKY-PRICE
Ramsgate, 1929

A Knight fork can be worth a great deal. Here three pieces are sacrificed to set up proper targets for the Knight.

1 Q–R3

Threatens mate on the move.

1	...	QxB
2	Q–R7 ch	K–B1
3	R–K1	

Restrains the King and again threatens him with immediate mate.

3	...	Kt–K4

Or 3 ... Kt–K2; 4 Q–R8 ch, Kt–Kt1 and 4 Kt–R7 is mate.

4	RxKt	QxR
5	Q–R8 ch	K–K2
6	QxR ch!	KxQ
7	KtxP ch	K–K2
8	KtxQ	

White wins. He is the exchange ahead, and there are no complications.

White to play

18

VOTRUBA

White's pieces are far apart but they co-operate beautifully to force a draw. The Bishop harasses Black's King on the black squares, while the Knights patrol the nine white squares outside the Bishop's scope.

The number of Knight forks the King can walk into is astonishing!

| 1 | B–K1 ch | K–B4 |

If 1 ... K–R5 or 1 ... K–Kt4; 2 Kt–B3 ch wins the Queen, while 1 ... K–Kt6 loses by 2 Kt–Q2 ch.

| 2 | B–B2 ch | K–Q3 |

On 2 ... K–Q4; 3 Kt–B6 ch is the winning Knight fork.

| 3 | B–Kt3 ch | K–K2 |

Moving 3 ... K–Q2 allows 3 Kt–B6 ch, while 3 ... K–K3 runs into 4 Kt–Kt5 ch.

| 4 | B–R4 ch | K–Q3 |

There is no escape by 4 ... K–K1 as 5 Kt–B6 ch catches the Queen nor by 4 ... K–B2 where 5 Kt–Kt5 ch does likewise.

| 5 | B–Kt3 ch |

"Care to go around again?" says the Bishop.

Drawn

White to play

19

MUNK-AMATEUR
Kassel, 1914

A Queen sacrifice opens the gates for a devastating double check.

1	Kt–B7 ch	K–R2
2	QxRP ch!	PxQ
3	Kt–Kt5 ch	K–R1

Knight and King have returned to their previous positions, but now the Rook has a clear road along the rank.

| 4 | R–R7 mate |

White to play

20

CAPABLANCA-SPIELMANN
San Sebastian, 1911

Black's overworked Queen gives Capablanca opportunities to sacrifice pieces almost impudently.

| 1 | B–B1 |

Giving up a Pawn to get his Bishop into active play.

| 1 | ... | RxBP |

Threatens mate.

| 2 | B–B4 |

A move with a four-fold purpose:
(a) The Bishop is developed.
(b) Mate is stopped.

(c) Black's Queen is attacked.

(d) Black's Rook is cut off from the defense.

2	...	Q–Q1
3	RxB!	Q–KB1

To prevent 4 QxP mate. If instead 3 ... QxR, 4 Q–B8 ch forces mate.

4	QxP ch	QxQ
5	R–K8 ch	Q–Kt1
6	B–K5 ch	

And White mates next move.

ently unrelated facts: Black's Bishop is unprotected, and his Queen must guard the back rank against mate.

4	Q–Kt4!

An attack on both pieces!

4	...	Q–B1

Obviously not 4 ... QxQ when 5 R–K8 ch forces mate.

5	QxB

And here too Black cannot take the Queen.

White wins a piece and the game.

White to play

21

MORPHY-MONGREDIEN
Paris, 1859

Morphy provides a lucid treatment of The Overworked Queen theme.

1	KtxKt	QxKt

Compulsory, as the Queen was under attack.

2	KR–B1	Q–Q1
3	RxR ch	QxR

Morphy now exploits two appar-

Black to play

22

POPOV-RIUMIN
Moscow, 1929

Black is happy to sacrifice Rook and Queen to maneuver White's King into position for a double check, a form of attack which is almost always fatal.

1	...	RxKt!
2	BxR	QxB ch!
3	KxQ	KtxQP ch
4	K–Kt4	

The only square open.

| 4 | ... | B–B1 ch |
| 5 | K–R4 | Kt–B6 mate |

Not content with mating, the sadistic Knight, while doing so, threatens White's Queen and Rook.

White to play

23

SALVIOLI-AMATEUR
Mailand, 1915

Brilliant moves are easy to find if there is a double check in reserve.

| 1 | KtxP! | BxQ |

On 1 ... KtxKt; 2 RxKt ch, and Black's loose pieces are in danger, while 1 ... B–K2 succumbs to 2 Kt–Q6 ch followed by 3 QxKt.

| 2 | KtxKt ch | K–B1 |

Now to lure the Queen away from the last rank....

| 3 | B–Q6 ch | QxB |
| 4 | R–K8 mate |

White to play

24

LAMPARTER-GREEN
Australia, 1938

White senses the possibility of a double check on the Knight file. Two pieces prevent a double check, Black's Knight on the Knight file and White's own Knight at K5. Watch how these obstructions are cleared away *without loss of time.*

| 1 | Kt–B6! |

An attack on the Queen. This gives Black no time to think about his King.

| 1 | ... | KtxKt |
| 2 | Q–R7 ch! |

And this check forces the Knight to vacate the file.

| 2 | ... | KtxQ |

If 2 ... K–B3, 3 Q–R6 ch mates on the move.

3 B–K5 ch   K–R3

"Even the laziest King flees wildly in the face of a double check."

4 B–Kt7 mate

White to play

25

TAVERNIER-GRODNER
Charleville, 1952

Chess has so many hidden resources in innocent-looking positions, that it tempts one to suggest a rule, "If you see a strong move, don't make it!"

1 B–Kt1

White, for example, cannot resist this pin, which seems to win on the spot.

1	. . .	P–R5 ch
2	K–Kt4	P–B4 ch!
3	RxP	

Forced, but now Black's Rook is no longer pinned.

3 . . .   R–Kt7 mate!

White to play

26

LANDSTATTER-AMATEUR
Zurich, 1950

Chess players often indulge in wishful thinking. "If I only had the opportunity," they say to themselves, "I could be as brilliant as any of the masters." The opportunities are often there, waiting to be seized. The chess master makes his chances by examining every move on the board—even the impossible ones!

1 Q–Kt7 ch!

Would you or I have made this move?

1 . . .   KxQ

The pinned Bishop cannot capture the Queen, but the King must.

| 2 | Kt–B5 ch | K–Kt1 |
| 3 | Kt–R6 mate | |

Sudden death! Black's Bishop
looks on helplessly.

White to play

27

ADELER-AMATEUR
Berlin, 1931

The King is always in danger facing an adverse Rook, no matter how
many pieces separate them. From
the diagrammed position, White
clears away the obstacles in four
moves and exposes Black to a fatal
attack by the Rook.

| 1 | KtxBP | PxKt |

Otherwise Black, a Pawn down, is
menaced with a Knight check at Q6.

| 2 | Kt–B6 ch | QxKt |
| 3 | Q–Q8 ch! | |

To dislodge the Bishop from the
King file.

| 3 | . . . | BxQ |
| 4 | B–Kt5 mate! | |

White to play

28

JANNY-KARDHORDO
Tamesvar, 1922

Before making the key move of
his combination, White undoubtedly
considered this procedure: 1 B–R6
ch, K–R1, and then said to himself,
"If not for Black's QRP I could continue with 2 B–B8, discovered check
and mate. I must therefore eliminate
the Rook Pawn at any cost."

1	QxP ch!	KxQ
2	R–QR3 ch	K–Kt2
3	B–R6 ch	K–R2
4	B–QB8 mate	

White to play

29

ALEKHINE-FLETCHER
London, 1928

Discovered check often lends it-self to hit-and-hold tactics, as Alek-hine shows in this attractive speci-men.

1	QxKt!	PxQ
2	BxP ch	K–R1
3	Kt–Kt6 ch	K–R2
4	KtxR ch	

It is necessary to remove the Rook before playing for mate.

4	...	K–R1
5	Kt–Kt6 ch	K–R2
6	Kt–K5 ch	K–R1
7	Kt–B7 mate	

White to play

30

TORRE-LASKER
Moscow, 1925

The windmill effect is pleasing— for White particularly so, as he brought off this combination against the mighty Lasker!

1   **B–B6!**

Threatens the King with 2 RxP ch followed by quick mate, and simul-taneously discovers an attack on the Queen.

1	...	QxQ
2	RxP ch	K–R1
3	RxP ch	

Before regaining his Queen, White picks up some extra material.

3	...	K–Kt1
4	R–Kt7 ch	K–R1
5	RxB ch	K–Kt1
6	R–Kt7 ch	K–R1
7	R–Kt5 ch	K–R2
8	RxQ	K–Kt3
9	R–R3	KxB
10	RxP ch	

And White wins.

Black to play

31

BLASEJ-MIKULKA
Correspondence, 1930

An unprotected piece is always in danger. White's Queen is separated from Black's by a Bishop and two Pawns. But how quickly these obstacles can be swept aside, exposing White to a discovered attack!

1   ...   KtxP!

Doubling the attack on White's pinned Knight.

2   PxKt

Capturing the Bishop instead loses immediately: 2 QxB, QxKt ch; 3 K–K1, R–Q8 mate.

2   ...   QxP ch
3   K–B2

The pieces are now in their proper places, and the conditions are favorable for the decisive stroke—check to the King, and discovered attack on the Queen.

3   ...   B–K8 ch

And Black captures the Queen next move.

Black to play

32

SEPP-SUNDBERG
Munich, 1936

White's Queen is vulnerable to attack, despite her control of the long diagonal, and apparent freedom. Only one flight square is actually open to the Queen. This circumstance (and the obligation to picture the effect of every check or capture) gives Black the idea for the winning combination.

1   ...   Q–K8 ch
2   RxQ   RxR ch
3   K–B2   RxKt

Black surrounds the Queen, and wins.

White to play

33

YOUNG-DORÉ
Boston, 1892

The smothered mate is a spectacular finish to a game. It can only be given by a Knight, the one piece that can leap over the heads of the guards around the King, and deal the final blow.

1   Kt–K5 ch   K–Q1

Forced: if 1 ... K–B1; 2 Q–
B7 mate.

2	Kt–B7 ch	K–K1
3	Kt–Q6 ch	K–Q1
4	Q–K8 ch!	RxQ
5	Kt–B7 mate	

White to play

34

NAJDORF-AMATEUR
Rafaela, 1942

Najdorf contributes a semi-smothered mate to The Treasury of Artistic Combinations.

1   **Q–R5**

The threat of 2 QxP mate explain
the next moves on each side.

| 1 | ... | BxP |
| 2 | RxB | QxR |

Still guarding the critical point.

| 3 | QxP ch! | QxQ |
| 4 | Kt–Q7 mate | |

White to Play

35

SELETSKY

A rare and unusual effect is ob-
tained when smothered mate is given
to a King surrounded by pieces only,
instead of pieces and Pawns.

| 1 | B–R6 ch | K–Kt1 |

Or 1 ... B–Kt2; 2 BxB ch, and
the King must move to a black
square and into a Knight fork.

2	Q–Kt3 ch	K–R1
3	B–Kt7 ch!	BxB
4	Kt–Q7	

Attacks the Queen, who must now
cover the last rank to prevent mate
by White's Queen, and Kt3, to guard
against mate by the Knight.

4	...	Q–Q1
5	Q–Kt8 ch!	QxQ
6	Kt–Kt6 mate!	

This is the final combination of a
remarkable endgame composition.

White to play   *White to play*

36   **37**

TCHIGORIN-ZNOSKO-BOROVSKY   BERGER
St. Petersburg, 1906

A smart bit of play disposes of the Rook, blockader of White's potential Queen.

The order of moves is important in planning a combination. In this one, White tries to win a Pawn, and then simplify by exchanging the surplus pieces.

1	R–K7 ch	K–Q3
2	B–Kt3 ch	KxR
3	BxR	B–B3

How now? Does White lose his precious Pawn?

4   **B–Q6 ch!**

Certainly not! Black must drop all business and get out of check.

Notice how clearance is made for the Pawn to advance *without loss of time*.

4	. . .	KxB
5	P–Kt8(Q) ch	

White wins.

The wrong way:

1	RxP ch	QxR
2	QxR ch	K–B2
3	QxQ ch	KxQ

Black captures the Pawn next move and draws.

The right way:

1	QxR ch	QxQ
2	RxP ch	K–K2
3	RxQ	KxR
4	P–Kt6	

White wins, since the order in which the exchanges were made drew the King away from his Pawn.

2

SIMPLE AND PLEASING

For surely, of all the drugs in the world, Chess must be the most permanently pleasurable.

Assiac

White to play

38

SOULTANBEIEFF-MENDLEWITZ
Huy, 1925

White has an idea for a combination, for the success of which two conditions are necessary: Black's Queen must be lured away from her present dominating position, and his Queen Rook must be restrained.

| 1 | R–KB1! | QxR |

If 1 ... P–R8(Q); 2 RxP ch wins instantly.

| 2 | Q–Kt4 ch | K–Kt1 |
| 3 | Kt–K7 ch | K–B1 |

| 4 | Kt–B8 ch! | |

Cuts off the action of Black's Queen Rook.

4	...	K–Kt1
5	R–Q8 ch	K–R2
6	Q–KR4 ch	K–Kt3
7	Kt–K7 mate	

White to play

39

SOULTANBEIEFF-LIUBARSKI
Liège, 1935

An unusual sacrifice culminates in an epaulette mate, Black's two Rooks

19

constituting the King's shoulder orna-
ments.

| 1 | R–B7 ch | K–K1 |

1 ... K–Kt1; 2 R(B7)–QB7
ch, K–R2; 3 RxKtP mate.

2	B–Kt5 ch	K–Q1
3	R(Kt7)–Q7 ch	K–K1
4	R(Q7)–K7 ch	K–Q1
5	R–K8 ch!	RxR
6	R–Q7 mate	

White to play

40

RICHARDSON-DELMAR
New York, 1885

A pleasing combination based on
the weakness of Black's vulnerable
back rank.

1	Kt–B6 ch!	PxKt
2	Q–B8 ch!	KxQ
3	B–R6 ch	K–Kt1
4	R–K8 mate	

White to play

41

PAVELCHIK-AMATEUR
Berlin, 1951

The heavy artillery makes no im-
pression on the open file, so White
discharges his Queen and Rook. This
enables Knight and Pawn to close in
on the King.

| 1 | RxB! | |

Square Kt6 is now clear for fleet-
ing occupation by the Queen.

1	...	RxR
2	Q–Kt6 ch!	RxQ
3	PxR ch	K–R1
4	Kt–B7 mate	

White to play

42

BOGOLYUBOV-AMATEUR
Zoppot, 1935

Strange as it may seem, White's King Rook mates at K7 in four moves! All the obstacles on the King file are made to disappear by a beautiful telescoping maneuver.

| 1 | RxP! | QxB(K3) |
| 2 | B–B5! | |

Discovering an attack on the Queen, and on the Bishop hiding behind the Queen.

2	...	QxQ
3	RxB ch!	QxR
4	RxQ mate	

Black to play

43

GYGLI-HENNEBERGER
Zurich, 1941

A great deal of material may sometimes be sacrificed for the sake of getting in one healthy check on an open file. A brilliant demonstration by Henneberger:

1	...	Kt–K7 ch
2	K–R1	QxKt!
3	PxQ	

The file leading to the King is now open, but how does Black make use of it? One of his Rooks is blocked by a Pawn, and the other would be captured if it checked.

| 3 | ... | R–R4 ch! |

This will displace the obstreperous Pawn (and clear the way for the other Rook).

| 4 | PxR | R–R5 mate |

White to play

44

SOULTANBEIEFF-LIUBARSKI
Liège, 1937

White reasons it out thus: "Two of my pieces attack Black's Bishop, which is pinned. It is defended by three pieces. If I can dispose of two of its protecting pieces, the Bishop will fall." So he entices one defender away, and destroys the other!

| 1 | B–B3! | QxB |

Refusing the offer costs the Queen Rook.

| 2 | QxKt ch! | |

To this, Black has no choice of reply.

2	...	RxQ
3	R(Q1)xB ch	K–B1
4	R–B7 ch	K–Q1
5	R(Kt7)–Q7 mate	

White to play

45

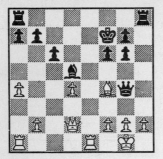

SOULTANBEIEFF-COURTENS
Visé, 1927

Black demonstrates that one can break into a position that seems bomb-proof, by giving away enough pieces.

1	B–Kt3	RxP!
2	KxR	R–R1 ch
3	K–Kt1	R–R8 ch!
4	KxR	Q–R6 ch

Exploiting the fact that the pinned Pawn may not capture.

5	K–Kt1	QxP mate

Black to play

46

AMATEUR-SOULTANBEIEFF
Liège, 1940

Black combines threats of mate on the last rank with pressure on an overworked Queen.

1 ...   Q–Kt7!

Threatens to invade the last rank with Queen or Rook.

2 Q–K4

Obviously 2 QxQ, R–Q8 ch is fatal.

2 ...   R–Q8 ch
3 Kt–K1

This explains White's previous move. From K4 the Queen keeps in touch with the Knight.

3 ...   Q–B7!

Decisive! White may not play 4 QxQ; his Queen can not remain at K4, nor move to any square of communication with the pinned Knight.

4   Resigns

Black to play

47

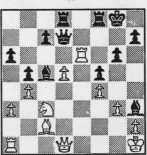

AMATEUR-SOULTANBEIEFF
Liège, 1943

The twist, à la Alekhine, comes at the end of the combination.

White's last move was 1 P–Kt4, a

strategical error, since it removes the Knight's support.

1	...	B–Kt5
2	Q–Q3	

The only move. If 2 Q–KB1, B–Q5; 3 Q–Q3, BxKt; 4 QxB, QxP ch, and Black wins a Rook.

2	...	QxR
3	PxQ	RxQ
4	BxR	B–B6 mate

White to play

48

MORAVEC

The finest combinations often arise out of positions that seem to offer no promise of excitement.

It would take a Sherlock Holmes though to figure out that checkmate will be given by the inconspicuous Rook Pawn.

The tempting 1 P–Kt7, threatening 2 R–Q8 ch, KxR; 3 P–Kt8(Q) ch, is refuted by 1 ... K–B3, and Black can force a draw.

1	R–Q8 ch!	KxR
2	P–Kt7	R–QKt5!

Attacks the dangerous Pawn. Black expects this continuation: 3 KxR, P–

B4 ch; 4 KxP, K–B2, followed by 5 ... KxP. The subsequent ending would then be a draw.

3	KxR	P–B4 ch
4	K–Kt5!	

Very clever, and the key to the win.

4	...	K–B2
5	K–R6	

Holds on to the Pawn. But hasn't Black a threatening passed Pawn?

5	...	K–Kt1

On 5 ... P–B5; 6 K–R7, P–B6; 7 P–Kt8(Q) ch wins at once.

6	K–Kt6	P–B5
7	P–R4	P–B6
8	P–R5	P–B7
9	P–R6	P–B8(Q)
10	P–R7 mate	

An exciting finish

White to play

49

LEVENFISH-FREYMANN
Leningrad, 1925

Sometimes one's own pieces stand in the way of effecting a mate. The trick is to get rid of the hindrance *without loss of time*.

1	BxP	PxB
2	RxP ch	K–Kt2

If only the Bishop at K4 did not stand in the way, White could mate by 3 Q–Kt6. The problem is to get rid of the Bishop without giving the King time to escape.

   3   B–Kt7!

The key! The Bishop attacks Black's Queen, simultaneously clearing the diagonal for a threat of mate.

   3   . . .   Resigns

White to play

50

POLLOCK-ALLIES
Buffalo, 1893

White blends a combination of beauty and power. Two sacrifices lend it beauty, and five checks in succession give it power.

1	Q–Q7 ch!	BxQ
2	Kt–Q6 ch	K–Q1
3	Kt–B7 ch	K–B1

4	R–K8 ch!	BxR
5	R–Q8 mate	

Black to play

51

AMATEUR-ANDRESEN
Christiania, 1914

White's King is cornered, but still needs subduing. Andresen dispatches him neatly with a four-move mating combination.

1	. . .	B–Kt7 ch!
2	RxB	Q–B8 ch
3	R–Kt1	Kt–Kt6 ch!
4	PxKt	Q–R6 mate

White to play

52

MARCO-SALTER
Czernowitz, 1929

White sacrifices a piece to get in a powerful Knight check. The final position is worth noting, as it occurs fairly often.

1   B–Kt5!   QxB

Black has no choice. If 1 ... Q–B1; 2 Kt–K7 ch is decisive.

2   Kt–K7 ch   K–R1
3   QxP ch!   KxQ
4   R–R1 mate

White to play

53

CASAS-PIAZZINI
Buenos Aires, 1952

The experienced combination player will detect points of resemblance between this and the previous diagram. The Rook file is closed here, and the Knight is unable to check at K7, but all this can change in a flash, and the familiar mating position appear.

1   QxP ch!   KxQ
2   PxB ch   K–Kt1
3   Kt–K7 mate.

Had Black played 2 ... K–Kt3, the response 3 Kt–K7 is the same mate in essence.

White to play

54

TRULTSCH-HEIDENREICH
Wurzen, 1935

Black survives a discovered check, followed by a double attack on King and Rook, but a simple exchange and Knight fork combination ruins him. It's all in the wrist!

1   P–K7 ch   RxQ
2   P–K8(Q) ch   Q–K1
3   Q–K6 ch   Q–Q2
4   QxQ ch   KxQ
5   Kt–K5 ch   K–K3
6   KtxR

White to play

55

KASHDAN-TENNER
New York, 1934

Kashdan slips out of a Knight fork

and wins—by a Knight fork, of course!

1 B–B7!   Q–K3

If 1 ... QxB; 2 BxP ch, K–R1; 3 QxB leaves an easily won ending for White.

2 **BxR**	**RxB**
3 **B–R4!**	**RxR**
4 **RxR**	**BxB**
5 **QxB**	**Kt–B6**

Tempting, and seems to promise some hope.

6 **QxKt!**	**QxQ**
7 **R–Kt8** ch	**K–B2**
8 **Kt–K5** ch	

White regains the Queen and wins.

White to play

56

PLATOV

An attractive ending, showing what may happen even if a harassed Queen escapes all the dangers which surround her.

1 R–R8 ch   **K–Kt4**

On 1 ... K–Kt5; 2 Kt–B6 ch wins the Queen by discovered attack.

2 Kt–Q6!

A threat on the Queen which forces. . . .

2 ...   Q–B3

Certainly not 2 ... QxR; 3 Kt–B7 ch, and the Queen is caught by the Knight fork.

3 Kt–B7 ch

Where shall the King move? If 3 ... K–Kt5 or 3 ... K–Kt3, the reply 4 Kt–K5 ch wins the Queen, while 3 ... K–B3 allows the skewer attack 4 R–R6 ch, and again White wins the Queen.

3 ...   K–B5

Saves the Queen, but. . . . 4 R–R4 is mate!

White to play

57

TARRASCH-AMATEUR
Munich, 1919

Tarrasch seems to be starting a combination against the pinned Knight, but it's the King he's really after.

1	PxP	KxP
2	R(R6)xKt	PxR
3	R–QB8 mate!	

Black to play

58

AMATEUR-CAPABLANCA
New Orleans, 1909

A pretty finish from an exhibition game, early in Capablanca's career.

1	. . .	R–K7
2	BxP	Kt–K5!
3	R–KB1	Kt–B7 ch
4	K–Kt1	

Forced, as 4 RxKt, R–K8 ch leads to mate.

4	. . .	Kt–R6 ch
5	K–R1	R–Kt7
6	Any	R–Kt8 ch
7	RxR	Kt–B7 mate

White to play

59

JANOWSKY-AMATEUR
New York, 1917

A Knight alone cannot force checkmate. But there are exceptions, as Janowsky demonstrates to a surprised opponent.

1	Kt–Kt4 ch	K–R1
2	K–B1	P–B6
3	K–B2	P–R7
4	K–B1	P–B7
5	KtxBP mate	

White to play

60

VOLLMER

White, who can hardly afford it, must lose his Knight. It is almost incredible that he can still escape with a drawn game!

| 1 | P–B6 ch | KxKt |

If Black spurns the Knight and moves 1 ... K–R1, then the reply 2 Kt–B8 actually leads to a win for White.

| 2 | K–Kt1! |

The key move! the natural 2 K–Kt3 loses after 2 ... K–R1; 3 KxP, B–R2; 4 K–Kt4, B–Q5; 5 P–R4, B–B6; 6 P–R5, BxP; 7 P–R6, B–B6 etc.

| 2 | ... | K–R1 |
| 3 | K–R1! | B–R2 |

Stalemate!

White to play

61

SELESNIEV

| 1 | P–R3 ch | K–Kt4 |

On 1 ... K–B4; 2 R–B8 ch followed by Queening the Pawn will compel Black to give up his Rook.

| 2 | P–R4 ch | K–Kt5 |
| 3 | R–KB8 |

Threatens 4 R–B4 mate.

| 3 | ... | R–Kt7 ch |
| 4 | R–B2 | RxR ch |

Forced, as the Rook cannot guard against the threat of mate, and restrain White's passed Pawn at the same time.

5	KxR	P–R7
6	P–Kt8(Q)	P–R8(Q)
7	Q–QB8 mate!

White to play

62

RINCK

Zig-zag combinations have a strange fascination (for me, at any rate).

1	Q–R8	K–Kt8
2	Q–R7 ch	K–R8
3	Q–Kt7	K–Kt8
4	Q–Kt6 ch	K–R8
5	Q–B6	K–Kt8
6	Q–B5 ch	K–R8
7	Q–Q5	K–Kt8
8	Q–Q4 ch	K–R8
9	Q–K4	K–Kt8
10	Q–K3 ch	K–R8
11	Q–KB3	K–Kt8
12	Q–B1 mate

3

BLENDING OF THEMES

> *Now we see wherein lies the pleasure to be derived from a chess combination. It lies in the feeling that a human mind is behind the game, dominating the inanimate pieces with which the game is carried on, and giving them the breath of life.*
>
> —Richard Réti

White to play

63

ZUKERTORT-ENGLISCH
London, 1883

A pin (supported invisibly) and a Knight fork can make beautiful music together.

1   **Q–Kt5!**   **QxQ**

The offer must be accepted. On 1 ... K–Q2; 2 P–B8(Q) ch, KxQ; 3 QxQ ch wins at once for White.

2   **P–B8(Q) ch**   **K–B2**

Or 2 ... Kt–Q1; 3 Kt–B7 ch, and White wins the Queen.

3   **QxKt ch**   **KxQ**
4   **Kt–B7 ch**

White regains the Queen and wins.

White to play

64

WADE-BENNETT
London, 1943

White's combination nets only a Pawn, but an extra Pawn is enough

29

(*ceteris paribus*, as Lasker used to say) to win the game.

| 1 | QxB! | | RPxQ |

Clearly, the Bishop Pawn, being pinned, may not capture.

| 2 | BxP ch | | RxB |
| 3 | R–R8 ch! | | |

Compels the King to take, and thereby set up the position for a Knight fork.

3	...		KxR
4	KtxR ch		K–Kt1
5	KtxQ		R–Q1
6	R–K6		

White holds on to the Pawn and wins.

White to play

65

RINCK

THE PIN AND THE SKEWER

Two pieces directly in line are always in danger of attack by

(a) The Pin, which threatens the piece standing in front, or

(b) The Skewer, which menaces the piece that is hidden.

In Rinck's masterly ending, Black's Queen (apparently so free) is forced into line with the King, and into a choice of deaths—by The Pin or The Skewer.

| 1 | R–R8! | | |

An unexpected attack which greatly restricts the Queen's movements.

| 1 | ... | | Q–R7 |

Alternatives and White's replies are:

1	...	QxR	2	B–B3 ch
1	...	Q–K3	2	R–R6 ch
1	...	Q–Q4	2	B–B3
1	...	Q–B5	2	R–B8 ch

White winning the Queen in each case.

| 2 | RxP! | | |

Another surprise!

| 2 | ... | | Q–Kt1 |

On 2 ... QxR; 3 B–K8 ch wins.

3	R–R8		Q–R2
4	B–Kt6		QxB
5	R–R6 ch		

White wins the Queen by The Skewer Attack.

Black to play

66

GRUNFELD-ELISKASES
Vienna, 1935

The practice of looking at every possible check or capture has brought many a fine combination into being. In this position, for example, Black checks three times in succession, allowing his opponent no choice of reply. The consequence is that Black can pick out a clear-cut winning line, with no variations to confuse the issue.

1	...	RxKt ch
2	RxR	RxR ch
3	KxR	Kt–B6 ch

In a way, this Knight fork was the only move Black had to visualize. He had to picture the King at R2 in position for the Knight's attack, and to see that the Knight could not be captured without unguarding the Queen.

| 4 | RxKt | QxQ ch |

Black wins.

White to play

67

KHOLMOV-ISAKOV
Krim, 1947

Positions where the pieces must depend on each other for support are susceptible to submarine attack. In this one a Rook sacrifice removes the under-pinning and Black's whole game collapses.

| 1 | P–R4 |

Attack on a convenient target—the pinned Bishop.

1	...	R–Kt5 ch
2	KxP	RxP
3	P–B4	

Again striking at the Bishop.

| 3 | ... | RxP |

While Black again removes the attacking Pawn. But note the position now: Black's Rook is supported by the Bishop, and the Bishop in turn by the King. If the King is forced away, everything will fall.

| 4 | RxP ch! | KxR |

If 4 ... K–R3 (refusing to capture) 5 R(Kt7)xB leaves White a Rook ahead.

| 5 | RxB ch | K–R3 |
| 6 | KxR | |

White wins.

White to play

68

TYLOR-WINTER
Hastings, 1933

A capture is generally met by an immediate recapture. Sometimes the recapture is delayed by a *zwischenzug*, an in-between move that generally upsets the opponent's plans, and often initiates a brilliant combination.

Black has just played ... RxR, and expects 1 RxR in reply. White crosses him up by paying no attention to the Rook. Instead he heads for the King with a combination leading to mate.

1 Q–R7 ch   K–B1
2 Q–R8 ch   K–K2
3 Kt–B5 ch!

White is not concerned with the fact that his Queen is attacked, and that his King is threatened with mate. At the moment Black's King is in check, and there is only one move open to him.

3 ...   PxKt
4 B–B5 mate!

White can win with a Knight fork and pin, but first he must make his own Knight disappear!

1 Kt–Kt6

Attack on the Queen.

1 ...   Q–KB2
2 Kt–K7 ch

Knight fork! Black must capture the beast.

2 ...   QxKt
3 QxR

The pin! White wins, as after 3 ... PxQ; 4 RxQ, K–B1; 5 QR–B7, the rest is child's play.

White to play

70

ZURALIEV-ROMANOV
Kalinin, 1952

A double pin prepares the way for a Queen sacrifice. The sacrifice sets Black's King up for a knockout, by discovered check.

1 Q–Kt5

White to play

69

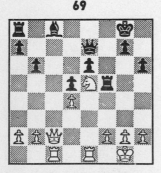

LEXANDROVICH-KRUMHAUSER
Berlin, 1951

Cross-pin and double attack on the Bishop. Black may not take the Queen, and certainly does not care for 1 ... BxB; 2 QxQ.

1 ...	P–Q4

Provides additional support for the Bishop.

2	Q–Kt7 ch!	BxQ
3	BxB ch	K–Kt1
4	B–B6 mate	

White to play

71

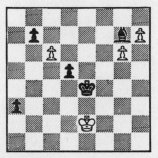

BERNHARDT

A couple of sacrifices pave the way for a blending of motifs—The Double Attack and The Skewer.

The obvious continuation 1 P–B7, P–R7; 2 P–B8(Q), P–R8(Q) provides no winning chances. White must be crafty!

1	P–R8(Q)	BxQ
2	P–Kt7	BxP

Now we have the position in the diagram, minus the two connected passed Pawns.

3	P–B7	P–R7
4	P–B8(Q)	P–R8(Q)
5	Q–Kt4 ch	

Drives the King into position for The Skewer Attack.

5 ...	K–K4
6 QxB ch	K–K5
7 QxQ	

White wins.

White to play

72

HOIT-AMATEUR

Chess can be brutal! Black's King and Queen are forced to move to the sixth rank, where a vicious Knight lies in wait, poised for the kill.

1	QxRP ch!	KxQ

Naturally, 1 ... RxQ; 2 RxQ ch, K–Kt3; 3 RxB is not an attractive alternative.

2	RxR ch	QxR
3	Kt–B5 ch	

White captures the Queen next move, and wins the ending.

White to play   *White to play*

73   **74**

RINCK   BRON

White's King Knight makes "the grand tour" and maneuvers the King and Queen into position for a pin and Knight fork combination.

| 1 | Kt–KB7 ch | K–K5 |

On 1 ... KxB; 2 Kt–B7 ch wins.

2	B–Q5 ch	K–B4
3	Kt–R6 ch	K–K4
4	Kt–Kt4 ch	K–B4
5	Kt–K3 ch	K–K4
6	Kt–B4 ch	K–B4
7	B–K6 ch	K–K5
8	B–B8!	Q–B3

If 8 ... QxB; 9 Kt(B4)–Q6 ch, PxKt; 10 KtxP ch wins for White.

9	B–Kt7!	QxB
10	Kt(B4)–Q6 ch	PxKt
11	KtxP ch	

White captures the Queen and wins.

The libretto reads as follows:
(1) Double attack
(2) Knight fork
(3) Pin
Stalemate Intermission
(4) Double attack
(5) Pin
(6) Knight fork
         Curtain

| 1 | P–B5 ch | QxP |

On 1 ... KxP; 2 Kt–K4 ch wins.

| 2 | Kt–R4 ch | PxKt |
| 3 | B–K3 | |

A pin invisibly supported. If 3 ... QxB; 4 Kt–B4 ch in reply wins the Queen.

| 3 | ... | K–R4! |

Very pretty! If White captures the Queen in haste, he stalemates Black's King.

| 4 | P–Kt4 ch! | QxP |

If 4 ... PxP e.p. or 4 ...
KxP, White captures the Queen and
wins.

5 **B–Q2**

The same dialogue as in the first
act, but the scene has been shifted
to another diagonal.

5 ...   QxB
6 **Kt–B4** ch

White captures the Queen and
wins.

White to play

75

HORWITZ AND KLING

White's pieces are widely scattered, yet they manage to create a
combination containing these ingredients:

(1) Pin—unsupported
(2) Sacrifice—1 Rook
(3) Double Attack—unprotected
(4) Knight Forks—choice of
The blend is potent.

1 **R–R4** ch   K–K4

On 1 ... K–B4; 2 R–R5 ch
wins the Queen.

2 **R–R5!**   P–B4

If 2 ... QxR; 3 Kt–B6 ch wins
the Queen.

3 **RxP!**   QxR
4 **P–Q4** ch!   QxP

Or 4 ... KxP, when 5 Kt–K6
ch is the decisive Knight fork.

5 **Kt–B6** ch

White captures the Queen next
move and wins.

4

A MIXED BOUQUET

----

*There are two classes of men; those who are content to
yield to circumstances, and who play whist; those who aim to
control circumstances, and who play chess.*

—Mortimer Collins

White to play

76

MIKENAS-LÉBEDEV
Gruzinske, 1914

1   RxKt!

Black may not recapture, as after
1 ... BxR; 2 Q–Q3 forces mate.

   1 ...   **K–Kt2**

   2   **Q–Q3!**

The Rook is still tabu. If 2 ...
KxR; 3 Kt–Kt4 ch, K–K2 (or 3 ...
K–Kt2; 4 Q–R7 mate) 4 Q–Q6 mate.

   2 ...   **P–KR4**

To stop White from moving 3 Kt–
Kt4.

36

   3   **P–KR4!**   **KxR**

What else could he do? On 3 ...
B–R3; 4 RxB, KxR; 5 Q–R7 is mate.

   4   **Kt–Kt4 ch!**

The Knight insists on moving to
Kt4!

   4 ...   **PxKt**

   5   **B–K5 ch!**   **KxB**

   6   **Q–Q4** mate

White to play

77

DENKER-FEIT
New York, 1929

An imaginative combination from a game won by Denker in his student days. Denker's own comment on it is, "This game is really unique. I was only fifteen when it was played, against an opponent who was known in those days as 'the titan of the interscholastics.' Since that time I have played a number of brilliant games, but none of them, it seems to me, can compare with this one for absolute purity and charm."

1 Q–R5

Denker, you will note, has already given up a piece. He is interested in mate, and nothing less.

| 1 ... | RxB! |

Black's best chance. If instead 1 ... BxB; 2 QxP ch, K–B2; 3 RxB ch, and White wins. Or if 1 ... B–KR3; 2 BxB, PxB; 3 QxP, RxR ch; 4 RxR, Q–K2; 5 R–B8 ch, QxR; 6 QxRP mate.

2	QxP ch	K–B2
3	B–Kt6 ch	K–B3
4	RxR ch	BxR
5	Q–R4 ch	B–Kt4
6	Q–K4!	B–K6 ch
7	K–R1	B–R6
8	R–B1 ch!	

Nothing stops our hero!

| 8 ... | K–Kt4 |

If 8 ... BxR; 9 Q–B5 ch, K–K2; 10 Q–B7 mate.

9 B–R7!

A quiet move after the fireworks.

| 9 ... | Resigns |

Just in time to avoid being mated, either by 10 Q–Kt6 or by 10 Q–R4.

White to play

78

DENKER-SCHWARTZ
New York, 1930

Given a position that is a win, a true chess player tries not to prolong the agony. He must finish off his opponent like an artist, not a butcher.

1 Q–Q5

Intending 2 RxB ch, RxR; 3 P–K7 ch, and mate in two more moves.

| 1 ... | K–B1 |

If instead 1 ... K–R1; 2 R–R5 ch, K–Kt1; 3 RxB ch!, KxR; 4 Q–Kt5 ch, K–B1; 5 R–R8 mate.

| 2 | RxB! | RxR |
| 3 | RxR | |

And wins. If 3 ... QxR; 4 Q–Q8 is mate, and if 3 ... KxR; 4 Q–Q7 ch, QxQ; 5 PxQ will leave White a Queen ahead after the imminent coronation.

White to play

79

DENKER-DAKE
Syracuse, 1934

Denker attacks dexterously, manipulating the pieces as though they were puppets on a string.

1   KtxP!

Planning this pretty continuation: 2 RxKt ch!, QxR; 3 QxQ ch, KxQ; 4 Kt–B5 ch, and White wins a Rook elegantly.

1   ...   BxP
Regains the Pawn and guards the critical B4 square.

2   Q–R4

Now the idea is 3 RxKt ch, QxR; 4 QxR, winning a piece.

2   ...   R–Kt3
3   R–QB1

White's pieces are so well posted that he has no less than four winning threats:

  (a) 4 Kt–B6
  (b) 4 RxKt ch, QxR; 5 R–B7 ch
  (c) 4 R–B7 ch, QxR; 5 QxKt ch
and mate next move

  (d) 4 Q–R8, and mate at QB8

3   ...   K–K1
4   RxKt ch!   QxR
5   Q–R8 ch   K–B2

If 5 ... Q–B1; 6 R–B8 ch wins the Queen, or if 5 ... K–Q2; 6 Q–B8 ch, K–Q3; 7 Q–Kt8 ch, and White mates in three.

6   Kt–B3!

A retreat, but a powerful one. White's threat of mate on the move can be averted, but not the decisive posting of the Knight at K5.

6   ...   Q–Q3
7   Kt–K5 ch   K–K2
8   R–B8!

Black can prevent the mate at KB8 by playing 8 ... R–B3, but then comes the epaulette mate by 9 R–K8.

8   ...   Resigns

White to play

80

SOULTANBEIEFF-BORODIN
Brussels, 1943

The combination with its problem-like ending will probably find a
place in many anthologies. This may
console M. Borodin, the victim of the
brilliancy.

1   P–K5!

Discovered attack! Black is forced
to exchange Bishops and thereby
help develop White's King Rook.

1   ...   BxB ch
2   RxB   BxP

The alternatives were:
(a) 2 ... PxP; 3 R–Kt1 ch,
K–R1; 4 Q–R6, and White wins a
piece.
(b) 2 ... B–Kt4; 3 R–KKt1,
P–KR3; 4 R–B6, and the threat of
5 RxB ch is overwhelming.

3   R–Kt1 ch   K–R1
4   Q–R6!

Threatens mate in three, starting
with 5 QxRP ch.

4   ...   RxKt
5   PxR   Q–R1

Crafty defense! The Rook is im-
mobilized by the pin, but Soultan-
beieff has a subtle rejoinder.

6   R–Kt2!

Frees the Rook, and renews the
threat of mate by 7 QxP ch, KxQ;
8 R–R3 mate.

6   ...   Resigns

The capture 6 ... QxR is countered by 7 QxR mate.

White to play

81

SOULTANBEIEFF-WERY
Liège, 1932

The mere act of Castling does not
assure a King perpetual safety. He
may still have to come out to the
middle of the board and face his
attackers.

1   B–R7 ch   KtxB

Preferable to 1 ... K–R1; 2
KtxP mate.

2   QxKt ch   K–B1
3   KtxBP!

Taking the Knight allows White
to mate in four: 3 ... KxKt; 4
Kt–K5 ch, K–B1; 5 Q–R8 ch, K–K2;
6 QxKtP ch, K–Q3; 7 Kt–B4 mate.

3   ...   Q–R4 ch
4   P–Kt4   QxRP
5   0–0   KxKt
6   Kt–K5 ch   K–K2
7   QxP ch   K–Q1
8   RxP!

The point of the combination!
Black must not be given time to

breathe. He may not play 8 ...
PxR on account of 9 KtxP mate in
reply, and he must do something
about the mate threats beginning
with either 9 R–Q6 ch or 9 RxB ch.

8 ...	Kt–K2
9 Kt–B7 ch	K–Q2
10 Q–K5!	KxR
11 Q–B5 ch	K–Q2
12 Q–Q6 mate	

White to play

82

SOULTANBEIEFF-DEFOSSE
Correspondence, 1941

Clever combinative play by White
imperils a Knight (that has rashly
gone Pawn-hunting) on one wing,
and the King himself on the other
wing.

1 KtxKP!	Kt–Kt3

Preferable to 1 ... PxKt; 2
BxP ch, followed by 3 BxKt, with
advantage to White.

2 KtxQ	KtxQ
3 R–Q4	KtxP

But this is greed, and merits
punishment.

4 BxP ch!	K–R1

On 4 ... RxB; 5 KtxR, KxKt;
6 R–Kt1, and White wins the exchange.

5 B–Kt3	P–QR4

To rescue the Knight by 6 ...
P–R5 and 7 ... P–R6.

6 Kt–B7 ch	K–Kt1
7 Kt–K5 ch	K–R1
8 Kt–Kt6 ch	PxKt
9 R–R4 mate	

White to play

83

DURAS-COHN
Carlsbad, 1911

The sparkling finale from a game
which was conducted brilliantly by
both players.

1 RxP ch!	KxR
2 Q–K7 ch	K–Kt3
3 R–Kt8 ch	K–B4
4 RxKt ch!	KxR

If 4 ... PxR; 5 Q–Q7 ch wins the Queen.

5   **Q–Kt7 ch**   Resigns

If 5 ... K–R4; 6 Q–R7 ch wins the Queen, or if 5 ... K–B4; 6 Q–Q7 ch does likewise.

White to play

84

STERK-MARSHALL
Pistyan, 1912

One of the rare times when the victim of a typical Marshall attack (including an under-promotion) is the maestro himself!

1   **P–Kt5**   Kt–B4
2   **P–Kt6**   R–K2
3   **Q–R5**   Kt–R3

To save the Knight, and also prevent the mate in two.

4   **QxKt!**

This must have given Frank J. a jolt.

4   ...   PxQ
5   **PxP ch**   K–R2

6   **P–B8(Kt) ch**   K–R1
7   **R–Kt8 mate**

White to play

85

BERNSTEIN-COHN
Hanover, 1902

Bernstein devises a pleasing combination, which begins with a Rook sacrifice and ends with a Rook sacrifice! The first one is brusque, the second is quiet and artistic.

1   **R–B7 ch!**   KtxR
2   **RxKt ch**   K–R1

If 2 ... K–R3; 3 Q–B2, KxKt; 4 Q–B4 ch, K–R5; 5 Q–R6 ch, KxP; 6 Kt–K3 mate.

3   **Q–B2!**

Attacks the Knight while threatening a deadly check at B6.

3   ...   Q–Q1
4   **Q–B6 ch**   QxQ
5   **PxQ**

White wins. There is no way to stop the second sacrifice 6 RxP ch followed by 7 Kt–B7 mate.

White to play

86

CANAL-AMATEUR
Budapest, 1934

Some people don't like to be pinned! Canal breaks a pin by force, giving away in the process two Rooks and his Queen. Seems expensive, but in return he gets a Bishop—and the King!

1	PxB!	QxR ch
2	K-Q2	QxR
3	QxP ch!	PxQ
4	B-R6 mate	

White to play

87

MIESES-AMATEUR
Metz, 1935

"Ahoy! Ahoy! Check!"
The White Knight in THROUGH THE LOOKING GLASS.

Mieses gives three checks in succession and disposes of any endgame complications.

| 1 | P-Kt4 ch | PxPe.p. |

If Black refuses to capture, then after 1 ... K-R5; 2 K-R2, P-R4; 3 R-KR6, and White mates next move.

| 2 | R-R4 ch! | PxR |

On 2 ... KxR; 3 RxP mate makes a delightful picture.

| 3 | R-Kt5 ch | QxR |
| 4 | PxQ | |

White makes a new Queen, and wins.

White to play

88

TIETZ-RAMISCH
Carlsbad, 1898

King wanderings are always interesting. In this one, Black's King must make a semi-circular tour to the King side to keep his appointment at Samarra.

| 1 | RxB! | KxR |
| 2 | QxP ch | KxQ |

Black must take the Queen, or lose his Rook.

| 3 | B–R4 ch | K–B5 |

If 3 ... KxB; 4 Kt–B3 forces checkmate.

4	P–Kt3 ch	K–Q6
5	B–Kt5 ch	K–K5
6	R–Kt4 ch	K–B4
7	Kt–K3 mate	

White to play

89

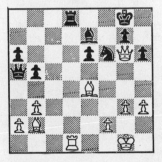

AHUES-AMATEUR
Berlin, 1907

While Black is kept busy warding off tactical threats, his King is drawn imperceptibly into a mating net.

| 1 | BxKt! | RxR ch |

After 1 ... BxB, the winning idea is 2 R–Q7!, RxR (otherwise 3 Q–R7 ch and mate next); 3 Q–K8 mate!

| 2 | K–R2 | B–B1 |

Here too, if 2 ... BxB; 3 Q–K8 is mate.

3	BxP!	BxB
4	QxKP ch	K–B1
5	B–Kt6	Resigns

Black cannot stop both mate threats, one at B7 and the other at K8.

Black to play

90

GERASIMOV-SMYSLOV
Moscow, 1935

From a tournament game played at the age of fourteen. The decisive combination deserves more than the usual grudging editorial tribute, "A creditable effort for a youngster." Smyslov conducts the final attack with courage, power and originality.

| 1 | ... | Q–B3 |
| 2 | B–KB1 | |

Smyslov's refutes 2 P–B3 thus: 2 ... Kt–Kt5; 3 P–Kt3, B–K6 ch; 4 K–Kt2, Kt–B7; 5 Q–K2, KtxB, and if White continues by 6 QxKt then 6 ... QxP ch; 7 K–R3, Q–R4 mate.

2	...	KR–Q1
3	Q–Kt3	Kt–Kt5
4	P–R3	R–Q6!

White cannot play 5 BxR as the Bishop must guard against mate, and if 5 QxR, B–R7 ch; 6 K–R1, KtxP ch; 7 KxB, KtxQ wins, White still being unable to capture the Knight.

| 5 | QxP | RxKRP! |

One of the points of the combination. Now 6 QxQ loses at once by 6 ... B–R7 ch; 7 K–R1, KtxP mate.

| 6 | B–Q4 |

Protects the tender spot, KB2. Smyslov is undisturbed though and completes his combination with the windmill idea.

6	...	B–R7 ch
7	K–R1	BxP ch
8	K–Kt1	B–R7 ch
9	K–R1	B–B2 ch
10	K–Kt1	BxQ

Black wins.

White to play

91

The mild-mannered Bronstein is one of the most fiercely aggressive players that ever lived. The combination that follows, played early in his career, is typical of his restless, resolute, resourceful style.

1	Kt–B3	PxP
2	QxP	BxP
3	B–Kt5 ch!	Kt–B3

Black does not fall for 3 ... B–K2, when 4 Q–B8 ch in reply would come like a shot.

| 4 | QR–K1! | P–B3 |

Carefully avoiding 4 ... QxB; 5 QxKt ch!, PxQ; 6 R–K8 mate.

5	BxKt ch	QxB
6	Q–K2	Q–Q5 ch
7	K–R1	B–Kt3

Guards against 8 Q–K8 ch, but Bronstein has other expedients.

| 8 | RxB ch! | K–B2 |

The alternative 8 ... RxR; 9 Q–K7 ch is clearly hopeless.

| 9 | BxP! |

Threatens the Queen by 10 Kt–Kt5 ch.

| 9 | ... | PxB |
| 10 | Kt–Kt5 ch! |

Delightful! The sacrifice of the Knight will enable Bronstein to sacrifice another piece later!

| 10 | ... | PxKt |
| 11 | QxKtP |

Indicating that he intends to continue with 12 R–K7 ch.

11 ...   R–K1

And Black of course prevents it. Bronstein's next move must have surprised him.

12 R–K7 ch!   RxR
13 Q–B6 mate

White to play

92

ROSSOLIMO-AMATEUR
Paris, 1944

In the space of six moves, there are three clearances (as though this were a composed problem) a couple of sacrifices, and a quiet move by the King. An astonishing combination!

1 RxKt!

Clears the diagonal for the Queen.

1 ...   PxR
2 QxP ch!   KxQ

If 2 ... PxQ; 3 Kt–B6 ch, K–R1; 4 R–Kt8 mate.

3 R–R1 ch   K–Kt3
4 K–B4!

Vacates the diagonal for operations by the Bishop. Mate now threatens by 4 B–R5 ch, K–R2; 5 BxP mate.

4 ...   Q–K3

Prepared to meet the threat by interposing his Queen.

5 R–R8!

A final clearance, it enables the Bishop to come in behind the Rook, and strike the final blow.

5 ...   Resigns

Black is a whole Queen ahead, but can do nothing to prevent mate by the Bishop.

White to play

93

SOMOV-NASIMOVICH

"Life imitates art," said Oscar Wilde. For art we have Somov-Nasimovich's composed ending, expressing beautifully a pin and Knight fork theme. Compare his combination with the following one, which occurred in life—in actual play.

1	B–Q6 ch!	PxB

On 1 ... QxB; 2 Kt–Kt5 ch wins the Queen.

2	K–B3

Threatens 3 R–R8 mate.

2	...	K–R7
3	R–Kt2 ch	K–R6

Forced, since 3 ... K–R8 allows 4 Kt–B2 mate.

4	R–Kt7!	K–R7
5	K–B2	K–R6
6	R–R7 ch	K–Kt5
7	Kt–B6 ch!	

White wins the Queen.

White to play

94

RAGOZIN-VERESOV
Moscow, 1945

From a tournament game, a rendition of the pin and Knight fork *motif*, initiated by a sacrifice of both Rooks.

Which is more brilliant, the combination from actual play, or the composed position?

1	RxB ch!	BPxR

If 1 ... KxR; 2 Q–Kt3 ch, K–R3; 3 R–B4, followed by 4 R–R4 mate.

2	R–B7 ch!	KxR
3	QxRP ch	K–K3

On 3 ... K–B1; 4 Kt–B4!, R(K1)–B1; 5 KtxP ch, K–K1; 6 Q–Kt8 mate.

4	QxKtP ch	K–K4
5	Q–Kt7 ch	KxP

Forced, since the reply to 5 ... K–K3 is 6 Kt–B4 mate.

6	Kt–B6 ch!	PxKt
7	QxQ	

White wins.

White to play

95

GERBEC-AMATEUR
Vienna, 1938

Black's Queen must be lured away, for Gerbec's combination to succeed. Two sacrifices, far from obvious, manage to do the trick.

1	RxR ch	KtxR

2 R–QR1!   QxR

Black must accept the offer. If instead 1 ... Q–Kt1; 2 P–Kt6, and Black must worry about 3 R–Q1, among other things.

3 P–K6!

Another gift which may not be refused. If, for example, 3 ... Q–R2 (the Queen must move, since it is attacked); 4 Q–Q7 ch, K–Kt1; 5 B–K5 ch, K–R1; 6 QxKt ch forces mate.

3 ...	QxB
4 Q–Q7 ch	K–Kt1
5 QxKt ch	K–R2

Unfortunately, the pinned Knight must not interpose.

| 6 P–Kt6 ch | K–R3 |
| 7 Q–R8 ch | K–Kt4 |

If 7 ... KxP; 8 Q–R5 mate.

| 8 Q–R5 ch | K–B5 |
| 9 Q–B5 mate | |

White to play

96

HART-ENDERS
Match, 1936

The Rook file, which promises winning possibilities, is blocked by White's own Pawn. An abrupt sacrifice opens the file for the convenience of the Rook.

1 Q–B6 ch	K–Kt1
2 Q–Kt7 ch!	RxQ
3 Kt–B6 ch	K–R1
4 PxR ch	KxP
5 R–R7 mate	

Black to play

97

MIKENAS-ARONIN
Moscow, 1950

An original combination, where Black works up a threat which endangers White's widely-separated King and Queen.

| 1 ... | Q–Kt8 ch |
| 2 R–B1 | |

If 2 Kt–B1, Q–K5; 3 P–B3, Q–K6 ch, and White's Rook falls.

| 2 ... | QxR ch! |
| 3 KtxQ | RxP |

Threatens the King at one end of the board, with mate, and the Queen at the other end, with a discovered attack.

4	Kt–Q3	R–B8 ch
5	KtxR	BxQ

And Black wins the ending easily with his passed Pawn.

White to play

98

KASPARYAN-AMATEUR
Moscow, 1936

A splendid combination which occurred, believe-it-or-not, in a simultaneous exhibition! A remarkable concoction, it contains a Queen sacrifice, a quiet King move, and a gentle but forceful threat of mate—by a Pawn.

1	RxKt	BxR
2	Q–B4 ch	K–Kt2
3	QxB ch!	KxQ
4	Kt–K5 ch	K–B4
5	Kt–Q3 ch	K–Q5
6	K–Q2!	Q–K3
7	P–B3 mate	

White to play

99

BEYER-WADE
New Zealand, 1940

The point of the combination is the *zwischenzug* that draws Black's King into a ruinous Knight fork.

1	B–R6	B–K4
2	KtxB!	BxQ
3	KtxB ch	K–R1

Black seems reasonably safe, as after 4 KtxR, Q–K2, his Queen attacks two pieces and threatens a third, by 5 ... Q–R5 ch.

4	B–Kt7 ch!

But this in-between move changes the picture!

4	...	KxB
5	KtxR ch	K–B1
6	KtxQ	

White wins.

Black to play

100

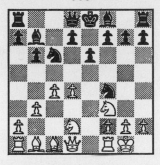

SEREDA-GAMBARASHVILLI
Tiflis, 1934

This exquisite combination is from a game almost completely unknown. For this and other happy discoveries I must thank a life-long addiction to serendipity.

| 1 | ... | KtxQP! |
| 2 | B–Kt2 | |

The Knight must not be taken. If 2 KtxKt, Q–Kt4; 3 P–Kt3, Kt–R6 mate!

| 2 | ... | Kt(Q5)–K7 ch |
| 3 | K–R1 | Q–Kt4! |

Threatens 4 ... QxP mate.

4   R–Kt1

White cannot take the Queen as after 4 KtxQ, BxP is mate.

| 4 | ... | Q–Kt5 |
| 5 | P–KR3 | Q–R4 |

Indicating that he intends to play 6 ... KtxRP (threatening 7 ... KtxP mate); 7 PxKt, QxP mate.

6	B–K4	BxB
7	KtxB	KtxRP!
8	Kt–R2	

If 8 PxKt, QxKt ch; 9 R–Kt2, QxP ch; 10 R–R2, Q–B6 ch; 11 R–Kt2, QxKt, and Black's extra Pawns guarantee the win.

Now comes a rare finish!

| 8 | ... | KtxP ch |
| 9 | KtxKt | Kt–Kt6 mate! |

White to play

101

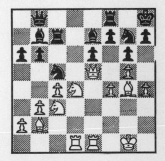

GEREBEN-TROIANESCU
Zoppot, 1951

The line-up on the long diagonal promises interesting doings. White is alert to the hidden possibilities in the position and comes through with a spectacular combination.

1   Kt–Q5!

Attacks a Rook on the Queen side, and threatens 2 QxKt ch!, KxQ; 3

Kt–B5 ch, K–Kt1; 4 Kt–R6—a beautiful mate on the King side.

1 ...   KR–B1

Gives the King a flight square and protects the Queen Rook from outright loss.

2 KtxKP

A brusque threat—3 QxKt mate.

2 ...   Kt(B4)xKt
3 BxKt

Revives the threat.

3 ...   B–B4 ch
4 K–R2   PxB
5 KtxR   RxKt

If 5 ... QxKt; 6 QxQ, RxQ; 7 R–Q8 ch, B–B1; 8 RxB mate.

6 R–Q7!

"Joli!" say Messrs. Kahn and Renaud.

6 ...   Resigns

White to play

102

TORRE-SHAPIRO
New York, 1925

Magnificent play by Torre, who produces a combination on a grand scale.

1 Kt–B6 ch!   BxKt

On 1 ... K–R1, the winning move is 2 Kt–Kt5 (threatening 3 KtxBP mate) when the capture of either Knight leads to quick mate.

2 PxB   P–Kt3
3 Q–R4   P–K4

Ready to meet 4 QxP with 4 ... QxBP.

4 PxP   BxKt

If instead 4 ... PxB, White intended the continuation 5 QxP, Kt–K3; 6 Kt–Kt5, and mate for Black is inevitable.

5 QxP!   Kt–K3
6 BxKtP!

The demolition of Black's King side is carried out inexorably.

6 ...   PxB
7 QxP ch   K–B1
8 PxB   Q–Kt2
9 P–B4   Kt–Q5

Hoping for 10 ... Kt–B6 ch, and drawing possibilities.

10 RxKt!   RxR
11 P–K6

With the evident purpose of playing 12 P–K7 ch next move, and forcing Black to give up his Queen.

11 ...   R–Q2

But not 11 ... R–K1; 12 Q–

R6 ch, K–Kt1; 13 P–B7 ch, and again Black loses his Queen.

12   R–K1!

Far stronger than 12 PxR, this faces Black with the threat of losing everything on the board by 13 P–K7 ch, RxP; 14 PxR ch, QxP; 15 RxQ, KxR; 16 Q–K4 ch, and White picks up the Rook in the corner.

12   ...   R–K1

Now comes a coup-de-grace or two.

13	QxR ch!	KxQ
14	PxR ch	K–Q1
15	R–K8 ch	KxP
16	R–K7 ch	K–B3
17	RxQ	KxR
18	P–B7	

And White wins.

Black to play

103

KOHLER-GRAF
Munich, 1934

It may be the feminine touch, but

Miss Sonia Graf dispatches her opponent with casual grace and polish.

1	...	Kt–Q4!
2	PxKt	

The alternative capture 2 KtxKt leads to immediate loss for White after 2 ... RxKtP when he must give up his Queen or be mated.

2	...	RxKt ch!
3	PxR	QxKP ch
4	K–Q1	

On 4 K-B1, RxP wins at once.

4	...	RxP
5	R–K1	

Now comes a neat version of the epaulette mate.

5	...	Q–Q7 ch!
6	QxQ	RxQ mate

Black to play

104

AMATEUR-TARTAKOVER
Paris, 1933

With four Queens on the board, the game should end in mate. And so it does, but none of the Queens does the mating!

| 1 | ... | Q–Q5 ch |
| 2 | K–Kt3 | |

Clearly if 2 K–K2, Q(Kt8)–Q8 is mate.

2	...	Q–Kt3 ch
3	Q–Kt4	Q(Kt3)xQ ch
4	PxQ	Q–K6 ch
5	K–R4	P–Kt4 ch
6	K–R5	

What a life for a King!

| 6 | ... | Q–K3 |
| 7 | Q–B5 ch | |

Does this win for White?

| 7 | ... | Q–Kt3 ch! |

Not at all!

| 8 | QxQ ch | PxQ mate! |

White to play

105

FOX-CASPER

Fox wins the game by a brilliant combination. Strangely enough (and this must have been disheartening) he could have forced mate by a couple of simple, prosaic moves. Herewith the two winning methods:

| 1 | B–Kt6! | QxB |

The capture is compulsory. If the Queen moves, say to Kt2 or Q2, then 2 BxKt, BxB; 3 KtxQP attacking the Rook and the King Bishop Pawn wins immediately.

| 2 | Q–Kt6! |

What a move!

2	...	RPxQ
3	Kt–K7 ch	K–R2
4	R–B3	Q–B4

In order to meet 5 R–R3 ch with 5 ... Q–R4, which returns the Queen but leaves Black with a won game.

| 5 | R–Q5! | Resigns |

After 5 ... QxR; 6 BxQ, mate by 7 R–R3 can no longer be delayed.

The sad part is that White could have spared himself the thought that went into working out the combination, beautiful though it is, and played instead:

1	Q–Kt5	P–Kt3
2	Q–R6	PxKt
3	B–Q4	

And White mates next move.

White to play

106

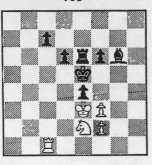

KAKOVIN

The discovery of this beautiful ending, more than anything else, influenced me to make a collection of remarkable endgame compositions. Part of this gallimaufry of strange and wonderful combination play has been published under the title of CHESSBOARD MAGIC!

From Kakovin's specimen you can see how this aspect of chess can hold you spellbound, to the detriment of your study of the Queen's Gambit Declined.

1	P–B4 ch	K–Q4

The alternative 1 ... K–B4 costs a whole Rook after 2 Kt–Q4 ch.

2	P–B5!	BxP
3	Kt–B4 ch	K–K4
4	R–Q1	

Threatens 5 R–Q5 mate.

4	...	P–B3

The only move to prevent instant mate.

5	R–Q5 ch!	

White gives check, anyway!

5	...	PxR
6	Kt–Q3 ch!	

Now he gives up the Knight!

6	...	PxKt
7	P–B4 mate!	

"Very pretty," you say, "but these things are artificial. They do not happen in actual play."

So here is a combination from a tournament game, whose finish bears a remarkable resemblance to the composed ending:

White to play

107

HROMADKA-OPOCENSKY
Kaschau, 1931

1	RxB ch!	PxR
2	Kt–Q3 ch!	PxKt
3	P–B4 mate!	

And if perchance, there are still some skeptics, here is the score of the entire game:

1	P–Q4	P–KB4	
2	P–K4	PxP	
3	Kt–QB3	Kt–KB3	
4	B–Kt5	Kt–B3	
5	B–Kt5	P–Q4	
6	BxKKt	KPxB	
7	Q–R5 ch	P–Kt3	
8	QxQP	B–QKt5	
9	Q–B4	BxKt ch	
10	PxB	B–Q2	
11	Kt–K2	P–QR3	
12	BxKt	BxB	
13	Q–K6 ch	Q–K2	
14	QxQ ch	KxQ	
15	K–Q2	P–QKt4	
16	P–KR4	K–Q3	
17	Kt–B4	QR–KB1	
18	K–K3	R–B2	
19	P–QR4	KR–KB1	
20	P–Q5!	BxP	
21	PxP	PxP	
22	KR–Q1	P–B3	
23	R–R6	K–K4	

On 23 ... K–B4, White ends it neatly by 24 RxB ch!, PxR; 25 Kt–K6 ch, K–B5; 26 R–B6 mate.

24 P–Kt4

Apparently intending 25 RxB ch, PxR; 26 R–K6 mate.

24 ... R–K1

Black parries the threat that he sees, but does not suspect that there may be a more subtle one.

Now we have the position in the diagram above, when Hromadka wound up the game in problem-like style.

25	RxB ch!	PxR
26	Kt–Q3 ch!	PxKt
27	P–B4 mate!	

White to play

108

CHRISTOFFEL-STAEHELIN
Zurich, 1952

In the art of combination play, the moderns are as ingenious as the old-timers. In this interesting example, White manipulates his pieces cleverly to assure the promotion of his Queen's Pawn.

1 Kt–K4

Protects the valuable Pawn, and is ready to continue with 2 B–Kt5, or perhaps 2 B–Kt6 and 3 B–B7.

1	...	RxR
2	RxR	R–QB1

Disputes the file, and prevents White from dominating the seventh rank by 3 R–B7. Further attack on the Pawn instead, by 2 ... B–B1, would cost the Queen after White's response 3 Kt–B6 ch.

3 R–B3!

Good position judgment. White intends to double on the file, and force his way into QB7.

3 ... P–B3

4	Q–B1	RxR
5	QxR	K–B2
6	Q–B7	

To evict the blockader. If Black now plays 6 ... QxQ, the continuation 7 PxQ, B–Q2; 8 BxKt, PxB; 9 P–B8(Q), BxQ; 10 Kt–Q6 ch wins a piece for White.

| 6 | ... | K–K1 |
| 7 | B–R6! | |

Sehr schön! Black cannot capture by 7 ... BxB, on account of the Knight fork 8 KtxP ch, nor with his Knight, since that exposes his Queen. Meanwhile, White threatens 8 BxB, QxB; 9 BxKt, winning easily.

| 7 | ... | QxQ |
| 8 | PxQ | B–Q2 |

Clearly if 8 ... K–Q2; 9 BxB leaves the pinned Knight unable to recapture.

| 9 | BxB | KtxB |
| 10 | P–B8(Q) ch | Resigns |

Black must give up his Bishop for the Queen.

White sacrifices his Queen. In return he gets only one little Pawn. But there are other than material considerations, such as the opportunity he has for giving three resounding double checks in succession.

| 1 | KtxP! | KxKt |
| 2 | P–Q5 | |

Attacks the Bishop while uncovering another attack on the Knight, which is now pinned.

2	...	B–Kt5
3	RxKt!	BxQ
4	R–Kt6 ch	K–R2
5	R–Kt7 ch	K–R1
6	R–R7 ch	K–Kt1
7	R–R8 mate	

White to play

110

BLACKBURNE-AMATEUR

How far ahead did Blackburne's calculations go in this combination? When he sacrificed a couple of exchanges at the beginning, did he

White to play

109

PLACE-AMATEUR
Paris, 1922

foresee the double self-block of the King at the finish?

| 1 | B–K8 | B–K3 |
| 2 | RxKt | PxR |

Definitely not 2 ... RxB; 3 R–B7 double check and mate, nor 2 ... PxB; 3 R–Q7 ch, KxR; 4 Q–Kt6 mate.

3	R–Q7 ch	BxR
4	Q–B7 ch	K–Q3
5	QxB(Q7) ch	K–B4
6	B–K3 ch	K–Kt5
7	QxP ch	K–R4
8	P–Kt4 ch!	BxP
9	B–Kt6 ch	PxB
10	QxR mate!	

Very nice! The blocking of two of the King's flight squares by sacrifices is rarely seen in practical play.

White to play

111

RAGOZIN-ROMANOVSKY
Leningrad, 1932

Even in the ending, with very few pieces on the board, there are all sorts of engaging finesses. Black's Rook is seduced from the pursuit of an attractive passed Pawn by a cute little trick.

| 1 | R–K7 | R–Q3 |

Forced, in view of White's threat of 2 RxKP, pinning and winning the Knight.

| 2 | RxKtP | Kt–Q2 |
| 3 | R–B7 | |

Vacates the file so that the passed Pawn can march up.

| 3 | ... | P–K4 |

Black must not capture the Pawn, as 3 ... KtxP is punished by 4 R–Kt7—instant mate.

| 4 | P–Kt7 | |

White intends to continue with 5 RxKt (eliminating the obstacle to the Pawn's promotion) RxR; 6 P–Kt8(Q).

4	...	PxB
5	RxKt	R–Kt3
6	R–Q6 ch!	

The last trump trick. White forces Black to capture, and then Queens his Pawn.

| ' 6 | ... | Resigns |

Black to play

112

HALLER-POLLOCK
St. Louis, 1890

"A charming termination to a beautifully played game," says Steinitz of this combination.

1 ...   KtxP
2 RxP

Capturing the Knight is quick suicide, as after 2 KxKt, Q–Q6 ch; 3 K–Q1, BxP is mate.

2 ...   K–Kt1
3 Kt–K5   Q–Kt4
4 Kt–QB3

Sets a fine trap, as Pollock himself points out. If Black plays the natural 4 ... QxP (threatening 5 ... Kt–Q5 mate) then 5 Kt–B6 ch, K–B1 (5 ... PxKt; 6 QxP mate); 6 R–R8 ch, K–Q2; 7 RxR ch, KxKt; 8 Q–K4 ch, followed by 9 QxKt wins for White.

4 ...   BxP!
5 B–Kt2

In order to give his King some room. White naturally avoids 5 KtxQ,

the response to which is 5 ... Kt–Q5 mate!

5 ...   Kt–Kt5 ch
6 K–B1   QxKt!
7 Resigns

After 7 QxQ (or 7 RxQ), Kt–Q6 ch followed by 8 ... KtxQ wins a piece and the game.

White to play

113

EUWE-FISCHER
New York, 1957

A combination especially interesting in view of the circumstances. A former Champion of the World faces the newest of the child prodigies. This time the irresistible force shatters the immovable body.

1 BxKt!

Euwe is not interested in keeping the two Bishops. He destroys the King Knight, the best defender of the King side.

1 ...   BxB
2 Q–Q3   KR–Q1

Gives the King room while protecting the Queen Pawn. If instead 2 ... KR–K1, then 3 Q–R7 ch, K–B1; 4 Kt(B3)xP, BxKt; 5 KtxB, and Black is threatened with mate on the move as well as loss of the Queen. The alternative defense 2 ... P–Kt3 succumbs to 3 KtxKtP!, PxKt (or 3 ... Kt–Kt5; 4 Kt–K7 ch and mate next move); 4 QxP ch, B–Kt2; 5 QxB(K6) ch, and White wins.

3 **QR–K1**   **Kt–Kt5**

Black has little hope of exchanging his Knight for White's dangerous Bishop, but he must give his Queen Pawn additional protection.

Two plausible alternatives were:
(a) 3 ... P–Kt3; 4 RxB, PxR; 5 QxP ch, B–Kt2; 6 QxP ch, K–R1; 7 Kt–Kt6 ch, K–R2; 8 Kt–K5 ch, K–R1; 9 Kt–B7 ch, K–Kt1; 10 KtxRP ch, K–R1; 11 Q–Kt8 ch!, RxQ; 12 Kt–B7 mate.
(b) 3 ... Kt–K2; 4 Q–R7 ch, K–B1; 5 Q–R8 ch, Kt–Kt1; 6 B–R7, K–K2; 7 Kt(B3)xP ch, RxKt; 8 KtxP ch, and White wins the Queen.

4 **Q–R7 ch**   **K–B1**
5 **P–QR3!**

It is important that the Knight be forced away from guarding the Queen Pawn.

5 **...**   **KtxB**
6 **Kt(B3)xP!**   **RxKt**
7 **KtxR**

Black's Queen is attacked, and immediate mate threatens his King. There is no defense: if 7 ... BxKt; 8 Q–R8 is mate, since control

of the King file prevents Black's King from escaping.

7 **...**   Resigns

Black to play

114

BARDA-KELLER
Moscow, 1956

Black has a grip on the adverse King side position, but how he will break through is not evident. But he does, and by means of a charming and original combination.

1 **...**   **QR–K1**
2 **B–B4 ch**   **K–R1**
3 **QxKtP**   **RxB!**
4 **PxR**   **B–B4!**

A quiet move, but a deadly one.

5 **Q–Q5**

White could not play 5 QxKt, the reply 5 ... B–K5 costing his Queen. The text move attempts to pin the Bishop, and prevent it from reaching K5. But Black has a beautiful hidden threat, which he proceeds to carry out.

5 **...**   **Q–Kt5 ch**
6 **K–B1**   **Q–R6 ch!**
7 **RxQ**   BxR mate!

5

COMBINATIONS IN THE NOTES

Combinations have always been the most intriguing aspect of chess. The master looks for them, the public applauds them, the critics praise them. It is because combinations are possible that chess is more than a lifeless mathematical exercise. They are the poetry of the game; they are to chess what melody is to music. They represent the triumph of mind over matter.

—Reuben Fine

White to play

115

TARRASCH-ALEKHINE
Pistyan, 1922

White is threatened with loss by 1 ... BxRP followed by 2 ... QxP mate. To meet this threat he played 1 K–R1. Against the alternative defense 1 Q–B6, Alekhine had prepared the following spectacular win:

1 Q–B6

Ready to parry 1 ... BxRP with 2 QxKP, which regains the Pawn and defends the critical square KKt2.

1	...	R–B6!
2	QxKP	B–Q4
3	Q–QR4	QxKtP ch!
4	KxQ	

A sacrifice which brooks no refusal. Now come three stunning double checks in succession to get the King into position for checkmate.

4	...	R–Kt6 ch
5	K–R2	R–Kt7 ch
6	K–R1	R–R7 ch
7	K–Kt1	R–R8 mate

59

Black to play

116

CAPABLANCA-SCHROEDER
New York, 1916

Black played 1 ... P–B4 and lost quickly. The move expected by Capablanca was 1 ... R–B2, against which he had planned the following superb combination:

1 ...	R–B2
2 P–R5	R(K1)–QB1
3 P–R6	B–Q3

The only way Black can free his pieces.

| 4 QxQ ch | KxQ |
| 5 RxR | RxR |

If 5 ... BxR; 6 R–B6 immobilizes Black completely!

| 6 RxR | BxR |
| 7 P–B4 | |

To keep the Bishop off the long diagonal.

7 ...	B–Q1
8 P–Kt4	B–B3
9 P–Kt5	B–R1
10 P–K4	K–Kt3

11 P–B5	PxP
12 PxP	K–B4
13 P–Kt6	PxP
14 PxP	K–Q3
15 P–Kt7 and wins	

Capablanca was awarded a brilliancy prize for this game.

White to play

117

RÉTI-TARTAKOVER
New York, 1924

After White's first move 1 Q–B3, it seems as though he must lose a Pawn by a combination he has overlooked. After the reply 1 ... KtxP, if he captures by 2 KtxKt, Q–Kt3 ch catches the unprotected Rook, and if he captures by 2 QxKt ch, K–R2 pins his Queen.

Actually, after 1 Q–B3, KtxP loses by a subtle counter-combination:

1 Q–B3	KtxP
2 R–Q6!	QxR
3 QxKt ch	K–R2
4 QxR ch	

Breaks out of the pin by force.

4	...	KxQ
5	Kt–B5 ch	K–B3
6	KtxQ and wins	

5	QxP ch	K–R1
6	B–B2	R–B4
7	R–Q3	

White wins.

Black to play

118

ALEKHINE-SELESNIEV
Pistyan, 1922

White to play

119

JOHNER-NIMZOVICH
Dresden, 1926

White's threat is 1 KtxBP followed by 2 RxP. Black defended against this by 1 ... B–B1, guarding the King Pawn. Had he played 1 ... B–Kt2 instead, in order to challenge White's Bishop at Q4, then the following combination would have occurred:

| 1 | ... | B–Kt2 |
| ◄2 | Q–Q3 | |

Gains time by the attack on the unprotected Queen Knight Pawn.

2	...	P–QR3
3	KtxKtP!	RPxKt
4	RxP!	PxR

If 4 ... Q–B2; 5 RxP ch, K–R1 (on 5 ... K–R2, White wins the Queen by discovered check); 6 R–R6 ch, K–Kt1; 7 Q–Kt6 mate.

White's actual move was 1 R–K2. Against an attempt to defend the King Knight Pawn by 1 B–Q2 and 2 B–K1, Nimzovich had prepared a profound combination:

1	B–Q2	R–Kt3!
2	B–K1	Kt–Kt5 ch!
3	PxKt	

If 3 K–Kt2, BxP; 4 QxB, Kt(Kt5)–K6 ch; 5 KtxKt, KtxKt ch, and Black wins the Queen.

3	...	PxP ch
4	K–Kt2	BxP
5	QxB	P–K6!

Threatens 6 Q–R6 mate, and there is only one move to prevent it.

| 6 | KtxP | |

The one move to save the King loses the Queen.

| 6 | QxKt | RxR ch |
| 7 | Q–B1 | R(Q1)–Q8 |

6 ...   KtxKt ch

Black wins.

Black wins the Queen.

White to play

121

White to play

120

MARSHALL-LASKER
Moscow, 1925

RAUZER-BOTVINNIK
U.S.S.R. 1931

Marshall's move was 1 P–KR3, to give his King some air. The tempting 1 Kt–K5 instead, would have led to catastrophe on the first rank, thus:

1	Kt–K5	QxR!
2	RxQ	Kt–Kt4
3	Q–Kt4	

The Queen must stay on the diagonal leading to K1.

3	...	R–Q8 ch
4	R–K1	P–QB4
5	Q–R5	P–QKt3

Making it impossible for the Queen to stay in touch with the Rook.

White's actual move was 1 RxKt, giving up the exchange, seemingly in desperation. Against the natural 1 K–Kt1 instead, Botvinnik had a winning line prepared, with a fine assortment of Knight forks, so:

| 1 | K–Kt1 | Kt–Kt5! |

Threatens mate.

| 2 | R–B3 | |

If 2 R–B1, Q–R7 ch; 3 K–B1, Kt–K6 ch wins the Queen.

| 2 | ... | Q–K8 ch |
| 3 | Q–B1 | |

On 3 R–B1, Q–K6 ch; 4 K–R1, Q–Kt6 forces mate at R7.

| 3 | ... | QxQ ch |
| 4 | RxQ | |

If 4 KxQ, Kt–R7 ch wins the exchange and the consequent ending
is easy.

4 ...   **Kt–K6!**

And White must lose the exchange
to save his Bishop.

Black to play

122

MAROCZY-MIESES
Teplitz-Schonau, 1922

Mieses played 1 ... R–B1, trying for a counter-attack. Had he
taken the Rook, the consequences
would have been as follows:

1 ...   **BxR**
2 **QxB**   **R–R3**

To prevent a deadly check by the
Bishop.

3 **P–K6!**   **R–Q1**

Or 3 ... Q–R6 ch; 4 B–Kt2,
QxKP; 5 QxQ, RxQ; 6 B–R3, K–B2;
7 BxR ch, KxB; 8 BxP, and the King
side Pawns decide the game.

4 **Q–KB5**   **Q–R6 ch**

5 **QxQ**   **RxQ**
6 **BxP**

Threatens mate!

6 ...   **R–Q3**
7 **K–Kt2!**

And wins the Rook, which has no
flight square.

White to play

123

BOLESLAVSKY-BISGUIER
Finland, 1952

White moved 1 Q–B7 and eventually won. Had he played 1 QxP
instead, to allow a pin and then
break it with a counter-pin, he would
have been trapped by a counter-
counter-pin!

Expressed more simply in chess
language, this is what would have
happened:

1 **QxP**   **R–KKt1**
2 **R–Q8**

Pins the Rook which pins his
Queen, and threatens 3 Q–Kt7 mate.

2 ...   Q–Kt8 ch!

There is no answer to this. White's pinned Queen may not capture, and after 3 K–Kt2, QxQ ch followed by 4 ... RxR does away with the white army.

Black to play

124

MARSHALL-JANOWSKY
Marienbad, 1925

Marshall's traps were subtle. Who would suspect that capturing the Queen Pawn (a move Janowsky shunned) could start a combination rolling which ends in a discovered check on the last rank?

1	...	QxQP
2	QR–Q1	Q–B4
3	Kt–Q3	Q–B6
4	KtxKt	BxKt
5	QxQ	BxQ
6	BxR	BxR
7	R–Q8	BxRP
8	R–R8	

Threatens mate. If Black replies

8 ... P–R3; 9 B–Kt4 ch wins the Bishop.

8 ...   B–B2

The Bishop is ready to interpose on a discovered check—but it's too late.

9	B–Q6 ch	B–Kt1
10	RxB ch	

White wins.

Black to play

125

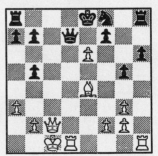

SPIELMANN-CAPABLANCA
Carlsbad, 1929

Capablanca's actual move was 1 ... Q–B1. Capturing by 1 ... QxP instead looks promising, since it gains a Pawn, and threatens to pin the Queen by 2 ... R–B1. The consequences would have been:

1	...	QxP
2	KR–K1!	R–B1
3	QxR ch!	QxQ ch
4	B–B6 dble. ch and mate!	

Black to play

126

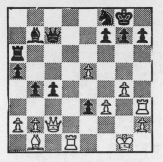

VIDMAR-TEICHMANN
Carlsbad, 1907

Black seems to have good winning chances with 1 ... QxP. If
then 2 QxBP, R–Q3; 3 R–K1 (or 3
RxR, P–K7); R–Q7, with a strong
attack. The threat is 4 ... BxP,
and a plausible continuation might
be 4 B–K4, R–Q5; 5 Q–K2, RxB;
6 PxR, QxKP; 7 RxKP, Q–R8 ch; 8
K–Kt2, Q–Kt7 mate.

All this is Tarrasch's suggestion,
but Marco quashes it completely.
This (he shows) is what really
would have happened to Teichmann:

1	...	QxP
2	QxRP ch!	KtxQ
3	R–Q8 ch	Kt–B1
4	R–R8 ch!	KxR
5	RxKt mate	

Black to play

127

ALEKHINE-POMAR
Gijon, 1944

Boy wonders are usually cautious
beyond their years. Thirteen year old
Pomar resists the impulse to capture
a fine-looking center Pawn, visualiz-
ing the following retaliatory combination by his opponent, the mighty
Alekhine:

| 1 | ... | BxP |

Black's actual move was 1 ...
Kt–Q2, and eventually he drew the
game.

| 2 | KtxB | KtxKt |
| 3 | Kt–B5 | |

Of course not 3 BxKt, BxKt, and
Black is a Pawn up.

| 3 | ... | Kt–KB3 |

On 3 ... Kt–Kt4; 4 KtxB ch,
RxB (4 ... QxKt unguards the
Queen Knight); 5 BxKt, and White
wins a piece.

| 4 | P–Kt5 | Kt–Q2 |
| 5 | Q–Q3 | |

Threatens 6 KtxB ch, RxKt; 7 QxRP ch, K–B1; 8 Q–R8 mate.

5	...	P–Kt3
6	KtxB ch	RxKt
7	QxQKtP	R–R1
8	P–Kt4	

White wins the Knight, which has no square of escape.

Black to play

128

SCHLECHTER-PERLIS
Carlsbad, 1911

Black is two Pawns behind. In the actual game he played 1 ... KtxP, regaining one of his Pawns. Suppose he had tried 1 ... B–K5 instead? He could then meet 2 PxP with 2 ... BxP, or 2 ... P–B7 with 2 ... Kt–QB3.

Here is how Schlechter would have trapped him:

1	...	B–K5
2	RxP!	RxR
3	P–B7!	

And wins. Black cannot parry the

two threats 4 PxKt(Q) ch and 4 P–B8(Q) ch, simultaneously.

White to play

129

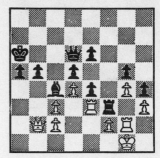

RABINOVICH-BOTVINNIK
U.S.S.R. 1939

In the actual game White played 1 K–R1. The natural desire in such cramped positions is to ease the pressure by exchanging some pieces. Had White tried that, starting with 1 RxR, the following would have occurred:

1	RxR	PxR
2	R–R2	P–R5
3	Q–Kt4	QxQ
4	PxQ	B–B8!
5	R–R1	

If 5 KxB, P–R6 wins at once.

| 5 | ... | B–Kt7 |
| 6 | R–R2 | P–R6 |

Black wins. White cannot extricate his King and Rook from their sad predicament.

Black to play   *Black to play*

130

PANOV-BOTVINNIK
U.S.S.R. 1940

131

SMYSLOV-BOTVINNIK
U.S.S.R. 1941

Black who is in check, has three moves at his disposal. He chose 1 ... K–K2! Obviously, taking the Rook would allow 2 Kt–K6 ch in reply followed by 3 KtxQ. But suppose Black had played 1 ... K–Kt3? The continuation:

1	...	K–Kt3
2	R–Kt1 ch	K–R4
3	QxR!	KtxQ
4	R–B5 ch	K–R3
5	R–B6 ch!	PxR

On 5 ... P–Kt3, White plays 6 Kt–B5 ch, as in the text.

6	Kt–B5 ch	K–R4
7	Kt–Kt7 ch	K–R3
8	Kt–B5 ch	

And White draws by perpetual check.

The natural move is 1 ... P–B7, and the three connected passed Pawns on the seventh rank look irresistible. Botvinnik restrained himself, and chose the modest move 1 ... R–B2. Here is what Smyslov had prepared against 1 ... P–B7:

1	...	P–B7
2	R–B7 ch	K–R1
3	R–B6	K–R2

Or 3 ... R–B2 (to interpose the Rook in reply to a check at R6); 4 R–R6 ch, R–R2; 5 P–R7, and White wins!

| 4 | R–B7 ch | K–R1 |

Not 4 ... K–R3; 5 R–Kt6 mate.

| 5 | R–B6 | |

White draws by repetition of moves.

Black to play   *Black to play*

132

133

ALATORSEV-RIUMIN
Moscow, 1935

SMYSLOV-EUWE
Moscow, 1948

Black's actual move was 1 ...
R–Q2. The alternative 1 ... K–
Kt1 would enable White to play a
combination whereby he sacrifices
his Queen at one end of the board
in order to win a piece at the other
end!

1	...	K–Kt1
2	Kt–QR5	K–R1
3	R–Kt3	R–QKt1

On 3 ... R–Q2; 4 KtxP wins a
Pawn.

4	QxKt ch!	PxQ
5	RxR ch	KxR
6	Kt–B6 ch	K–B2
7	KtxQ	BxKt
8	BxKt	

White wins.

Euwe played 1 ... Q–Kt2 at
this point. Had he tried to drive off
White's Queen instead by 1 ...
Q–K3, this would have taken place:

1	...	Q–K3
2	RxP!	QxQ
3	RxR ch	Kt–B1
4	RxKt ch	K–K2
5	R–B7 ch	K–K3

On 5 ... K–K1; 6 B–Kt5, P–
B3; 7 PxP, and White wins easily.

6	RxQBP ch!	QxR
7	Kt–Q4 ch	K–Q4
8	KtxQ	KxKt
9	R–Q8	

White wins.

Black to play   *Black to play*

134   **135**

BOLESLAVSKY-KASPARYAN
U.S.S.R. 1954

ALEKHINE-ROSSELLI
Zurich, 1934

Black played 1 ... P–K5 to save himself from loss by 2 BxP, QxB; 3 QxQ, KtxQ; 4 RxB mate.

Had he moved 1 ... K–B2 instead, the following would have been Boleslavsky's winning combination:

1 ...	K–B2
2 BxP	KtxB

On 2 ... QxB; 3 RxB ch, KxR; 4 QxQ ch, and the pinned Knight is helpless to recapture the Queen.

3 RxB ch	K–Kt3
4 B–B1	

White continues by 5 P–Kt4, and wins the pinned Knight.

Rosselli played 1 ... BxKt at this point. Had he tried to win the Bishop Pawn instead, it would have cost a piece, or if he were stubborn, his Queen.

1 ...	PxBP
2 PxBP	BxP ch
3 RxB!	RxR
4 P–Kt5	

Black must give up the Knight. If he moves it away, say to Q2, 5 Kt–B6 ch wins his Queen by discovered attack.

White to play

136

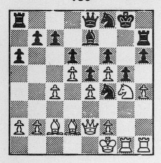

ALEKHINE-JOHNER
Zurich, 1934

Black has just played Kt–B5, threatening the Queen. It is White's move:

1   Q–B3!

Apparently a routine move, to escape the Knight's attack.

Alekhine points out that White is actually planning a Queen sacrifice leading to mate, thus:

2	BxKt	KPxB
3	QxP!	KtPxQ
4	KtxRP ch	K–R1
5	R–Kt8 mate	

This explains why Johner replied 1 ... K–Kt2, the kind of move that often looks meaningless at first glance.

Black to play

137

BOTVINNIK-SMYSLOV
Match, 1954

White has just played 1 R–Kt8 pinning the Knight. Smyslov's reply to this was 1 ... K–Q1. The natural move 1 ... K–Q2, to free himself from the pin would have led to loss as follows:

1	...	K–Q2
2	Kt(B4)–K5 ch	PxKt
3	KtxP ch	K–Q1 (or Q3)
4	Kt–B7 ch	K–Q2
5	KtxR	

And White has won the exchange.

White to play

138

JOHNER-NIMZOVICH
Dresden, 1926

White's actual move was 1 R–K3. The natural 1 Kt–Q2, to attack the King Pawn a third time, would have involved him in the following:

1	Kt–Q2	B–B1!
2	KtxP	Q–B4
3	Kt–B2	QxRP ch!
4	KtxQ	Kt–Kt5 mate!

Black to play

139

Buenos Aires, 1911

Black's actual move was 1 ... P–QR3. He resisted the temptation to seize the outpost K5 with his Knight. Against this aggressive move Capablanca had planned to continue thus:

| 1 | ... | Kt–K5 |
| 2 | PxP | BxBP |

If 2 ... KtxP(B4); 3 BxP ch, KxB; 4 Q–R5 ch, K–Kt1; 5 Kt–Kt5, and Black will be mated.

| 3 | P–QKt4 | B–Kt3 |

On 3 ... B–Q3; 4 BxKt, PxB (or 4 ... BxKt; 5 BxP ch, KxB; 6 Q–R5 ch, K–R1; 7 Kt–Kt5 and

White wins); 5 QxB wins a piece for White.

4	P–Kt5	B–Q2
5	BxKt	PxB
6	QxB	

White has won a piece.

White to play

140

London, 1922

White's move at this point was 1 B–Q2. Accepting the offer of the Bishop instead would have led to a beautiful loss by this profound combination:

1	PxB	Kt–B5
2	Q–K3	KtxP
3	Q–Kt5	

Clearly not 3 KxKt, Q–Kt5 ch; 4 K–R1, BxKt ch, and White loses his Queen, and shortly thereafter his King.

3	...	QxQ
4	KtxQ	Kt–B5
5	PxKKtP	

Or 5 P–B7 ch, RxP; 6 KtxR, Kt–R6 mate.

5 . . .	R–B3
6 B–Kt5	Kt–R6 ch!

Much faster than Tartakover's recommendation 6 . . . R–Kt3.

| 7 KtxKt | R–Kt3 ch |
| 8 Kt–Kt5 | RxKt mate! |

Black to play

141

EUWE-ALEKHINE
Match, 1937

Black can capture the Bishop with check. But which way shall he take? Capturing with the Queen looks plausible as he can pin the Rook next move. Here is what would happen, though:

| 1 . . . | QxB ch |
| 2 K–R2 | R–Kt7 |

Looks good, but White turns the tables (as the Victorian novelists used to say) with:

3 Q–K5!

White wins! The threats of 4 QxP mate and 4 QxR mate cannot both be parried.

(Alekhine's actual move was 1 . . . RxB ch, which regained the piece, won the game, the match and the Championship of the World.)

Black to play

142

EUWE-SMYSLOV
Moscow, 1948

Black, who has lost a Pawn, moved 1 . . . Kt–K2. Had he tried to equalize by capturing the Queen Knight Pawn, the game would have gone as follows:

1 . . .	QxQKtP
2 QxKt(B8)	RxQ
3 RxR ch	B–B1
4 B–R6	Q–Kt1
5 RxB ch	QxR
6 BxQ	KxB

White has gained a piece, and wins.

Black to play

143

KERES-SMYSLOV
Leningrad-Moscow, 1937

White's last move was 1 B–B5, with the remarkable threat of 2 B–K6 followed by 3 QxKtP ch. Smyslov's reply was 1 ... PxP. Had he taken the Bishop, this is what would have happened:

1 ...　　　　　　　PxB
2 KtxP(B5)　　　Q–B2

If 2 ... Q–Kt3; 3 Kt–K7 ch wins the Queen, or if 2 ... Q–KB3; 3 Kt–K7 ch, and mate comes next move at R7.

3 Kt–K7 ch　　　K–Kt2
4 Q–R7 ch　　　K–B3
5 Kt–Kt8 ch!　　RxKt
6 QxBP mate

Black to play

144

ANDERSSEN-MORPHY
Paris, 1858

Anderssen has captured a piece, and Morphy must recapture. Which Knight shall he take? Off-hand, 1 ... QxKt(K4) is not inviting, since 2 KtxKt ch, QxKt; 3 Q–R7 ch allows White to invade Black's King side position. Nevertheless, Morphy

took the Knight at K4. The capture of the other Knight would have plunged him into one of the deep Anderssen traps:

1 ...　　　　　　　QxKt(Q4)
2 Kt–B6　　　　　R–K5

The only way to protect the Bishop.

3 RxB!　　　　　RxR
4 Kt–K7 ch

White wins the Queen.

White to play

145

RESHEVSKY-BRONSTEIN
Zurich, 1953

Reshevsky played 1 Q–Kt4. It must have been hard to resist taking a Pawn with check instead, but Sammy must have seen the sequel:

1 QxP ch　　　　K–Q1
2 Q–R8 ch　　　K–B2
3 Q–R5 ch

Once you start checking it's hard to stop.

3 ...　　　　　　　B–Kt3

And White must give up his
Queen or be mated.

White to play

146

ALEKHINE-WEST
ALEKHINE-WEST
Portsmouth, 1923

The conscientious master wants to
win logically, in the quickest way
possible. Accuracy must not be sacrificed for the sake of brilliancy.

In this position, for example, Alekhine won quickly by 1 BxKt, KPxB;
2 Kt–B6 ch, and Black resigned,
since 2 ... K–B2 allows White
to mate in three beginning with 3
RxP ch, while 2 ... K–B1 is
hopeless after 3 Q–R7.

This is how Alekhine would have
preferred to win:

| 1 | B–Q1 | Kt–Kt5 |

This move, though plausible, is
not forced, which is why Alekhine
did not go in for the combination.

2	Q–R7 ch!	KxQ
3	RxP ch!	RxR
4	Kt–B6 ch	K–Kt3
5	B–R5 mate!	

Black to play

147

SZABO-BOLESLAVSKY
Zurich, 1953

Players sometimes abandon a
game when there are still opportunities for fascinating combinative play.
In this position, as a case in point,
the annotator of the tournament
book, Bronstein, shows this fine combination Black might have tried to
realize before consenting to a draw:

1	...	R–K1
2	Q–Q2	Kt–K5
3	QxP	

The losing move, but a tempting
one to make.

| 3 | ... | KtxKBP! |
| 4 | QxQ | |

Clearly, if 4 KtxKt, QxQ; 5 RxQ,
R–K8 mate.

| 4 | ... | KtxR ch |
| 5 | K–B1 | |

If 5 QxB, R–K8 mate!

| 5 | ... | Kt–K6 ch |
| 6 | K–Kt1 | |

On 6 K–K2, Kt–B4 ch discovers
an attack on the Queen.

6 ...	Kt–B4 ch

Black wins the Queen and the game.

Black to play

148

ALEKHINE-RESHEVSKY
Avro, 1938

Reshevsky moved 1 ... K–Kt2 at this point and eventually got into a losing position.

At the conclusion of the game, Reshevsky demonstrated an ingenious line he could have played, which draws by perpetual check, or forces a win if the opponent insists on making another Queen.

1 ...	KtxKt!
2 PxKt	Q–Q5!
3 Q–K8 ch	K–Kt2
4 P–Q7	Q–Q7 ch
5 K–R3	Q–Q6!

White's King must now return to Kt2 and allow a perpetual check. Promoting to a Queen instead offers Black an opportunity for a pretty win:

6 P–Q8(Q)	Q–B8 ch
7 K–R4	P–Kt4 ch
8 QxP ch	

Or 8 K–R5, Q–R6 mate.

8 ...	PxQ ch
9 K–R5	

On 9 KxP, Q–B3 ch; 10 K–R5, Q–R3 is mate.

9 ...	Q–B3!

And White will be mated.

White to play

149

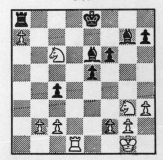

YATES-SULTAN KHAN
Hastings, 1932

The wins that are missed in practical play often turn up in the notes to the games. The sparkling combinations that might have won are not lost to us forever. We can still enjoy them in the annotations of competent critics.

It was White's turn to move, and bothered somewhat by time-pressure, he played 1 Kt–K4. The win he missed runs as follows:

1 R–Q8 ch!

Intending to exchange Rooks, and rid the board of the piece that blockades his passed Pawn.

| 1 | ... | RxR |
| 2 | KtxR | |

Black has no time to take the Knight, now that the passed Pawn is free to move on.

| 2 | ... | B–Q4 |

Saves the Bishop and keeps the Pawn under surveillance.

3 Kt–K6!

Attacks one Bishop and threatens the other—by 4 Kt–B7 ch.

3	...	K–B2
4	Kt–B7	B–B3
5	P–R8(Q)	

And wins, since Black must give up a piece for the Queen.

White to play

150

GELLER-NAJDORF
Zurich, 1953

White's actual move was 1 K–Q3. He could have won quickly by this line of play:

1	PxP ch	KxP
2	PxB!	RxR
3	P–B6	R–Kt1
4	P–B7	R–QR1
5	P–B8(Q)	RxQ
6	Kt–K7 ch and wins	

White to play

151

CAPABLANCA-BOGOLYUBOV
Moscow, 1925

Rarely did Capablanca miss the quickest way to win, no matter how complicated the position. At the conclusion of his game with Bogolyubov, Capablanca pointed out this magnificent combination which could have ended their exciting struggle in a blaze of glory:

| 1 | R–R3 ch | K–Kt5 |
| 2 | K–Kt2! | KtxP |

The alternative is 2 ... Kt–B4; 3 Kt–R6 ch, RxKt; 4 RxR, Kt(B4)xP; 5 KtxKt, KtxKt; 6 R–Q5!, and Black cannot prevent 7 P–R3 mate!

3	R–Q5!	KtxKt
4	R–R4 ch!	PxR
5	Kt–R6 ch!	RxKt
6	P–R3 mate!	

An exquisite combination.

6

CONVINCING THE KIBITZERS

If a combination forcing a win has been found, nothing avails the opponent, for the demonstration of the win can be grasped. In Life it is different. There the struggles are not so indubitably terminated as in a game. The game gives us a satisfaction that Life denies us. And for the Chess player, the success which crowns his work, the great dispeller of sorrows, is named "combination."

—Emanuel Lasker

White to play

152

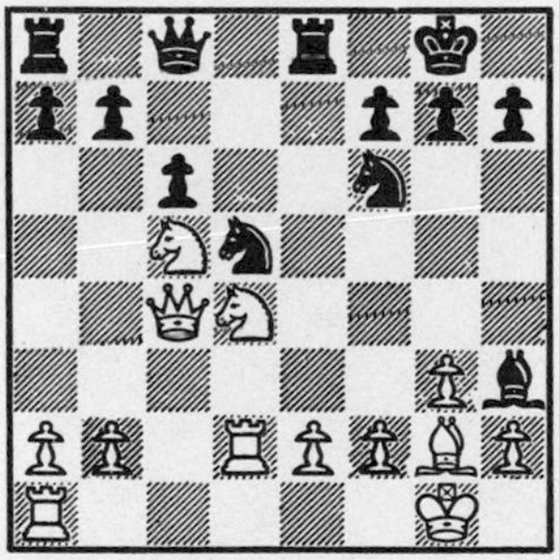

RÉTI-ALEKHINE
Baden-Baden, 1925

Reti played 1 B–B3 at this point. Exchanging Bishops instead, in order to win a Pawn would have led to a brilliant combination, with Reti at the losing end of it:

1	BxB	QxB
2	KtxKtP	Kt–KKt5!

Menacing mate in two.

3	Kt–KB3	Kt(Q4)–K6!
4	PxKt	KtxKP

White's Queen is attacked, while mate threatens his King.

5	QxP ch	K–R1

Naturally, 5 ... KxQ; 6 Kt–Kt5 ch; winning the Queen is unthinkable.

6	Kt–R4	R–KB1
7	Q–R5	R–B8 ch

Black mates next move.

Black to play   *White to play*

153

NIMZOVICH-ALEKHINE
Vilna, 1912

154

NIMZOVICH-ALEKHINE
Vilna, 1912

It was Alekhine's move, and he played 1 ... B–Q3, refusing White's offer of a Pawn. Accepting it would have involved him in a lovely combination (from Nimzovich's standpoint) ending in mate, as follows:

1	...	PxP
2	PxP	KtxP
3	RxKt!	QxR
4	QxP ch	Kt–Q2

The alternative is 4 ... R–Q2; 5 BxR ch, K–Q1 (or 5 ... KtxB; 6 Q–K8 mate); 6 B–B7 ch, KxB; 7 Kt–Kt5 ch winning the Queen.

5	Q–QB6 ch!	PxQ
6	B–QR6 mate!	

From the same game, another combinative jewel, this time with Alekhine planning the glorious finish. It is Nimzovich's move:

1   P–B3!

Preventing, believe-it-or-not, a Queen sacrifice leading to mate! Let us retract this move, and see what Black threatened.

1	...	KtxB
2	RxKt	QxKtP
3	R–QKt1	QxKt ch!
4	KxQ	Kt–K5 mate

There may be some who deplore the fact that neither this combination nor the previous one really came about. To me the fact that both players were aware of the tactical possibilities (including the scintillating Queen sacrifices) adds luster to the game as actually played. It is the mark of a great player to anticipate the combinations of his opponent as well as devise them himself.

White mates next move, Black being singularly helpless to prevent it.

Black to play

156

TARRASCH-GOTTSCHALL
Dresden, 1892

Black to play

155

CAPABLANCA-NIMZOVICH
Bad Kissingen, 1928

The natural move for Black is 1 ... K-R1, to seize the open file with his Rook. Instead of this, Nimzovich played 1 ... BxKt. Let us see what would have happened had Nimzovich yielded to instinct:

1 ...   K-R1
2 Kt-K4

Intending 3 KtxP followed by 4 QxP mate.

2 ...   B-K2
3 Kt(B3)--Kt5   PxKt
4 Kt-B6   BxKt
5 B-K4

Threatened with mate on the move, Gottschall defended by 1 ... P-Kt3. The alternative 1 ... Kt-B1 would have subjected his King to an unusual smothered mate, thus:

1 ...   Kt-B1
2 PxP   BxP
3 Kt-Kt5

Threatens 4 KtxBP mate.

3 ...   KtxP

Now comes a superb finish!

4 QxP ch!   KtxQ
5 KtxBP ch!   KtxKt
6 Kt-Kt6 mate!

Black to play

White to play

157

158

BOTVINNIK-BOLESLAVSKY
U.S.S.R. 1945

MARSHALL-LASKER
Match, 1907

The kibitzers must have groaned
at the thought of Botvinnik missing
the powerful 1 Kt–K5. It threatens
Black with loss by 2 RxP ch, K–R1;
3 KtxP mate, as well as 2 QxKtP ch,
K–R1; 3 KtxP ch, forcing Black to
give up his Queen. But there is a
subtle combination which would
have refuted this winning attempt:

The ubiquitous kibitzer might be
inclined to play 1 ... RxP, on the
theory that you take first and philos-
ophize afterwards, but this is the
retribution that Marshall would have
exacted:

1	Kt–K5	Kt–B3!
2	RxP ch	QxR
3	KtxQ	R–R8 ch
4	K–R2	Kt–Kt5 ch
5	K–R3	KtxP ch
6	K–R2	R–R8 mate

1	...	RxP
2	QxR ch!	RxQ
3	RxR ch	K–R2
4	R–R8 ch	KxR
5	KtxP ch	K–Kt1
6	KtxQ and wins	

Botvinnik's actual procedure was
simple and strong: 1 Q–Q4 ch, K–
R2; 2 Kt–B6 ch, KtxKt; 3 QxKt, K–
Kt1; 4 K–R2, R–KB1; 5 QxQBP,
K–Kt2; 6 Q–Q6, Q–Kt8; 7 Q–Q4 ch,
K–R2; 8 P–B6, and Black resigned,
since 8 ... R–KR1 loses by 9
QxR ch, KxQ; 10 P–B7.

Lasker avoided the Marshall
swindle, played 1 ... Kt–K5, and
eventually won the game.

Black to play   *Black to play*

159

LASKER-CAPABLANCA
Match, 1921

160

SPIELMANN-ELISKASES
Match, 1932

The friendly kibitzer might spot an opportunity for Capablanca to win a piece by a pretty combination, as follows:

1	...	Kt–Kt5
2	R–Q2	R–Kt8
3	Kt–Kt2	RxKt
4	RxR	Kt–Q6 ch

This wins a piece, but not the game! Capablanca saw this line of play—and the continuation:

5	K–K2	KtxR
6	K–Q2	K–B1
7	K–B2	

White corners the Knight and draws! Capablanca's actual move was 1 ... R–Kt8, and he wins the Knight Pawn. On 2 K–K1, Kt–R4 assures it, and if 2 K–K2 (which was what Lasker played) 2 ... RxP wins the Pawn at once.

Black's actual move was 1 ... KPxP, after which White broke into his position by 2 P–K6, PxP; 3 KtxKP. Any kibitzer worth his salt would have suggested the alternative capture by 1 ... KtPxP, to keep the center compact. Here is how lightning would have struck the black game:

1	...	KtPxP
2	KtxKP!	PxKt(K3)
3	B–R5 ch	K–B1
4	B–R6 ch	K–Kt1
5	Q–Kt4 ch!	

Beautiful!

| 5 | ... | PxQ |
| 6 | B–B7 mate! | |

Black to play

161

FLOHR-BOTVINNIK
Match, 1933

White has just captured a Pawn. How shall Black recapture? If 1 ... KtxP; 2 B-B8 wins the Queen side Pawns, while 1 ... QPxP leaves White with a protected passed Pawn. Almost without hesitation a kibitzer would select 1 ... BPxP as the best of the three ways to regain the Pawn. White's continuation, on that reply, is surprising:

| 1 ... | BPxP |
| 2 K-B3 | |

Uncovers an attack on the Rook Pawn.

| 2 ... | P-R4 |
| 3 B-Kt5 ch | K-K1 |

On 3 ... Kt-B3; 4 B-B8 is decisive.

    4 B-R6!

And White wins a piece! Black's Knight at Kt2 has no move, and the King cannot protect the Knight without abandoning the other.

In the actual game, Botvinnik played 1 ... QPxP, choosing the least of the evils.

White to play

162

FOX-CAPABLANCA
New York, 1906

It was Fox's turn to play. He moved 1 P-KR3, and the game continued by 1 ... Kt-B7 ch; 2 KtxKt, BxKt; 3 R-K2, PxP!; 4 RxB, P-K5, and Capablanca eventually won.

Ringside critics who are quick to point out a player's errors the moment he loses, might suggest that White try opening the file instead by 1 PxP, with some tactical threats.

Against this, Capablanca was prepared to unfold this impressive combination:

| 1 PxP | KtxP(B5) |
| 2 Kt-K7 ch | |

Or 2 RxR ch, RxR; 3 Q-QB3 (to attack the Bishop, since 3 Q-KB3,

QxKt; 4 QxKt(B4), QxQ; 5 BxQ, R–K8 falls into mate), QxKt; 4 QxB, Kt–K7; 5 B–K3, RxB; 6 KtxR, Kt–B7 mate.

2	. . .	RxKt!
3	PxR	KtxQ
4	PxR(Q) ch	QxQ
5	PxKt	Q–R5
6	P–KR3	Q–Kt6
7	PxKt	Q–R5 mate

A quiet move, but a strong one. There are two threats of mate on the move!

5	KtxR	R–Q5!

Again facing White with two threats of instant mate.

6	RxP	B–Q1 ch
7	R–B6	BxR mate

White to play

163

EUWE-ALEKHINE
Match, 1937

It was Euwe's turn to play, and he evaded Black's threat (1 . . . RxP mate) by moving 1 K–R4.

The kibitzing spectator would be inclined to suggest 1 BxKt followed by 2 B–B4, attacking both Rooks on the white squares. Anticipating this possibility, Alekhine had an interesting combination prepared in which he places both of his Rooks *en prise!*

1	BxKt	PxB
2	B–B4	RxP ch
3	K–Kt4	P–B4 ch
4	K–Kt5	K–Kt2!

White to play

164

BOTVINNIK-BRONSTEIN
Match, 1951

Botvinnik's actual move was 1 R–K1. Well-meaning advisers would undoubtedly recommend the removal of Black's powerful passed Pawn.

Had White heeded them, this would have been the consequence:

1	KtxQP	BxKt
2	BxB	KtxB
3	RxKt	P–Kt3!

This unobtrusive move wins a piece, or forces mate!

4	Kt–Q6

Other moves by the Knight do not affect the result.

4 ...   Kt–K6!

Black wins! White is powerless to save his Rook and prevent 5 ... R–B8 mate simultaneously.

Black to play

165

LASKER-TARRASCH
Match, 1908

The actual game went 1 ... BxKt; 2 QxQ, RxQ; 3 PxB, and Black remained a Pawn behind. Eventually he drew a hard ending. Somebody or other watching the game must have suggested 1 ... QxQ instead, to regain the lost Pawn immediately. Tarrasch in his notes to the match, demonstrates how this would have cost a piece:

1 ...	QxQ
2 KtxQ	BxP
3 QR–Kt1	B–QR6
4 Kt–B7	R–Kt1
5 BxKt	

White wins a piece, the pinned Pawn not daring to recapture.

White to play

166

TARRASCH-SCHLECHTER
Match, 1911

Tarrasch's actual move was 1 Kt–K2, which seems rather circuitous. "Why not," says our kibitzer, "dispute possession of the Queen file in a straightforward way, and equalize without any difficulty?"

The answer is, and this seems incredible, that against this Black has a combination which ends in a win by Queening a Pawn!

1 QR–Q1	KR–Q1
2 RxR	RxR
3 R–Q1	KtxKt!
4 RxR	

Certainly not 4 PxKt, RxR ch, and White gets mated.

4 ...	PxR
5 PxKt	BxKt
6 PxB	P–QR4!
7 K–B1	P–R5
8 PxP	PxP
9 K–K1	P–R6

And Black wins. The Pawn cannot be headed off!

Black to play

167

TARRASCH-SCHLECHTER
Match, 1911

White has just moved his Queen to B5, attacking two pieces. The plausible reply is of course 1 ... Kt–K3, rescuing both pieces in the simplest way. If Black had played this instinctively, he would have fallen into a beautiful mating combination, as follows:

1	...	Kt–K3
2	Q–R7 ch	K–B1
3	Q–R8 ch	K–K2
4	RxP ch!	KxR
5	B–Kt6 ch!	KxB

Or 5 ... K–K2; 6 Q–K8 mate.

6   Q–R5 mate!

The game continuation was 1 ... Q--R2 ch; 2 K–R1, Q–K6; 3

QxR, QxRP ch; 4 K–Kt1, Q–Kt6 ch, and Schlechter drew by perpetual check.

White to play

168

ALEKHINE-BOGOLYUBOV
Match, 1929

This is the sort of position in which the master clearly *must* make the move the kibitzer has in mind. How can anyone overlook 1 P–Q7, a move which wins on the spot?

Against that though, Black has a problem-like refutation:

1	P–Q7.	R–Q8 ch
2	K–Kt2	

At this point everyone expects Black to play 2 ... KtxP, to prevent the passed Pawn from Queening.

2	...	KtxR!
3	P–Q8(Q)	Kt–B5 mate!

7

BOOMERANG COMBINATIONS

There is no other game so esteemed, so profound and so venerable as chess; in the realm of play it stands alone in dignity.

—Ely Culbertson

There are times when a player does not look far enough ahead. He works out a combination which wins material or threatens mate, and then to his horror the combination boomerangs, and the win he counted on turns out to be a loss.

Here are a few interesting case histories:

Black to play

169

MARSHALL-SWIDERSKI
Nuremberg, 1906

86

Black saw a golden opportunity to capture a Pawn, force an exchange of Queens, and then win a simple ending.

1	...	QxP ch
2	KxQ	Kt–K6 ch
3	K–B3	KtxQ

The boomerang:

4 P–B4!

Now the Knight cannot escape!

4	...	K–Kt1
5	K–K2	

White wins.

Black to play   *White to play*

170

ALEKHINE-COHN
Stockholm, 1912
(variation)

1 ...   Q–R5

Threatens 2 ... QxP mate.

2 Kt–B3!

To parry the threat and drive the Queen off.

2 ...   B–B4 ch
3 K–R1   Kt–B7 ch
4 RxKt

Forced, as 4 K–Kt1 allows Black to capture the Queen *with check*.

4 ...   QxR

Wins the exchange but now comes The boomerang:

5 Kt–K4!

And wins! The Queen is attacked, and has no square of escape.

171

ALEKHINE-STERK
Budapest, 1921
(variation)

1 P–K5   Kt–Kt5
2 Kt–KKt5

Threatens 3 QxP mate.

2 ...   P–Kt3
3 KtxKP

Looks good: the Knight attacks Queen and Rook, and if 2 ... PxKt; 4 BxP ch followed by 5 BxKt (Kt4) wins.

The boomerang:

3 ...   Q–R5!
4 P–KR3   Q–Kt6!

And Black mates by 5 ... QxKtP or 5 ... Q–R7.

Black to play

172

HORWITZ-POPERT
Hamburg, 1844

| 1 ... | B–Kt1 |
| 2 RxP | P–B3 |

Attacks the Rook with a Pawn, and discovers a third attack on White's pinned Bishop. Despite the double threat there comes

The boomerang:

3 R–KR5!	QxR
4 QxP ch!	PxQ
5 BxP mate	

White to play

173

KUBART-BLECHSCHMIDT
Bautzen, 1949

| 1 | Kt–B4 |

Does he overlook the pin on his Knight?

1 ...	B–K6
2 P–Kt7 ch	K–K2
3 R–Kt6	RxR
4 KtxR ch	K–B2

Black anticipated this continuation, and now expects to capture the passed Pawn, with winning chances.

The boomerang:

| 5 Kt–K7! |

Threatens to Queen the Pawn next move.

| 5 ... | KxP |
| 6 Kt–B5 ch | |

White removes the Bishop next move and wins.

Black to play

174

RICHTER-AMATEUR
Berlin, 1930

| 1 ... | R–R8 ch |

2   KxR   PxP

Apparently Black will Queen the
Pawn, but Richter has everything in
hand.

> The boomerang:

3   R–KB5!   KxR
4   P–Kt4 ch   KxP
5   K–Kt2

White wins.

Black to play

175

HARTLAUB-AMATEUR
Berlin, 1913

1   . . .   BxKtP
2   BxB   Kt–B5 ch

Has White fallen into a trap?

3   K–R2   KtxQ

> The boomerang:

4   RxP ch   K–R1
5   R–Kt8 ch!   KxR
6   R–Kt1 ch

And Black will be mated.

White to play

176

NIELSEN-AMATEUR
Denmark, 1930

1   R(Kt2)–Q2   BxP
2   PxB   RxKtP

Attacks the Bishop while threatening mate.

3   B–Kt3!   RxB

Black's combination has succeeded
in that he has wound up two Pawns
ahead. But he no longer threatens
mate, and the displacement of his
Rook gives White the time he needs
for

> The boomerang:

4   P–K6!   R(Kt6)–Kt4

No better is 4 ... PxP; 5 P–
B7, and the Rook (at Kt1) is helpless. It cannot prevent White's Pawn
from advancing and at the same
time protect its fellow Rook.

5   R–Q8 ch!   RxR
6   RxR ch   KxR
7   PxP

White wins, as his Pawn cannot be headed off.

White to play

178

Black to play

177

1 ...	P–QR3
2 KtxP	PxKt
3 KtxKt ch	

Fine expects the play to continue thus: 3 ... PxKt; 4 QxQ ch, KxQ; 5 BxP ch followed by 6 BxR, and White has won the exchange. He gets a jolt though with

The boomerang:

3 ...	QxKt!
4 BxQ	B–Kt5 ch
5 Q–Q2	

Unfortunately forced.

5 ...	BxQ ch
6 KxB	PxB
7 PxP	B–K3

And Black wins.

1 KtxP	BxKt
2 BxB	

Confident that Black may not recapture since 2 ... KtxB is met by 3 QxR!, RxQ; 4 RxR ch followed by mate.

2 ...	KtxB!
3 QxR	

The boomerang:

3 ...	KtxKP ch
4 K–R1	

On 4 K–B1, QxP is mate.

4 ...	KtxBP mate!

White to play

179

BLACK-BIGELOW
New York, 1935

1 P–B3	PxP
2 BxP ch	KxB
3 QxQ	PxP ch
4 K–K2	PxR(Q)

Black is satisfied with the turn of events. He has lost his Queen, but now has acquired a new one. Nevertheless he falls a victim to

The boomerang:

5 Kt–Kt5 ch	K–Kt3
6 Q–K8 ch	K–R3
7 Kt–K6 ch	P–Kt4
8 BxP mate	

White to play

180

ALEKHINE-LEVENFISH
St. Petersburg, 1914
(variation)

1 KtxBP	RxKt

On 1 ... BxQ; 2 KtxQ ch, K–R1; 3 KtxKt wins for White.

2 BxR ch	

The right move is 2 Q–B4!, which wins the exchange after 2 ... B–R4; 3 QxKt.

2 ...	KxB
3 Q–B4 ch	

The boomerang:

3 ...	B–K3
4 QxKt	B–Q4!

Surrounds the Queen, and wins

Black to play

181

RUBINSTEIN-TARRASCH
Gothenberg, 1920
(variation)

1 ...	QxP ch
2 RxQ	BxR ch
3 K–R1	Kt–B7 ch

Intending to meet 4 K–Kt1 with 4 ... Kt–K5 ch followed by 5 ... KtxQ with the exchange ahead. Or if 4 RxKt, R–K8 ch forces mate.

The boomerang:

4   QxKt!   BxQ
5   B–Kt2 ch

And the Bishop mates, capturing any pieces thrown in its path.

Black to play

182

KOMKE-MAI
Berlin, 1931

1   ...   P–Kt5

Sets a trap for White: if 2 RxB (counting on 2 ... KxR, when 3 B–Kt5 ch followed by 4 BxR wins for White) 2 ... RxB ch!; 3 KxR, KxR, and Black's unstoppable passed Pawn assures him the win.

But he gets crossed up! White reverses the order of moves and wins.

The boomerang:

2   B–B4 ch   K–B1
3   RxB ch   KxR
4   B–Kt5 ch   K–K2
5   BxR

And wins, since the Pawn is stopped dead in its tracks.

The conscientious student will note in all this, that the capture with check takes precedence over a mere capture.

Black to play

183

ROSSOLIMO-AMATEUR
Paris, 1944

1   ...   BxP ch
2   KxB   Q–R5 ch
3   K–Kt1   R–KR1

With a threat of mate that looks irresistible. Apparently White must give up his Queen by 4 QxR ch, and lose slowly but surely.

The boomerang:

4   Q–Kt7 ch!   K–K2

Or 4 ... KxQ; 5 KtxB ch, K–B3; 6 KtxQ, RxKt, and White is a piece ahead.

5   Q–K5 ch   K–Q2

The alternatives are:
(a) 5 ... K–B1; 6 QxR(Kt8) ch, K–Kt2 (or K2); 7 KtxB ch followed by 8 KtxQ.

(b) 5 ... K–Q1; 6 QxR(Kt8) ch, K–Q2 (or 6 ... B–B1; 7 Q–B7 ch, K–K1; 8 QxB ch winning); 7 QxP ch, K–Q1; 8 Q–Kt8 ch, K–Q2; 9 QxR (the simplest); QxQ; 10 P–Kt7, and White wins.

6 Q–Q6 ch!

White wins: if 6 ... KxQ, by 7 KtxB ch, if 6 ... K–B1, by 7 Q–B7 mate, and finally if 6 ... K–K1, by 7 QxR ch.

The threat of a Knight fork is the key to White's attack throughout.

White to play

184

LASKER-RAGOZIN
Moscow, 1936

1 PxP   BxP
2 RxP

One of those rare occasions when Lasker captures a Pawn without calculating all the consequences. Ragozin refutes the move by a combination profound and beautiful.

The boomerang:

2 ...   Kt–Kt5!

Discovered attack—to begin with.

3 R(K5)xB   RxR

Not 3 ... KtxQ; 4 RxR, Q–B3; 5 R(Q7)–Q6, Q–B4; 6 B–Kt6, KtxP ch; 7 K–R2, and White wins.

4 BPxKt   BxKt

Killing off the protector of White's Rook.

5 RxR   BxB

White's Rook is attacked and he is also threatened with a pin by 6 ... B–Kt3.

6 R–Q6

After which, Black chases the Rook in order to get in the pin by the Bishop.

6 ...   B–B2
7 R–KB6

Naturally White avoids the tempting 7 R–Q7 (pinning the Bishop, and threatening to win by 8 QxP ch) because of 7 ... B–R7 ch; 8 KxB, QxR.

7 ...   B–Q1
8 R–Q6

The attempt to release himself by 8 Q–B3 fails after 8 ... Q–R2 ch; 9 Q–B2, QxQ ch; 10 RxQ, B–Kt3, and the Rook is pinned.

8 ...   B–K2
9 R–Kt6

The last place of refuge on the sixth rank.

9 ...   QxR!

The point! Black wins the exchange with this temporary sacrifice.

| 10 | QxQ | B–B4 ch |
| 11 | QxB | RxQ |

And Black won the ending.

White to play

185

FLOHR-ROMANOVSKY
Moscow, 1935
(variation)

1	PxP	R–B1
2	B–K3	KtxBP
3	BxKt	Kt–Q2
4	KR–Q1	RxB

The right move is 4 ... Q–B2. Now Black gets a lesson in the art of pinning and unpinning pieces.

The boomerang:

| 5 | Q–Q3 | R–B2 |
| 6 | Kt–K5 | P–B3 |

Black must lose a piece, but he hopes to regain it by a pin.

| 7 | KtxKt | R–B2 |
| 8 | Kt–B5! | |

Breaks the pin. If now 8 ... QxQ; 9 KtxQ leaves White a piece ahead with an easy win.

| 8 ... | | Resigns |

White to play

186

ALEKHINE-CAPABLANCA
Match, 1927
(variation)

1	KtxKt	QxKt
2	R–QB1	R–QB1!
3	KtxP	

Apparently winning a Pawn. Black's Knight is pinned on the rank and on the file—or is it?

The boomerang:

| 3 ... | | Kt–K6! |

Threatens 4 ... QxP mate, and also discovers an attack on the Queen (to say nothing of the Rook).

4	QxQ	RxR ch
5	K–R2	Kt–B8 ch
6	K–Kt1	Kt–Q7 ch
7	K–R2	KtxQ

Black wins.

White to play

187

RABINOVICH-NIMZOVICH
Baden-Baden, 1925
(variation)

1	BxP	P–KR5!
2	R–Kt4	PxB
3	RxP	Q–B4
4	RxB	

Wins a couple of Pawns, but loses the game.

The boomerang:

| 4 | ... | Q–K5 ch |
| 5 | Q–Kt2 | |

If 5 R–Kt2, P–R6 wins a whole Rook.

| 5 | ... | R–Q8 ch |
| 6 | Kt–Kt1 | P–R6! |

The impudent Pawn cannot be touched by either of White's pinned pieces!

| 7 | QxQ | KtxQ |

And wins. White's only move to prevent 8 ... KtxP mate is 8 R–Kt2, giving up his Rook.

White to play

188

RASMUSSON-NIEMI
Helsingfors, 1938

1	PxP	KtxP
2	BxP ch	KxB
3	Q–B2 ch	

Expecting to capture the Knight next move, gaining a Pawn by the combination. To White's astonishment he is plunged in the next few moves into an assortment of pins and unpins.

The boomerang:

3	...	Kt–Q6
4	R–Q1	B–R3
5	Kt–K1	

Triple attack on the Knight which is pinned on the file and the diagonal.

| 5 | ... | Q–B1! |
| 6 | Q–Kt1 | |

Maintains the pin. If instead 6 QxQ, QRxQ; 7 KtxKt, KR–Q1!, and suddenly it is White's Knight that is pinned!

6 ...	R–Q1!
7 KtxKt	K–Kt1!

So that White's newly-pinned Knight cannot break loose by dis-covering check.

8   P–B3

To vacate the square B2, and free himself from the pin by 9 Kt–B2.

8 ...	Q–Q2
9 Kt–B2	

At last, but there is a final surprise.

9 ...	QxR ch!
10 KtxQ	RxKt ch
11 K–B2	B–Q6!

And White's Queen is trapped!

White to play

189

DURAS-TCHIGORIN
Nuremberg, 1906
(variation)

1 RxB	KtxR
2 P–Kt5	QxKtP
3 Kt–B4	Q–R5
4 KtxKt	

Winning two pieces for a Rook. The Queen Knight's escape is cut off, but since it attacks two pieces, it will capture the Bishop before it dies.

The boomerang:

4 ...	Q–R6 ch
5 K–B2	Q–R7 ch
6 K–K3	QxKt
7 KtxB	

If 7 KtxR, RxKt, and Black is two Pawns ahead.

7 ...	KR–Q1
8 Kt–B6	

Or 8 Kt–Kt6, QR–Kt1, and the Knight does not get out alive.

8 ...	Q–B5 ch
9 K–K2	QxKt
10 BxKt	P–Kt4

Shuts in the Bishop. Black will continue by 11 ... R–KKt1 and 12 ... R–Kt3, capture the Bishop, and win with the exchange ahead.

Black manipulates the pieces ex-pertly in this interesting combination.

8

THE OLD MASTER
Adolf Anderssen

There's not the mystery in ten murders that there is in one game of chess.
—Detective Linley in *Two Bottles of Relish.*

In a world where almost everybody played dull, stodgy, unimaginative chess, Anderssen came along to liven things up with his brilliant sacrifices and fiery King side attacks. He manipulated the pieces with bewildering skill, and created most ingenious combinations in pursuit of one objective—mate to the King. To that end, others might try to win pieces, but Anderssen gave them away lavishly. For Anderssen, amassing extra material had no point. He was interested in mate—preferably by means of an artistic combination.

Here are some of my favorites:

White to play

190

ANDERSSEN-DUFRESNE
Berlin, 1851

Anderssen, aiming for the mate, finds an ingenious way to break into the adverse King's position.

| 1 | BxKt | PxB |

If 1 ... BxB; 2 KtxB, PxKt (on 2 ... RxKt; 3 KtxP ch, QxKt; 4 QxR wins the exchange); 3 R–K6, Q–B2; 4 R–K7 (threatens 5 QxP mate); QxR; 5 Kt–B6 ch, and White wins the Queen.

| 2 | R–K7! | |

Threatens mate on the move.

| 2 | ... | P–Kt3 |

If 2 ... QxR; 3 Kt–B6 ch exploits the pin to win the Queen.

3 Q–R4

Shifts the attack to the Rook Pawn, and forces a loosening of Black's position.

3 ...   P–R4

Black may not play 3 ... QxR, as the Knight check in reply wins his Queen.

4 Kt–B6 ch   K–B1

On 4 ... K–R1; 5 R–R7 mates.

5 Kt–Kt5

With two powerful threats: 6 R–B7 mate, and 6 Kt(Kt5)–R7 mate.

5 ...   R–Q2

Obviously the reply to 5 ... QxKt is check by the remaining Knight at R7, winning the Queen and the game.

6 Kt(Kt5)–R7 ch   K–B2
7 RxR ch   KxR
8 R–K1!

Refraining from the tempting discovered check, White prevents the King's escape to the King side.

8 ...   Resigns

Black has no defense to the threat 9 R–K7 ch, which wins the Queen or forces mate. If he tries 8 ... R–K1; then 9 Kt–K5 ch, K–Q3; 10 Q–B6 ch, K–K2; 11 KtxP ch, K–Q1; 12 Q–B8 mate. Or if 8 ... B–B1; 9 Kt–Kt8 ch, K–B2; 10 Q–Q7 ch, KxKt; 11 Kt–B6 ch, and Black must give up his Queen or be mated next move.

White to play

191

ANDERSSEN-KIESERITZKY
London, 1851

This is the crucial position from what has come to be known as "The Immortal game."

Disregarding the threat against his Rook, Anderssen nonchalantly sails in with his Knight.

1 Kt–Q5!   QxP

Rather than retreat, the Queen counter-attacks. Now both Rooks are threatened.

2 B–Q6!

A magnificent move! Black's Bishop is cut off from the defense, as later will be his Queen.

2 ...   BxR

If 2 ... QxR ch; 3 K–K2, QxR; 4 KtxP ch, K–Q1; 5 B–B7 mate. Or if 2 ... BxB; 3 KtxB ch, K–Q1; 4 KtxP ch, K–K1; 5 Kt–Q6 ch, K–Q1; 6 Q–B8 mate.

3 P–K5!

White gives up another Rook! It is worth a great deal to keep Black's

Queen (practically his only developed piece) out of play.

3 ...   QxR ch
4 K–K2   Kt–QR3

Guarding against the threat of 5 KtxP ch, K–Q1; 6 B–B7 mate. If instead 4 ... B–Kt2; 5 KtxP ch, K–Q1; 6 QxP, Kt–KR3; 7 Kt–K6 ch, K–B1; 8 Kt–K7 mate.

Now comes what Lasker describes as "a glorious finish."

5 KtxP ch   K–Q1
6 Q–B6 ch!

Anderssen throws in his Queen for good measure.

6 ...   KtxQ
7 B–K7 mate

White to play

192

ANDERSSEN-DUFRESNE
Berlin, 1852

Anderssen's combination against Kieseritzky was called "The Immortal," but the one he sprung on Dufresne has a pretty good longevity record, too. It started going the rounds more than a hundred years ago, and it's still being quoted in today's anthologies.

Anderssen's enthusiastic admirers gave it a name in keeping with its grandeur of conception. They called it "The Evergreen Partie."

1 Kt–B6 ch!

An attack on King and Queen which leaves Black no option.

1 ...   PxKt
2 PxP   R–Kt1

Black's King Knight is pinned, so he counter-attacks by threatening 3 ... QxKt followed by 4 ... QxKtP mate.

3 QR–Q1!!

This, which Lasker calls "one of the most subtle and profound moves on record," certainly deserves two exclamation marks.

3 ...   QxKt

Black goes about his business, blissfully unconscious of the fact that he will now be polished off in brilliant style.

4 RxKt ch!   KtxR

If 4 ... K–Q1; 5 RxQP ch, K–B1 (... KxR; 6 B–K2 dis. ch wins the Queen); 6 R–Q8 ch!, KtxR (... RxR permits 7 PxQ); 7 Q–Q7 ch!, and White wins as in the actual play.

5 QxP ch!!

Magnifique!

5 ...   KxQ
6 B–B5 dble ch

Both of White's checking pieces are unprotected, but both cannot be taken at once! Black's King must move, as the only way to get out of check.

6   ...   K–K1

If 6 ... K–B3; 7 B–Q7 is mate.

7   B–Q7 ch   K–Q1
8   PxKt mate

White to play

193

ANDERSSEN-DE RIVIÈRE
Paris, 1858

Anderssen revelled in wide-open positions where both Kings faced the threat of sudden death. In this combination Anderssen's King fearlessly moves all the way up the board to help the Queen to mate!

1   B–K3   KR–B1 ch
2   K–K2   Q–R4 ch

Black's Queen must stay on the Rook file to prevent a fatal Rook check.

3   P–Kt4   Q–R7 ch

4   R–B2   RxR ch
5   BxR   R–KB1

More pressure on the pinned piece. But it is Black who is in danger!

6   R–R1!   RxB ch
7   K–Q3

Not 7 K–K1, R–K7 ch; 8 QxR, QxR ch, and Black wins.

7   ...   R–Q7 ch
8   K–B4   RxP ch
9   K–Q5   B–B3
10 K–K6!   BxP
11 K–B7

Threatens 12 Q–Kt6 mate.

11 ...   R–B7 ch
12 K–Kt8   Resigns

If 12 ... P–Kt3 (to stop 13 Q–R7 mate); 13 Q–K7 wins, or if 12 ... R–B1 ch; 13 KxR, QxR; 14 QxQ ch, K–Kt3; 15 Q–K4 ch, K–R3; 16 K–Kt8, P–Kt3; 17 Q–R1 mate!

An amusing finish.

White to play

194

ANDERSSEN-AMATEUR
Breslau, 1860

The classic custom of announcing

mate in a certain number of moves seems sadistic to me. But when the mate is as pretty as this, much may be forgiven.

White announced mate in five:

1	QxKtP ch!	KtxQ
2	RxP ch	K–R1
3	R–Kt8 dble ch!	KxR
4	R–Kt1 ch	Q–Kt4
5	RxQ mate	

Black to play

195

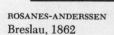

ROSANES-ANDERSSEN
Breslau, 1862

Anderssen's weakening of his opponent's position is a lesson in technique, and his sacrificial combination is sheer delight.

1 . . .   B–Q5

Threatens mate on the move.

2 P–B3   QR–Kt1

Again threatening 3 ... QxP mate.

3 P–QKt3

If instead 3 B–K1, B–K6 ch; 4 B–Q2, QxP mate.

3 . . .   KR–Q1!

A quiet move whose purpose is to keep White's King from escaping by way of the Queen file.

4 Kt–B3

If 4 PxB, QxQP followed by 5 ... Q–R8 mate.

4	. . .	QxP!
5	PxQ	RxP
6	B–K1	B–K6 ch
7	Any	R–Kt8 mate

Black to play

196

ROSANES-ANDERSSEN
Breslau, 1863

Anderssen's combination subtly exploits the circumstance that White's Queen must guard the square K2 against a Rook check, while keeping an eye on the all-important Queen Pawn.

1 . . .   Q–Kt3

Threatening 2 ... B–K4—further attack on the Pawn.

2 Kt–R4   Q–R3

An attack on the Knight, which is incidental to the real threat—mate in four by 3 ... Q–K7 ch; 4 QxQ, RxQ ch; 5 K–Kt1, R–K8 ch; 6 K–B2, R–B8 mate.

White cannot meet this by 3 P–B4 (cutting off Black's Queen along the diagonal while protecting his own Knight) as 3 ... QxKt; 4 QxQ, R–K7 ch involves him in the mate as before.

3   Kt–B3   B–K4!
4   P–R4

Clearly 4 PxB, Q–Kt3 ch; 5 K–K1, Q–Kt8 ch; 6 K–Q2, Q–K6 mate is unthinkable.

Anderssen finds another means of utilizing the black diagonal.

4   ...   Q–B8 ch!
5   QxQ   BxQP ch
6   B–K3   RxB

Threatens 7 ... R–K7 dble ch and mate.

7   K–Kt1   R–K8 mate!

White to play

197

ANDERSSEN-MAYET
Berlin, 1865

Anderssen would dearly love to check at R7 with his Queen, so his Knight engages in a duel with the Knight controlling that square.

1   Kt–R7!

Threatening 2 KtxKt ch, PxKt; 3 Q–R7 ch and mate next move.

1   ...   Kt–K1

White's own Knight blocks the critical square, so he continues.

2   Kt–B8!

Again threatening the fatal check.

2   ...   Kt–B3

And again Black covers the square.

3   Kt–Q7!

Now the Knight attacks from the other side, and renews the threat of mate in three.

3   ...   B–K3

Trying to get rid of one of White's minor pieces, or at least to block the action of the Rook on the King file.

4   RxB!

To this there is no answer. If 4 ... PxR; 5 BxP is mate. Meanwhile, Black is still faced with 5 KtxKt ch followed by quick mate.

4   ...   Resigns

White to play

198

ANDERSSEN-ZUKERTORT
Breslau, 1865

The Knight does some fancy stepping in this combination.

1   **QxKt!**   **RxQ**

If 1 ... PxKt; 2 QxR, PxB; 3 B–R6, Q–K2; 4 QR–K1, and White wins.

2   **Kt–B6** ch   **K–K2**
3   **KtxR** ch!

First the Rook! The Knight will come back later to pick up the Queen.

3   ...   **K–K1**
4   **Kt–B6** ch   **K–K2**
5   **KtxQ**

And White wins.

White to play

199

ANDERSSEN-ALEXANDER
Hamburg, 1869

Anderssen's second move is quiet, but it indicates that all sorts of Knight forks lurk in the background.

1   **RxP!**

With a threat against the King by 2 R–K7 ch, K–Q1; 3 R–B8 mate, and against the Queen by 2 R–B8 ch.

1   ...   **BxR**
2   **Q–B3!**

The threat is obvious. Black must protect his Bishop or move it.

2   ...   **BxKt**

What else was there? If 2 ... Q–Q2; 3 Kt–B6 ch wins the Queen, or if 2 ... Q–K3; 3 KtxP ch does likewise. On a Bishop move (to K3 or Kt1); 3 Q–B8 ch, K–Q2; 4 Q–Kt7 ch, K–B3; 5 Kt–K7 ch is the winning Knight fork.

3   **BPxB!**

Strange how completely helpless Black is to parry the threat of 4 Q–

B8 ch followed by the Rook mate!
Should his Queen move closer to
help out, say to Q1 or Q2, it leaves
mate open at B7 or B8.

White to play

200

ANDERSSEN-PAULSEN
Vienna, 1873

Anderssen's combination threatens
to win material, and enables him to
simplify into an easily won ending.

| 1 | Kt(K4)–B6 ch! | PxKt |
| 2 | KtxP ch | K–B2 |

Obviously if 2 ... K–R1; 3
RxP ch and mate next move.

| 3 | RxP ch | B–Kt2 |

If instead 3 ... K–Kt3, White
forces the win by 4 Q–KB3, Q–K3;
5 Q–R5 ch, K–B4; 6 Q–Kt4 ch, K–
Kt3; 7 P–B5 ch, QxP; 8 Q–R5 mate.

4	RxB ch	KxR
5	KtxR ch	K–B1
6	QxQ ch	BxQ
7	KtxP	

And White wins.

9

KING OF CHESS

Paul Morphy

An ancient writer said that if there were no flowers and moon and. beautiful women, he would not want to be born into the world. I might add that if there were no pen and ink and chess and wine, there was no purpose in being born a man.

—Chang Chao

From the age of twelve, Morphy dazzled the world with the brilliance of his combination play, the fertility of his ideas and the vividness of his imagination. It is no wonder that admirers of attacking play consider him the most famous player that ever lived.

More than any other master of his time, Morphy realized the importance of sound positional play in the opening, quick development of the pieces, and avoidance of premature attack. The combinations which he evolved had the merit of being sound as well as brilliant.

Black to play

201

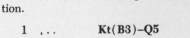

New York, 1857

A short, but astonishing combination.

1	...	Kt(B3)–Q5
2	Q–K4	Kt–KKt6!
3	QxQ	Kt(Q5)–K7 mate!

"Very pretty," you might say, "but was there a better defense than 2 Q–K4?"

Let's look at the alternatives:

If 2 Q–Q3, Kt–KKt6!; 3 QxKt (Kt3), Kt–K7 ch, and Black wins the Queen.

If 2 Q–R4, P–Kt4; 3 QxB, Kt–K7 ch; 4 K–R1, KtxB; 5 R–Kt1, R–Q8!

105

(threatening 6 ... QxP mate); 6 P–Kt3, Q–B3 ch, and mate next move.

If 2 R–Q1, Kt–K6! (threatens the Queen, the Rook, and mate on the move); 3 QxQ, Kt–K7 ch; 4 K–R1, RxR mate.

8 ...	Kt–B6 ch
9 K–Kt2	KtxQ ch
10 K–Kt1	Kt–B6 ch
11 K–Kt2	KtxR

And Black wins.

Black to play

203

SCHULTEN-MORPHY
New York, 1857

Black to play

202

SCHULTEN-MORPHY
New York, 1857

Anticipating a technique applied so successfully by Alekhine, Morphy puts a surprise twist to an apparently routine combination.

1 ...	RxB!
2 PxR	BxKt
3 RxB	QxP ch
4 K–K1	Q–Kt8 ch
5 K–Q2	R–Q1 ch
6 K–B3	Q–B4 ch

More forceful than the obvious 6 ... QxQ.

| 7 K–Kt2 | Kt–R5 ch! |
| 8 K–Kt1 | |

If 8 PxKt, Q–Kt5 mate!

Morphy's combination is the crowning point of a game which, says König, "has become a classic. It is one of the few early examples in which no improvement, either of opening theory or execution of attack has been advanced."

1 ...	RxB!
2 KtxR	Kt–Q5
3 Q–Kt1	BxKt ch
4 K–B2	Kt–Kt5 ch
5 K–Kt1	

If 5 K–Kt3, Kt–B4 ch followed by mate, or if 5 K–K1, Q–R5 ch; 6 P–Kt3, Q–K2, and White's King must stand where he is and wait for the mate.

5	. . .	Kt–B6 ch!
6	PxKt	Q–Q5 ch
7	K–Kt2	Q–B7 ch
8	K–R3	QxBP ch
9	K–R4	Kt–R3
10	R–Kt1	Kt–B4 ch
11	K–Kt5	Q–R4 mate

Black to play

PAULSEN-MORPHY
New York, 1857

Morphy's first combination "in the grand style" against a master player. Steinitz deemed it worthy of being embossed in letters of gold on the cover of his MODERN CHESS IN-STRUCTOR.

| 1 | . . . | QxB! |

This must have made the natives sit up and take notice.

2	PxQ	R–Kt3 ch
3	K–R1	B–R6
4	R–Q1	

If 4 R–Kt1, RxR ch; 5 KxR, R–K8 ch, and mate next move.

| 4 | . . . | B–Kt7 ch |

5	K–Kt1	BxP dis. ch
6	K–B1	B–Kt7 ch
7	K–Kt1	B–R6 dis. ch
8	K–R1	BxP
9	Q–B1	

White must give up his Queen, but his troubles are not over.

9	. . .	BxQ
10	RxB	R–K7
11	R–R1	R–R3
12	P–Q4	B–K6!

Black wins. If 13 BxB, R(R3)xP ch; 14 K–Kt1, R(K7)–Kt7 mate.

The critics later pointed out that Morphy missed quicker wins at his 6th and 7th moves. This does not lessen Morphy's achievement. The combination he analyzed assured a clear win, and nothing was to be gained by trying to shorten the process.

Black to play

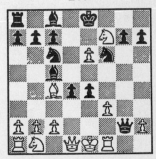

BARNES-MORPHY
London, 1858

Morphy's combination makes short work of one of London's strongest players.

1 ...   Kt–QKt5

Threatens to win the Queen by
2 ... KtxP ch.

2 Kt–R3   BxP!

Now threatening 3 ... BxKt,
winning a piece as well as 3 ...
BxB; 4 KtxB, KtxP ch, forcing
White to give up his Queen.

3 BxB   Kt–Q6 ch!
4 QxKt

Played with a heavy heart, but 4
PxKt, B–Kt5 ch; 5 Q–Q2, QxQ mate
is even worse.

4 ...   PxQ
5 0–0–0

If instead 5 R–B2 (to stop 5 ...
Q–K7 mate); Q–Kt8 ch; 6 R–B1,
Q–K6 ch; 7 K–Q1, Q–K7 ch and
Black wins.

5 ...   BxKt
6 B–Kt3

He must stop 6 ... QxBP mate,
and if he tries 6 PxP, then 6 ...
QxKtP mate is the penalty.

6 ...   P–Q7 ch
7 K–Kt1   B–B4
8 Kt–K5   K–B1

Making way for the Rook to work
on the open file.

9 Kt–Q3   R–K1
10 KtxB   QxR!

Ready to end it after 11 RxQ by
11 ... R–K8 ch; 12 RxR, PxR(Q)
mate.

11 Kt–K6 ch

Does he think Morphy will blunder into 11 ... K–K2, allowing
12 RxQ?

11 ...   RxKt

And Barnes is convinced.

Black to play

206

ST. AMANT
F. DE L'A.   -MORPHY
Paris, 1858

Morphy's second move, cutting
the lines of communication, is even
prettier than the Bishop sacrifice
with which he begins the combination.

1 ...   BxP!

A sacrifice which must be accepted, in view of Black's threat 2
... BxP dis. ch; 3 K–Kt3, Q–Kt4
ch; 4 K–R2, Q–R5 ch and quick
mate.

2 PxB   R–Q6!

Attacks the Rook Pawn a third
time, and cuts off the Queen.

3 QxR

If 3 BxR, QxP ch; 4 K–Kt1, Q–Kt7 mate.

3 ...	KtxQ
4 BxKt	Q–Q3 ch
5 P–B4	QxB

And Black wins.

White to play

207

MORPHY-AMATEUR
New Orleans, 1858

Every piece takes part in this combination, one of Morphy's neatest.

| 1 RxP! | BxR |
| 2 RxB | RxR |

If instead 2 ... K–Kt1, White forces an exquisite win by 3 RxR ch, KxR; 4 Q–B6 ch, K–K1 (if 4 ... K–Kt1; 5 P–K7, Q–B1; 6 Q–K6 ch!, QxQ; 7 PxQ, and the passed Pawn cannot be stopped); 5 Q–R8 ch, K–K2; 6 Kt–B5 ch, RxKt; 7 PxR, and there is no way to prevent mate by the Pawn!

| 3 QxR ch | Q–Kt2 |

If instead 3 ... R–Kt2; 4 Kt–B5, P–B5 (or 4 ... K–Kt1; 5

KtxP ch, K–R1; 6 Q–B8 ch followed by mate); 5 P–K7, and White wins.

| 4 Q–Q8 ch | Q–Kt1 |
| 5 P–K7 | R–K4 |

Stops the Pawn from advancing, but White has a Knight on the sidelines ready to leap into action.

| 6 Kt–R5 | RxP(K5) |

Black actually threatens mate!

| 7 P–K8(Q) |

Two pieces attack the new Queen, but if either piece captures, the reply 8 Q–B6 ch wins on the spot.

7 ...	R–K8 ch
8 QxR	QxQ
9 Q–B3 ch	K–Kt1
10 Q–Kt7 mate

This is from one of four blindfold games played simultaneously by Morphy.

White to play

208

MORPHY-FORDE
New Orleans, 1858

Another of the famous Morphy attacks, where he subjects the adverse King to a raking cross-fire.

1	RxP ch!	KxR
2	P–Q4 ch	K–K3
3	P–Kt4	

White to play

209

Threatens mate on the move. This is far better than 3 Q–K4 ch, K–B3 when White regains a piece but loses the initiative.

| 3 | ... | P–Kt3 |
| 4 | Q–K4 ch | K–B2 |

MORPHY-AMATEUR
New Orleans, 1858

The difference is apparent: if now 4 ... K–B3; 5 Q–K5 ch wins, as the King cannot escape to Kt3, Black having blocked that square with a Pawn.

The threats are all on the King side, but the ultimate victim of Morphy's combination is an innocent Knight away over on the Queen side.

| 5 | BxKt ch | K–Kt2 |
| 6 | B–K7 | |

1   P–K6

Threatening an immediate win of material by 2 P–K7.

| 1 | ... | PxP |
| 2 | KtxKP | |

Attacks the Queen, which dares not move as 6 ... Q–K1 allows 7 Q–K5 ch, followed by mate.

Direct attack on one Rook, and indirect (by 3 Kt–B7) on the other.

2	...	BxKt
3	RxB	Q–B1
4	RxKt!	PxR
5	QxKtP	

6	...	R–K1
7	Q–K5 ch	K–R3
8	P–Kt5 ch	K–R4
9	B–B3 ch	B–Kt5
10	Q–Kt3	Q–Q2
11	Q–R3 mate	

Threatening mate on the move.

5	...	Q–B4
6	RxP!	QxQ
7	RxR ch	K–R2
8	B–Kt8 ch	K–R1
9	B–B7 dis. ch	K–R2

One of four blindfold simultaneous games.

10 BxQ ch   KxB
11 B–B4

A second attack on the pinned Knight, which wins a piece and the game.

From one of four games played simultaneously by Morphy, blindfold.

White to play

210

MORPHY-AMATEUR
New Orleans, 1858

Morphy's combination demonstrates the power exerted by two Bishops operating on adjacent diagonals.

1 R–K8!   QxR
2 QxR!   Q–K2

Naturally, the reply to 2 ... PxQ is 3 BxP mate.

3 QxKtP ch!   QxQ
4 P–B6   QxP ch

The alternative 4 ... Q–B1 leads to 5 P–B7 dis. ch, Kt–K4; 6

PxKt, P–KR4; 7 P–K6 dis. ch, K–R2; 8 B–Q3 ch, K–R3; 9 R–B6 ch, K–Kt4; 10 R–Kt6 ch, K–B5; 11 K–B2 (threatening 12 P–Kt3 mate); P–R5; 12 R–Kt4 mate.

5 KxQ   BxP ch
6 KxB   P–KR4
7 R–KKt1

And White wins. A fine combination from a set of four simultaneous blindfold games.

White to play

211

MORPHY-AMATEUR
New Orleans, 1858

The finish of this combination, to one who has not seen this idea before, is nothing short of amazing. Note please that Morphy has given the odds of a Rook.

1   Q–B7

This cuts the King off from his army and threatens 2 Kt–K4 mate.

1 ...   B–K3

2	BxB	KtxB
3	Kt–K4 ch	K–Q4
4	P–B4 ch	KxKt
5	QxKt	Q–Q5

The Queen comes down to help out, since the King cannot get back.

6	Q–Kt4 ch	K–Q6
7	Q–K2 ch	K–B7
8	P–Q3 dis. ch	KxB
9	0–0 mate!	

Black to play

212

BIRD–MORPHY
London, 1858

This is probably the finest of Morphy's combinations. A Rook is sacrificed at one side of the board for the astonishing purpose of sacrificing the Queen at the other!

Bird must have appreciated Conway's comment, "When one plays with Morphy the sensation is as queer as the first electric shock, or first love, or chloroform, or any entirely novel experience."

1	...	R–Kt1
2	0–0–0	

Plausible, in that the King reaches safety while protecting the Knight Pawn.

2	...	RxBP!

Startling—and the prelude to a move even more startling.

3	BxR	Q–QR6!
4	P–B3	

Naturally, if 4 PxQ, BxQRP is mate. Or if 4 Q–B3 (to drive Black's Queen off), B–B5 ch; 5 R–Q2, QxQ; 6 PxQ, P–K6, and Black wins. On 4 Q–Kt5 (to give the King room), QxP ch; 5 K–Q2, B–Kt5 ch; 6 K–Q3, Q–R6 ch!; 7 B–Q3 (if 7 K–B4, B–Q3 ch wins), B–R3; 8 KR–Kt1, B–KB1! wins for Black.

4	...	QxRP
5	P–Kt4	

White must stop 5 ... RxP; 6 QxR, B–R6.

5	...	Q–R8 ch
6	K–B2	Q–R5 ch
7	K–Kt2	

White should have played 7 K–B1 to escape the effects of the next sacrifice.

7	...	BxP!
8	PxB	RxP ch

The difference is that Black's Rook comes in with a check. If the King were at B1 instead, White could now counter-attack with 9 Q–Kt5, mean-

while providing the King with an
exit leading to the King side.

9   QxR

This is forced. The alternative 9
K–B1 allows mate in two.

9   ...   QxQ ch
10   K–B2

On 10 K–R2 Black wins by 10
... P–B4! 11 R–QKt1 (if 11 PxP,
P–Q5 12 RxP, B–K3 ch 13 K–R1,
Q–R6 ch 14 K–Kt1, P–K6 wins)
Q–R4 ch, 12 K–Kt3 (12 K–Kt2, Q–
Q7 ch) B–Q2, and all the threats
cannot be met.

10   ...   P–K6!

When it came to giving away
Pawns to open lines for an attack,
Morphy's generosity was unparal-
leled.

11   BxP   B–B4 ch
12˙   R–Q3

On 12 B–Q3, Q–B5 ch wins the
Bishop.

12   ...   Q–B5 ch
13   K–Q2   Q–R7 ch
14   K–Q1

If 14 K–K1, BxR 15 BxB, Q–R8
ch and Black wins the King Rook.˗

14   ...   Q–Kt8 ch

And Black wins.

White to play

213

MORPHY-BAUCHER
Paris, 1858

The first part of the combination
(winning a piece) does not convince
Black. So Morphy reveals the second
part, the execution of mate.

1   R–R3

Threatens 2 RxP ch and mate next
move.

1   ...   P–R3

If instead 1 ... R–K1; 2 Q–R5,
P–R3; 3 KtxKtP, KxKt; 4 R–Kt3 ch,
followed by mate in two.

2   Q–Q2

Now threatening 3 RxP ch.

2   ...   K–R2
3   QxB   B–Q3

Ordinarily, a player would resign
after losing a piece. But this was one
of eight blindfold games, and
Morphy might overlook that his
Queen is *en prise*.

| 4 | RxP ch! | KxR |
| 5 | R–Q3! | |

The blindfolded player sees the position clearly. Black is welcome to the Queen!

| 5 | ... | K–R4 |
| 6 | Q–B7 ch | |

And White mates after 6 ... P–Kt3 by 7 Q–R7 ch, K–Kt5; 8 Q–R3 mate.

White to play

214

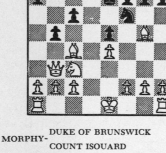

MORPHY– DUKE OF BRUNSWICK
COUNT ISOUARD
Paris, 1858

This, the most famous of Morphy combinations, has been reprinted a million times. Morphy enthusiasts will resent seeing again a theme so familiar to them, but howl if it were omitted!

So here once more is the scintillating finish of the game Morphy played with his titled opponents while watching "The Barber of Seville"

from the Duke's box at the Opera House.

1	KtxP!	PxKt
2	BxKtP ch	QKt–Q2
3	0–0–0!	

Everything with gain of tempo! Castling on the Queen side enables White's Rook to attack the pinned Knight immediately.

| 3 | ... | R–Q1 |
| 4 | RxKt! | |

Again, the speediest, most effective way to capture. Black's recapturing Rook will be held fast by a pin.

| 4 | ... | RxR |
| 5 | R–Q1 | |

Threatening very strongly 6 BxR ch.

| 5 | ... | Q–K3 |

Unpins the Knight so that he may answer 6 BxR ch with 6 ... KtxB, and tries also to bring about an exchange of Queens.

White has an attractive continuation in 6 BxKt, QxQ (if 6 ... PxB; 7 BxR ch wins the Queen); 7 BxR mate! A pretty enough win for anybody—but Morphy! He puts his own stamp of elegance on the combination by terminating it thus:

6	BxR ch	KtxB
7	Q–Kt8 ch!	KtxQ
8	R–Q8 mate	

White to play

215

MORPHY-HARRWITZ
Match, 1858

The key to the combination on the King side is a preliminary attack on the base of Black's Pawn chain in the center, a procedure recommended by Nimzovich, a master strategist who appeared long after Morphy's time.

1 **P–B5!**   **RxBP**

If 1 ... PxP; 2 QxP ch wins the exposed Rook at once. Or if 1 ... R–Q2; 2 PxP, BxP; 3 KtxB, R(Q2)xKt; 4 RxKP, Q–Q2 (Q–Kt4; 5 R–K8 ch, K–Kt2; 6 Q–K7 ch, K–R3; 7 Q–R4 ch, K–Kt2; 8 R–B7 ch, KxR; 9 Q–K7 mate); 5 R–K8 ch, R–Kt1 (K–Kt2; 6 R–K7 ch wins the Queen); 6 Q–K5 ch, Q–Kt2; 7 RxR ch, KxR; 8 Q–K8 ch and mate next move.

After Black's actual move, the Rook having been lured away, his Bishop is protected only by the Queen. This is a salient point in the combination, as we shall see.

2 **RxP** ch!

A brilliant sacrifice, made possible only by the subtle preceding move.

2 ...   **KxR**

Forced, as the Bishop was doubly attacked.

3 **Q–R5** ch   **K–Kt1**
4 **KtxB** ch   **K–Kt2**

If 4 ... QxKt; 5 QxR ch, K–R1 (Q–Kt2; 6 Q–K8 ch, K–R2; 7 R–B7 wins the Queen); 6 R–B7, and Black must give up his Queen to avoid mate.

5 **Kt–B5** ch   **K–Kt1**

Other King moves allow a discovered check winning the Queen.

6 **KtxP**   Resigns

The Queen must move, after which 7 QxR ch is fatal.

White to play

216

MORPHY-THOMPSON
New York, 1859

The finish of a Knight-odds game. Morphy's attack on a pinned piece (a natural target) leads to his Rook reaching the seventh rank. This in turn enables Morphy to sacrifice his Queen and mate with a Bishop.

1	P–K5	Kt–K1
2	Q–R4	Q–Kt5
3	P–K6	

A third attack on the Bishop, meanwhile cutting off Black's Queen from its defense.

| 3 | ... | Kt–B3 |
| 4 | RxB ch | K–B1 |

If 4 ... K–K1; the quickest way is 5 R–QB7 dis ch, K–Q1; 6 P–K7 mate.

| 5 | Q–B6 ch! | PxQ |
| 6 | B–R6 mate | |

White to play

217

MORPHY-LEWIS
Philadelphia, 1859

Control of the center and possession of a couple of open files entitles Morphy to look for a decisive combination—and being Morphy, he finds it!

| 1 | R–KKt3 |

Threatens 2 QxRP.

| 1 | ... | K–R2 |
| 2 | R(B1)–B3 | R–KKt1 |

To prevent 3 RxP ch, KxR; 4 R–Kt3 ch, K–R2; 5 R–KR3, P–KB4; 6 Q–Kt6 ch winning. If instead 2 ... P–Kt3; 3 KtxKtP, PxKt; 4 RxP is decisive.

| 3 | Kt–R3! |

Intending 4 Kt–Kt5 ch, K–R1; 5 RxP, Q–Q1; 6 QxP ch, PxQ; 7 R–R7 mate.

| 3 | ... | P–Kt3 |
| 4 | Kt–Kt5 ch! | QxKt |

On 4 ... K–Kt2; the reply 5 KtxP (even stronger than 5 RxP ch) with threats against the Rook Pawn and Knight Pawn is convincing.

| 5 | RxP ch | K–R1 |

If 5 ... R–Kt2; 6 RxQ (simpler than 6 RxR ch, KxR; 7 RxQ which also wins), PxQ; 7 R(Kt5)xR ch, and Black can turn down his King.

| 6 | QxQ | PxQ |
| 7 | R–KR3 mate! | |

10

TACTICIAN BY INSTINCT

William Steinitz

The delight in gambits is a sign of chess youth. . . In very much the same way as the young man, on reaching his manhood years, lays aside the Indian stories and stories of adventure, and turns to the psychological novel, we with maturing experience leave off gambit playing and become interested in the less vivacious but withal more forceful maneuvers of the position player.

—Emanuel Lasker

It took a long time for Steinitz to realize the validity of Lasker's remarks. Early in his life, Steinitz, who revelled in the excitement of combination play said of his own style, "I did not play with the object of winning directly, but to sacrifice a piece." Late in his career Steinitz discovered what we know now, that position play—the art of placing pieces where they will be most effective—is the best possible preparation for releasing accumulated energy in the explosion of a combination.

White to play

218

STEINITZ-MONGREDIEN
London, 1862

"The finest combination played in the tournament," said Anderssen of this sparkling King side attack. Anderssen, winner of the tournament, was somewhat of a connoisseur of combination play himself.

1	P–KKt4	PxP
2	RxP!	KtxKt
3	BPxKt	KxR
4	QxP	R–KKt1

If 4 ... Q–K1; 5 Q–R5 ch, K–Kt2; 6 B–R6 ch, K–Kt1; 7 BxP wins for White.

117

| 5 | Q–R5 ch | K–Kt2 |
| 6 | Q–R6 ch | |

Of course, 6 QxP ch, K–R1 leaving White's Queen pinned, would be a terrible blunder.

| 6 | ... | K–B2 |
| 7 | Q–R7 ch | K–K3 |

If 7 ... R–Kt2; 8 BxP ch, K–B1; 9 Q–R8 ch, R–Kt1; 10 B–R6 mate.

| | 8 Q–R3 ch | |

The King must not escape to the Queen side.

8	...	K–B2
9	R–B1 ch	K–K1
10	Q–K6	R–Kt2
11	B–KKt5	Q–Q2

Or 11 ... B–B1; 12 Q–B6 ch, B–Q2; 13 QxKtP ch, RxQ; 14 BxP mate.

12	BxP ch	RxB
13	QxR ch	K–Q1
14	R–B8 ch	Q–K1
15	QxQ mate	

White to play

There are tricks of the trade in combination play. Note how Steinitz pauses to tighten his grip on an open file before capturing an unprotected Knight.

1	KtxRP	KtxKt
2	RxKt	KxR
3	Q–R5 ch	K–Kt1
4	R–R1	

Threatens mate on the move. The natural capture by 4 QxKt allows Black time to reorganize his forces by 4 ... Q–B3, after which a clear win for White is not evident.

| 4 | ... | R–K1 |
| 5 | QxKt | Q–B3 |

To stop 6 QxP mate.

6	BxP ch!	QxB
7	R–R8 ch	KxR
8	QxQ	

And White wins.

White to play

219

STEINITZ-MONGREDIEN
London, 1863

220

STEINITZ-ROCK
London, 1863

From a Rook-odds game. Steinitz's Queen sacrifice forces Black's King to walk down the white squares to his doom.

1	R–K1 ch	B–K3
2	PxB!	KtxQ
3	PxP dble ch	K–Q2
4	B–K6 ch	K–B3
5	Kt–K5 ch	K–Kt4
6	B–B4 ch	K–R4
7	B–Kt4 ch	K–R5
8	PxKt mate	

Black to play

221

AMATEUR-STEINITZ
London, 1864

"One of the loveliest Queen sacrifices in all chess literature," says Reinfeld of Steinitz's combination and the remarkable move that sets it in motion.

| 1 | ... | Q–R5! |
| 2 | KtxQ | |

White must take the Queen. If instead 2 QxB, R(B1)xKt crashes through.

| 2 | ... | BxP! |

Threatens 2 ... R–B8 mate.

3 Kt–Kt6 ch

Or 3 P–KR3 (to give the King room), R–B8 ch; 4 K–R2, B–Kt8 ch; 5 K–R1, Kt–B7 mate.

3	...	PxKt
4	P–KKt3	R–K7 ch
5	K–R1	RxR ch
6	K–Kt2	R–Kt8 ch
7	K–R3	Kt–B7 ch
8	K–R4	R–B5 ch!

This is the beautiful move which Steinitz had to see in his mind's eye before starting the combination.

9 PxR

If 9 K–Kt5, R–Kt5 is mate.

| 9 | ... | R–Kt5 mate |

White to play

222

STEINITZ-VAN DER MEDEN
London, 1865

Steinitz has not only given Knight-odds, but sacrificed two pieces to work up an attack on Black's King. Now comes a combination that begins with a crashing Rook sacrifice and ends with a curiously quiet Queen move.

1	RxKt ch!	KxR
2	B–Q4 ch	K–B2
3	R–B1 ch	K–Kt1
4	Q–K5	B–Kt2
5	Q–Q5 ch	Q–K3
6	Q–KKt5	Q–KR3
7	Q–Q8 ch	B–B1
8	Q–K8!	

White wins. If Black tries 8 ... Q–Kt2 (the only move to guard against mate while protecting the Bishop) White wins by 9 BxQ, KxB; 10 R–B7 ch, K–R3; 11 R–B6 ch!, K–Kt4; 12 Q–K5 ch, and mate next move.

Black to play

223

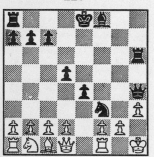

King wanderings are always attractive. Steinitz uses all his pieces in this one, including his Queen's Rook away over in left field!

1	...	QxRP ch!
2	PxQ	RxP ch
3	K–Kt2	R–R7 ch
4	K–Kt3	B–Q3 ch
5	K–Kt4	R–R5 ch
6	K–B5	R–R4 ch
7	K–Kt6	

If 7 K–B6, B–K2 ch; 8 K–K6, R–K4 mate.

7	...	R–Kt4 ch
8	K–R6	B–B1 ch
9	K–R7	K–B2
10	R–R1	B–Kt2

And the Queen Rook mates next move.

Black to play

224

AMATEUR-STEINITZ
The Hague, 1873

A daring combination by Steinitz in which he allows his King to be chased about in order to do some King-chasing himself.

1	...	QxKtP!

Allows an attack beginning with a double check!

2	Kt–Q6 ch	K–Q1

3	Q–K8 ch	K–B2
4	QxQB ch	KxKt
5	R–Q1	Kt–R3!

Offering a Rook which White must accept.

6	QxR	K–B2

Clearing a path for the Bishop. The threat is now 7 ... B–Kt5 ch with a discovered attack on the Queen.

7	QxRP	B–Kt5 ch
8	K–K2	QxBP ch
9	K–B3	Q–B4 ch
10	K–Kt3	

If 10 K–K2, Q–K5 mate.

10	...	B–Q3 ch
11	K–R4	Q–Kt4 ch
12	K–R3	Q–R4 mate

White to play

225

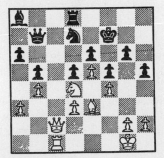

STEINITZ-SELLMAN
Baltimore, 1885

By means of the open file and control of the black squares (the latter concept a mystery to all of his con-

temporaries) Steinitz fashions a combination involving *zugzwang* to crush his opponent to death.

Zugzwang: the compulsion to move when one has nothing but losing moves left.

1	Q–B7!	Q–Kt1

On 1 ... QxQ; 2 RxQ, K–K2 (the only move any of Black's pieces can make!); 3 B–B2, and the threat of 4 B–R4 (with or without check) leaves Black helpless.

2	B–B2!	

Threatens to win the exchange by 3 B–R4.

2	...	Q–Kt3
3	Kt–B3	

The Knight retreats (meanwhile discovering an attack on the Queen) in order to advance.

3	...	QxQ
4	RxQ	

White now threatens 5 B–R4, attacking the protector of the pinned Knight.

4	...	K–K1

A move dictated not only by caution (to unpin the Knight) but also by necessity (the King being the only piece that can move without immediate loss).

5	Kt–Kt5	Kt–B1
6	B–B5!	

Threatens mate on the spot!

6	...	Kt–Q2
7	B–Q6	Resigns

If 7 ... Kt–Kt3 (only the Knight and Rook can move) 8 KtxP, with two threats of mate on the move, wins at once. Or if 7 ... R–Kt1; 8 RxKt, KxR; 9 BxR finishes Black off.

White to play

226

STEINITZ-TCHIGORIN
Havana, 1892

Activity in the center seduces Tchigorin into expecting an obvious recapture there, but disaster strikes suddenly elsewhere.

1 P–Q4	PxP
2 KtxP	BxKt
3 RxB!	KtxR

Ready to reply to 4 BxKt ch with 4 ... R–B3 giving back the exchange, but Steinitz has other plans —involving Tchigorin's King.

4 RxP ch!	KxR
5 Q–R1 ch	K–Kt2
6 B–R6 ch!	K–B3
7 Q–R4 ch	K–K4
8 QxKt ch	

And White mates next move.

White to play

227

STEINITZ-BARDELEBEN
Hastings, 1895

Late in his career, no longer World Champion, no longer the most-feared chess master, Steinitz played a combination that might properly be called "The Steinitz Immortal." It is one of the grand combinations of chess literature.

1 Q–Kt4	P–KKt3

If 1 ... R–KKt1; 2 Kt–Kt5 ch, K–K1; 3 Q–R5 ch, P–Kt3; 4 QxRP, R–KB1; 5 Kt–K6, R–KKt1 (5 ... R–B2; 6 Q–R8 ch wins) 6 Kt–B5, and the attack on the Queen as well as the threat of 7 QxR mate wins for White.

2 Kt–Kt5 ch	K–K1
3 RxKt ch!	K–B1

If 3 ... QxR; 4 RxR ch wins at once, or if 3 ... KxR; 4 R–K1 ch, K–Q3 (4 ... K–Q1; 5 Kt–

K6 ch, K–K2; 6 Kt-B5 ch wins the Queen); 5 Q–Kt4 ch, K–B2; 6 Kt–K6 ch, K–Kt1; 7 Q–B4 ch, R–B2; 8 KtxR, QxKt; 9 R–K8 mate.

Four of White's pieces are *en prise* and he is threatened with mate—but he forces a win!

4   R–B7 ch!   K–Kt1

Clearly if 4 ... QxR; 5 RxR ch wins easily, and if 4 ... K–Q1; 5 QxQ is mate.

5   R–Kt7 ch!   K–R1

Again if 5 ... QxR; 6 RxR ch, RxR; 7 QxR ch, Q–B1; 8 QxQ ch leaves White a piece ahead, while 5 ... KxR loses at once by 6 QxQ ch followed by 7 RxR. Finally, on 5 ... K–B1; 6 KtxP ch, KxR (6 ... K–K1; 7 QxQ mate); 7 QxQ ch is fatal.

6   RxP ch!   Resigns

After 6 ... K–Kt1 there is a remarkably brilliant mate in ten moves, as Steinitz announced and demonstrated at the time: 7 R–Kt7 ch, K–R1 (7 ... K–B1; 8 Kt–R7 ch wins as in the previous note); 8 Q–R4 ch, KxR; 9 Q–R7 ch, K–B1; 10 Q–R8 ch, K–K2; 11 Q–Kt7 ch, K–K1; 12 Q–Kt8 ch, K–K2; 13 Q–B7 ch, K–Q1; 14 Q–B8 ch, Q–K1; 15 Kt–B7 ch, K–Q2; 16 Q–Q6 mate.

This little man has taught us all to play chess.

—Adolf Schwarz

11

LARGE-SCALE OPERATOR

Harry N. Pillsbury

----

*There must have been a time when men were demi-gods—
or they could not have invented chess.*

—Gustav Schenk

Pillsbury was the first master to realize that combinations directed at the
opponent's King were affected by conditions outside of that immediate area.
Control of the center was an important factor, while possession of the square
B5 on the Queen side (remarkable concept!) could be decisive in effecting
mate on the King side. Pillsbury's combinations were often large-scale pro-
ductions, involving operations on the whole board. Réti put it aptly when
he said, "Pillsbury is most wonderful when he sets himself out to exploit
weaknesses in the hostile position. Then does his play on big lines assert
itself; not content with storing up small advantages, he always finds the
right method for destroying his opponent's position root and branch."

White to play

228

PILLSBURY-WALBRODT
Boston, 1893

The young expert overwhelms the
European master with an assortment
of pins, Knight forks and discovered
attacks.

1 Kt–Q5!	Q–B1

If 1 ... KtxKt; 2 PxKt, Kt–
Kt1; 3 B–KKt5 with a pin and discovered attack on the Queen.

2	RxKt!	BxR
3	R–B1	K–B1
4	RxB	Q–K1
5	BxP	QxP
6	B–KKt5	P–R3

Black avoids 6 ... KtxP; 7 R–B4 losing a Knight, or 6 ... QxQP; 7 Kt–K7 ch, K–Q1 (7 ... KtxKt; 8 QxQ); 8 KtxKt ch, losing his Queen.

7   R–B7

Threatens 8 RxB, KxR; 9 Kt–B6 ch, winning the Queen.

| 7 ... | Q–Kt3 |
| 8 **Q–B4** | **P–Kt4** |

Suspecting nothing, but what can he do? If he moves the Bishop to K3 then 9 R–B6, Q–Kt1; 10 RxB, QxR; 11 Kt–Kt6 ch wins the Queen. Or if he protects the Bishop by 8 ... R–R2 (not 8 ... Q–K3 on account of 9 Kt–Kt6 ch, nor 8 ... Kt–Kt1 when 9 Kt–K7 ch wins) then 9 RxR, QxR; 10 Q–B8 ch forces mate.

| 9   **RxB!** | **KxR** |

Black must accept the sacrifice as 9 ... PxB loses by 10 RxP ch followed by 11 RxKt.

| 10   **Q–Kt4** ch | **K–K1** |

Again forced, as 10 ... Q–K3 costs the Queen after 11 Kt–B6 ch.

11 **KtxP** ch	**K–B1**
12 **Q–B4** ch	**K–Kt2**
13 **Kt–K6** ch	**K–R2**

Distressing, but then so is 13 ... K–Kt1; 14 Kt–B8 ch.

| 14 **B–Q3** | **Resigns** |

The pin of his Queen coupled

with the threat of mate on the move convinces Walbrodt.

White to play

229

PILLSBURY-TARRASCH
Hastings, 1895

The final combination from one of the greatest games in all chess history, won against Tarrasch, then the world's leading tournament player. For the unknown Pillsbury it was a marvellous achievement and presaged his winning the tournament, despite the presence in it of such giants as Lasker, Steinitz, Tarrasch, Tchigorin, Schlechter and Teichmann.

1   KtxB!

Before proceeding on the King side Pillsbury disposes of two pieces that might help defend the King. He kills off the Bishop and draws the Rook away from the open Rook file.

| 1 ... | RxKt |
| 2 **Kt–R6** | |

Threatens 3 R–Kt8 mate.

2 ...   R–Kt2

If instead 2 ... R–K1; 3 Q–
Kt3 forces mate at Kt7 or Kt8.

3 RxR   KxR
4 Q–Kt3 ch!   KxKt

On 4 ... K–B1; 5 Q–Kt8 ch
picks up the stranded Rook.

5 K–R1!

A quiet move, making room for
the Rook on the Knight file. The attractive 5 R–B4, threatening 6 R–R4
mate, allows Black to escape. He
plays 5 ... R–Kt8 ch, and either
draws by perpetual check, or forces
White to exchange Rooks.

5 ...   Q–Q4
6 R–KKt1   QxBP

Black must give up the Queen to
prevent mate.

7   Q–R4 ch   Q–R4
8   Q–B4 ch   Q–Kt4
9   RxQ   PxR
10 Q–Q6 ch   K–R4
11 QxKt   P–B7

A last despairing hope. Pillsbury
might fall for 12 Q–B7 ch, K–R3;
13 QxR, P–B8(Q) ch, or for 12 Q–
B6, R–Kt8 ch; 13 K–Kt2, P–B8(Q).
But Pillsbury puts an end to such
wild dreams.

13 QxP mate

White to play

230

PILLSBURY–POLLOCK
Hastings, 1895

In an ending with scanty material
on the board, Pillsbury creates effects
with bits of things—a Knight occupy-
ing QB5, an open file, a centralized
King. An artist needs little to work
with, to enchant us.

1 K–K3!

To centralize his King Pillsbury
gives up two Pawns and allows his
opponent two connected passed
Pawns!

1   ...   RxP ch
2   K–Q4   RxKKtP
3   Kt–B5!

Very strong! It stops 3 ... R–
QKt6· (to head off White's passed
Pawn), it prevents the check at Q6,
and hinders Black from playing 3
... R–Kt7, when the reply 4 KtxB
wins a piece for White. The Knight's
dominating position at QB5 also has
a strong influence on the King side
as we shall see.

3	...	P–R5
4	P–Kt4	P–R6

Intending to continue with 5 ... R–Kt7; 6 R–Q1 (if 6 KtxB, RxR ch; 7 KtxR, P–R7 and Black wins); P–R7 and the threats of Queening the Pawn by 8 ... R–Kt8 or 8 ... R–Q7 ch assure the win for Black.

5   R–QR2

A threat of mate, which has priority over anything else.

5	...	K–Kt1
6	R–R8 ch	K–R2
7	P–K6!	PxP

If 7 ... P–R7; 8 PxP, P–R8(Q); 9 R–R8 ch, KxR; 10 P–B8(Q) ch and mate next move.

8	KtxB	PxKt
9	P–B7	R–KB6

Naturally if 9 ... P–R7; 10 P–B8(Q) threatening mate, wins for White.

10	P–B8(Q)	RxQ
11	RxR	P–Kt4

If 11 ... P–R7; 12 R–B1 followed by 13 R–KR1 will remove the reckless Pawn.

12	KxP	P–Kt5
13	R–B1	P–K4

If 13 ... P–R7; 14 R–KR1, P–Kt6; 15 K–B3 wins, or if 13 ... P–Kt6; 14 R–KR1, P–Kt7; 15 RxP ch, K–Kt3; 16 R–Kt3 ch disposes of the passed Pawns.

14	P–Kt5	P–Kt6

Against 14 ... K–Kt3 White plays 15 P–Kt6, P–Kt6 (if 15 ... K–R4; 16 P–Kt7 wins); 16 K–B3, P–Kt7; 17 R–KKt1, and the passed Pawns fall.

15	R–KR1	Resigns

White to play

231

PILLSBURY–GUNSBERG
Hastings, 1895

Pillsbury's striking combination results in his obtaining two connected passed Pawns in the center. So impressed was Fine by the beauty of Pillsbury's play that he accorded ten exclamation marks to Pillsbury's first four moves, in annotating the position for BASIC CHESS ENDINGS.

1   P–B5!

To get at the Queen Pawn, White attacks the base of the Pawn chain Q4 and K3.

"White's play from here to the end is of the highest order," says Lasker.

1	...	P–Kt4

If 1 ... KPxP; 2 PxP, PxP (on 2 ... P–Kt4; 3 Kt–Kt4 wins the Queen Pawn); 3 Kt–B4, followed by 4 KtxQP gives White two connected passed Pawns.

2 Kt–Kt4!   P–QR4
3 P–B6!

White's reply to 3 ... PxKt will be 4 P–B7 followed by Queening the Pawn.

3 ...   K–Q3
4 PxP!

Now the winning idea after 4 ... PxKt is 5 P–K7, KxP; 6 P–B7, and the Pawn cannot be stopped.

4 ...   KtxP
5 KtxKt   KxKt

After this it looks as though White's advanced Pawn is lost, and with it the game and first prize in the tournament. But Pillsbury has a few surprises left.

6 P–K4!

"The key to the remarkable combination." (Lasker)

6 ...   PxP
7 P–Q5 ch!

Suddenly the position is transformed! White has two connected passed Pawns safe from harm (if 7 ... KxP; 8 P–K7 wins) while Black's King Pawn is doomed.

7 ...   K–Q3
8 K–K3   P–Kt5
9 KxP   P–R5
10 K–Q4   P–R4

Against 10 ... K–K2, a more stubborn defense, White wins nicely by 11 K–B4, P–Kt6; 12 PxP, P–R6; 13 K–B3, P–B4; 14 PxP, P–R4; 15 P–Kt4, P–R7; 16 K–Kt2, P–R8(Q) ch; 17 KxQ, P–Kt5; 18 P–Kt5, P–R5; 19 P–Kt6, P–Kt6; 20 PxP, PxP; 21 P–Q6 ch, KxQP (if 21 ... K–B3; 22 P–Q7, K–K2; 89 P–B6 ch, K–Q1; 24 P–B7 wins); 22 P–Kt7, K–B2; 23 P–K7, P–Kt7; 24 P–Kt8(Q) ch, KxQ; 25 P–K8(Q) ch, followed by halting the Pawn.

11 PxP   P–R6
12 K–B4   P–B4
13 P–R6   P–B5
14 P–R7   Resigns

White to play

232

PILLSBURY–WINAWER
Budapest, 1896

An illustration of what Hoffer termed, "The proverbial combination expected by the stronger player who sees farther ahead than his opponent."

1 Kt–K5!   BxP

2 **BxP!**   **BxP**

Black is playing with fire, but
what can he do? If 2 ... PxB;
3 Q–Kt3 ch, K–B1 (or R1); 4 Kt–
Kt6 ch discovers an attack on his
Queen.

3 **QxB**   **PxB**
4 **Q–KB4**

Again menacing the Queen by 5
Q–Kt3 ch followed by 6 Kt–Kt6 ch.

4 ...   **Kt–Q4**
5 **QxP!**   **P–B3**

On 5 ... QxKt White forces
the win by 6 B–R7 ch (Note the
technique in this sort of position:
Not 6 Q–R7 ch, and the King escapes
by way of K2), K–R1; 7 B–Kt6 ch,
K–Kt1; 8 Q–R7 ch, K–B1; 9 QxP
mate.

6 **P–B4**   **R–K2**

If 6 ... PxKt; 7 Q–Kt6 ch,
K–B1; 8 PxP ch, K–K2; 9 R–B7
ch wins, and if 6 ... Q–Kt2;
7 Q–R5, B–Q2 (Black's Rook was
attacked); 8 R–B3 followed by 9
R–KKt3 is convincing.

7 **Kt–Kt6!**   Resigns

The Rook was attacked, but it
dared not move away:
If 7 ... R–B2 (self-block); 8
Q–R8 mate
If 7 ... R–R2 (self-block); 8
Q–B8 mate
If 7 ... R–Kt2; 8 Q–R8 ch,
K–B2; 9 Q–B8 mate
If 7 ... R–Q2; 8 Q–B8 ch, K–
R2; 9 Q–R8 mate

If 7 ... R–K1 (self-block); 8
Q–R8 ch, K–B2; 9 Q–R7 mate

Black to play

233

MC CONNELL-PILLSBURY
New Orleans, 1898

A beautiful piece of play by Pillsbury from a little-known game.

1 ...   **P–QR4!**

Notice how a great master creates
attacking opportunities. Not only
does the Pawn threaten to advance
and break up White's King side position, but it also opens up a file for
the Queen's Rook.

2 **Q–B4**

To unpin the Queen Knight. If
instead 2 K–Kt1 (to follow with 3
Kt–Q5, breaking the pin by force),
P–R5; 3 Kt–Q5, BxQ; 4 KtxQ ch,
PxKt; 5 RxB, PxP, and White is helpless against the effects of 6 ... PxP
ch followed by 7 ... R–R8 ch.

2 ...   **P–R5**
3 **PxP**

To prevent 3 ... PxP; 4 PxP, RxKt!; 5 KtxR, R–R8 mate.

3 ...   RxP

Black threatens 4 ... RxKt!; 5 KtxR(R4) (if 5 KtxR(K2), R–R8 is mate), RxP ch; 6 K–Kt1, B–Q3, and White's Queen is surrounded.

4   Kt–Kt3

On 4 KtxR, RxKt; 5 P–B3, R–B7 ch; 6 K–Kt1, B–Q3 and White falls into the loss in the previous note.

4 ...   R–R8 ch
5   K–Q2

On 5 Kt–Kt1, RxKt ch; 6 KxR, BxP ch discovers an attack on the Queen.

5 ...   B–Q3!

This is the killer in all cases!

6   QxB(B5)   QxP ch
7   Q–Q3   B–B5 mate

Black to play

234

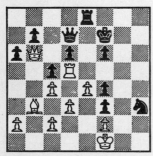

An attack that is met by a counter-attack may be old-fashioned but it's exciting. Here it results in a fine combination with a lusty finish.

1 ...   Q–Kt5
2   K–K1

The King must run. If instead 2 QxP ch, R–K2, and White is threatened with loss of the Queen as well as mate on the move.

2 ...   KtxP!
3   RxQP

Naturally, White avoids 3 KxKt, Q–Kt7 ch followed by mate.

3 ...   RxP ch!

The Rook forces his way into the position.

4   K–Q2

If 4 PxR, Q–Kt8 ch; 5 K–Q2, KtxP ch; 6 K–Q3, Q–K6 mate.

4 ...   R–K7 ch
5   K–B1

On 5 K–B3, Kt–Q8 mates neatly.

5 ...   R–K3!

A good clearance move, enabling Pillsbury's Queen and Rook to operate on the King file.

6   QxP ch   R–K2
7   Q–Q5 ch   K–Kt2
8   R–Q8   Q–K3

White can now exchange Queens and go into a drab, hopeless ending, or pursue his attack—and lose gallantly.

9   Q–R5

Janowsky takes a chance, risking everything on his threat of 10 Q–R8 ch, K–Kt3; 11 R–Kt8 ch, K–B4; 12 Q–R5 mate.

9 ...   Q–Q8 ch

Pillsbury gets there first!

10	K–Kt2	Kt–Q8 ch
11	K–B1	Kt–B6 ch
12	K–Kt2	Q–Kt8 ch!
13	KxKt	

If 13 K–R3, Q–B8 is a nice mate.

| 13 | ... | Q–R8 ch |
| 14 | K–Q2 | Q–K8 mate |

White to play

235

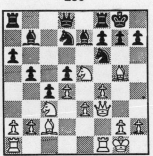

PILLSBURY-MARCO
Paris, 1900

Paying no attention to the threats to his Queen side, Pillsbury crashes through with an attack which destroys Black's King side. He lets a Knight be taken on one wing as a curtain-raiser to his sacrifices on the other!

1   Q–R3!

Threat: 2 KtxKt, QxKt (if 2 ... KtxKt; 3 QxP mate); 3 BxP ch, K–R1 (3 ... KtxB; 4 QxQ); 4 B–B5 ch, and White wins the Queen.

1	...	P–Kt3
2	P–B5!	P–Kt5
3	PxP!	RPxP

If 3 ... PxKt; 4 BxKt (threatens 5 QxP mate), KtxB; 5 RxKt, BPxP; 6 BxP, PxB; 7 RxP mate!

4   Q–R4   PxKt

Black is no better off with 4 ... KtxKt; 5 PxKt, PxKt; 6 PxKt, B–Q3; 7 Q–R6, and mate stares him in the face.

5   KtxKt!

Weakens Black's King Knight by taking away its support.

| 5 | ... | QxKt |
| 6 | RxKt! | P–R4 |

Naturally 6 ... BxR; 7 BxB is fatal, death coming on the black squares.

| 7 | QR–KB1 | R–R3 |
| 8 | BxP! | |

With a threat of mate by the Queen. Black is forced to take the Bishop.

8	...	PxB
9	RxR ch	BxR
10	RxB ch	KxR
11	Q–R8 ch	K–B2
12	Q–R7 ch	K–B1

Other moves allow instant mate by the Queen.

13   QxQ   Resigns

Black cannot prevent 14 B–R6 ch followed by mate.

White to play

236

PILLSBURY-JUDD
St. Louis, 1901

A combination is in the air. But in order to get all the machinery (a Queen, two Rooks and a Knight) going, it needs the keen thrust of a Pawn.

1   P–KKt4!   Kt–Q5

If 1 ... Kt–Kt2; 2 P–Kt5 (2 Kt–Q6 does not win the exchange as 2 ... Q–K2 pins the Knight), R–Kt1; 3 Kt–B6 ch, K–R1; 4 R–Q7, and White has a winning advantage.

2   RxKt!   PxR
3   Kt–B6 ch   K–R1

If 3 ... RxKt; 4 RxR ch, K–Kt2; 5 Q–B8 mate, or if 3 ... K–Kt2; 4 KtxR ch wins a piece.

4   RxR

This too wins a piece: 4 ...

PxR; 5 KtxR, or 4 ... RxR; 5 Q–B8 mate.

4   ...   Resigns

White to play

237

PILLSBURY-GUNSBERG
Monte Carlo, 1902

Pillsbury's combination starts with a Rook sacrifice which ties Black up in knots. A series of exchanges then clears the board for the triumphal march of Pillsbury's passed Pawn.

1   RxP!   PxR
2   Kt–B4   B–QKt2

To help the unfortunate Knight. The power of White's pin can be seen in the way any move of Black's Knight is punished at once by 3 QxRP mate.

3   R–Kt3 ch   B–Kt2
4   R–R3   B–R1

If 4 ... B–KB1; 5 QxBP, R–Q2; 6 KtxKt, BxKt; 7 BxB ch, K–R1 (7 ... RxB; 8 QxRP mate); 8 BxR, QxB; 9 QxR wins for White.

5	QxP	Q–Q2
6	KtxKt!	BxKt

The beauty of Pillsbury's combination can be seen in this alternative line: if 6 ... QxQ; 7 Kt–K7 ch, K–B1; 8 KtxQ, R–QB2 (if 8 ... R–Q2; 9 R–Kt3 threatening mate forces 9 ... B–Kt2; 10 KtxB, RxKt; 11 B–R6 winning a Rook); 9 R–Kt3, K–K1; 10 B–K6, R–B2 (to interpose on a Rook check); 11 BxR ch, KxB; 12 Kt–Q6 ch and White wins.

7	QxB	QxQ
8	BxQ	R–KB1
9	B–R6	

Intending 10 R–Kt3 ch, B–Kt2; 11 RxB ch, K–R1; 12 BxR, winning.

9	...	B–Kt2
10	BxB	KxB
11	R–Kt3 ch	

Not at once 11 BxR, KxB, and the King is closer to the center.

11	...	K–R1
12	BxR	RxB
13	K–B2	R–B2
14	K–K2	R–B5
15	K–Q3	P–Kt4
16	R–K3	R–R5
17	P–Q5!	RxP
18	P–Q6	R–R3
19	R–K6	

Threatens 20 P–Q7, RxR; 21 P–Q8(Q) ch.

19	...	K–Kt2

No better is 19 ... R–Kt3; 20 P–Q7, R–Kt1; 21 R–K8 ch, winning.

20	P–Q7	RxR
21	P–Q8(Q)	

White wins.

White to play

238

Hanover, 1902

A combination with more than its share of eye-catching moves. For example: Pillsbury breaks loose from a pin by permitting an enemy Pawn to attack two of his pieces!

1	B–Q5!	Q–B4
2	RxKt ch!	KxR

Clearly, 2 ... RxR; 3 B–Q6 ch winning the Queen is unthinkable.

3	QxP	PxB

If 3 ... R–KB1; 4 R–K1 ch, K–Q2; 5 B–K6 ch, K–K1; 6 BxP ch, K–Q2; 7 Q–Kt4 ch forces mate.

4	QxR ch	K–Q2
5	QxP	K–B1
6	QxP	P–Q5
7	Q–K6 ch	R–Q2

8	Q–Kt8 ch	R–Q1
9	Q–Kt4 ch	R–Q2
10	B–K3!	

Allows the Pawn to attack two pieces. It dares not capture though, the penalty for 10 ... PxB being 11 QxR ch, and an easy win for White.

| 10 | ... | BxP |
| 11 | RxP | Resigns |

White to play

239

PILLSBURY-WOLF
Monte Carlo, 1903

One of Pillsbury's most attractive combinations despite the fact that he misses a problem-like winning move—an offer of a piece that can be captured in five different ways!

1 R–B4

Bringing up the reserves to help assault the King's position.

1 ... R–Kt1

Black intends to move the Rook to Kt3 where it will attack the Queen, and help defend the vulnerable point, the King Knight Pawn.

2 BxP!

The Bishop cannot be captured. If 2 ... RPxB; 3 R–R8 is mate. Or if 2 ... KtxB (2 ... BPxB; 3 QxKt mate); 3 RxKt ch, RPxR; 4 R–R4, and mate will follow at R8.

2 ... R–Kt3

This looks good, since the Queen is attacked, as well as the Bishop behind the Queen. But Pillsbury has two excellent replies—the move he actually makes and the one he misses!

3 QxR(Kt6)

Better than this is 3 Kt–K6! (threatening 4 Q–Kt7 mate) which is brilliant, and (more to the point) immediately decisive. The proof:

If 3 ... PxKt; 4 QxKt mate.

If 3 ... KtxKt; 4 BxRP ch, K–B1; 5 Q–R8 mate.

If 3 ... R(K2)xKt; 4 BxBP ch, QxB; 5 QxQ ch, K–R1; 6 QxKt mate.

If 3 ... BxKt; 4 BxRP ch, KtxB; 5 RxKt, KxR; 6 R–R4 ch, K–Kt1; 7 R–R8 mate.

If 3 ... R(Kt3)xKt; 4 BxRP ch, KtxB; 5 R–Kt4 ch, K–B1; 6 Q–R8 mate.

3 ... KtxB

On 3 ... QxQ White wins by 4 BxRP ch, KtxB; 5 RxQ.

4 Q–KB6 R–K1

After 4 ... KtxR; 5 PxKt, Black is helpless against the threat of 6 R–R5 followed by 7 R–Kt5 ch.

5 **R–B1**

White prepares to regroup his heavy pieces.

5	...	**B–K3**
6	**Q–Kt5**	**K–R1**
7	**Q–R5**	**Kt–B1**
8	**KtxB!**	

The Knight coming from the Queen side strikes the decisive blow!

8 ... **RxKt**

Or 8 ... KtxKt (8 ... PxKt; 9 QxR); 9 RxRP ch, K–Kt1; 10 R–R8 ch and mate next move.

9 **RxR**   Resigns

The continuation 9 ... KtxR (9 ... PxR; 10 RxKt ch); 10 RxP is hopeless for Black. He could not then parry the simultaneous attack on his King and Queen.

12

MAN OF METHOD
Siegbert Tarrasch

It is not a move, even the best move, that you must seek, but a realizable plan.

—Eugene Znosko-Borovsky

Thousands of experts owe their understanding of chess to Tarrasch. Tarrasch's own games are marvellous examples of strategy in the classical tradition, and the combinations that he created as a result of his careful preliminary planning are not flashy, but precise, economical and sound to the core. Good as the games were, Tarrasch's notes to them were even better. Tarrasch held no secrets back. He explained in full detail everything that was going on, and patiently described the reasons for the moves he made or rejected. Tarrasch holds the title of The Great Teacher of Chess, with very few worthy contenders in sight.

White to play

240

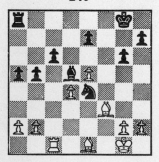

TARRASCH-ALAPIN
Nuremberg, 1892
136

Tarrasch surrounds the centralized Knight and threatens to win it. Black's King rushes to save the Knight, only to find himself caught (unjust reward of a kind act!) in a mating net.

1 P–KR4

Takes away the Knight's last flight square.

1	...	K–B2
2	R–B2	K–K3
3	R–K2	K–B4
4	P–Kt4 ch	K–B5
	5 K–Kt2!	

To this there is no reply. White's

threat of 6 RxKt, BxR; 7 B–Q2 mate cannot be parried.

7	Kt–K2 ch!	K–Kt3
8	R–B6 ch!	KxR
9	B–Kt5 ch	K–Kt3
10	Kt–B4 mate	

White to play

241

TARRASCH-ROMBERG
Nuremberg, 1893

From a Rook-odds game. One hardly knows which to admire more, Tarrasch's brilliant sacrifices, or the elegant maneuvering of his Knights as they administer mate.

1 **Kt–Q5!**

Threatens a quick finish by 2 Kt–B6 ch, PxKt; 3 QxKt, PxKt (to prevent 4 QxP mate); 4 P–B6, and White mates at Kt7.

1 . . .		K–R1
2	P–B6	B–KKt5
3	PxP ch	KxP
4	QxKt ch!	KxQ
5	Kt–K6 ch!	K–R4

If 5 . . . K–Kt3; 6 R–B6 ch, K–R4; 7 R–R6 mate.

6 Kt(Q5)–B4 ch   K–R3

On 6 . . . K–R5; 7 P–Kt3 mates instantly.

White to play

242

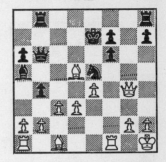

TARRASCH-TCHIGORIN
Match, 1893

A clever Rook sacrifice is the prelude to a picturesque finish—the epaulette mate.

1 **Q–R5**

Threatens 2 RxP!, QxR (2 . . . KxR; 3 Q–Kt5 mate); 3 B–Kt5, winning the Queen by a pin.

1 . . .		Kt–Kt3
2	RxP!	KxR
3	B–Kt5 ch	K–Kt2

If 3 . . . K–K4; 4 B–K7 ch, P–B4; 5 QxP mate.

| 4 | Q–R6 ch | K–Kt1 |
| 5 | R–KB1 | R–KB1 |

To prevent 6 BxP mate.

6 B–KB6   QxB

Even great masters hate to resign.

7 RxQ

And wins. Black has no defense against 8 RxKt ch, RPxR; 9 QxP mate.

White to play

243

TARRASCH-SCHEVE
Leipzig, 1894

In an accurately calculated combination attention must be paid to the little things—such as the little Rook Pawns.

1 B–Q6!

This will lure the Queen away from the defense of the Knight Pawn.

| 1 ... | QxB |
| 2 RxP ch | K–B1 |

2 ... K–R1 allows 3 QxP ch!, KtxQ; 4 R–Kt8 mate.

3 RxP ch!

It is important to destroy this Pawn!

| 3 ... | K–K2 |
| 4 RxR ch | KxR |

| 5 R–Kt7 ch | K–K1 |
| 6 QxKt | Resigns |

If 6 ... Q–B1; 7 Q–Kt6 ch (White could not make this move with Black's Rook Pawn still on the board), K–Q1; 8 R–Kt8 and the pin wins the Queen.

White to play

244

TARRASCH-JANOWSKY
Ostend, 1907

Despite the presence of so many heavy pieces on the board, Tarrasch evolves a combination with as pretty a set of Pawn moves as I've ever seen.

1 P–Kt4!

Intending to break in by 2 P–Kt5. If Black tries to stop this by 1 ... K–R3 he falls into a beautiful loss by 2 P–Kt7, (a vicious attack on both of Black's Rooks), KxKtP; 3 Q–Kt6 mate!

| 1 ... | Q–K2 |
| 2 P–Kt5 | PxP |

Forced, as otherwise 3 PxP ch is disastrous.

| 3 | QxR ch | RxQ |
| 4 | RxR | QxR |

This is forced; if 4 ... Q–Q3; 5 R(B2)–B7 ch, K–R3; 6 R–R8 mate. Or if 4 ... Q–B4; 5 P–Q4 attacks the Queen, unpins the Rook and renews the threat of mate in two.

5 P–R6 ch!

The point! The hasty 5 RxQ, KxR would leave a drawn ending.

| 5 | ... | K–Kt1 |
| 6 | P–R7 ch! | Resigns |

After 6 ... K–Kt2 White finally takes the Queen and wins.

Black to play

245

SPIELMANN–TARRASCH
San Sebastian, 1912

Tarrasch wins this by an idea rarely found in actual games. It is the problem-like Indian theme, where the piece that is to give mate has its line of action shut off by another piece!

1 ... QxB!

| 2 | RxQ | RxR |
| 3 | P–Kt4 | |

To give the King a flight-square from the Rook's mate threat.

The natural continuation 3 ... B–Q3 allows the following defense: 3 ... B–Q3; 4 B–K3, P–Kt3; 5 Q–R4, P–Kt4; 6 Q–R5, KtPxP; 7 Q–B7 ch, and White can force a draw by perpetual check. Tarrasch finds another Bishop move—a brilliant key to the combination.

3 ... B–B8!

White faces these possibilities:
(a) 4 K–Kt1, B–K6 ch; 5 K–R2, BxP ch; 6 B–Kt3, R–R8 mate.

(b) 4 B–K1, BxP ch; 5 K–Kt1, B–Kt6, and White must give up his Queen to prevent mate.

(c) 4 K–Kt3, P–Kt3; 5 Q–R4, BxP ch; 6 KxB, P–Kt4 ch, and the Pawn's double attack wins the Queen.

Spielmann of course resigned.

Black to play

246

NIMZOVICH–TARRASCH
St. Petersburg, 1914

A two-Bishop sacrifice is the feature of this sparkling combination.

Tarrasch would have been awarded the first brilliancy prize except for the fact that Lasker had won a game by a somewhat similar idea 25 years previously!

1	...	BxP ch!
2	KxB	Q–R5 ch
3	K–Kt1	BxKKtP!

This must have come as a shock!

4   P–B3

If 4 KxB, Q–Kt5 ch; 5 K–R1, R–Q4; 6 QxP, R–R4 ch!; 7 QxR, QxQ ch; 8 K–Kt2, Q–Kt4 ch, and Black picks up the Knight and wins.

| 4 | ... | KR–K1 |

Much more to the point than the unimaginative 4 ... BxR. Black's threat is 5 ... R–K7 followed by 6 ... Q–R8 mate.

5	Kt–K4	Q–R8 ch
6	K–B2	BxR
7	P–Q5	

With the hope of a counter-attack along the long diagonal. Naturally, he avoids 7 RxB, which loses the Queen after the reply 7 ... Q–R7 ch.

| 7 | ... | P–B4! |
| 8 | Q–B3 | |

Threatens mate on the move. There was no hope in 8 Kt–B6 ch, K–B2; 9 KtxR, RxKt, and White can hardly escape being mated.

| 8 | ... | Q–Kt7 ch |
| 9 | K–K3 | RxKt ch! |

Chess is not for the kind-hearted.

| 10 | PxR | P–B5 ch |

Intent on winning by the line of play he analyzed, Tarrasch misses a mate in three, beginning with 10 ... Q–Kt6 ch.

11	KxP	R–B1 ch
12	K–K5	Q–R7 ch
13	K–K6	R–K1 ch
14	K–Q7	

If 14 K–B6, Q–R5 is mate.

| 14 | ... | B–Kt4 mate |

White to play

247

TARRASCH-SATZINGER
Munich, 1915

A fascinating tour by the Knight which retreats to the first rank and works its way up the board into the heart of Black's position to execute the mate. Oh yes, there is a Queen sacrifice too, but then everybody sacrifices Queens nowadays.

1   Kt–Q1!

It's hard to picture the importance of the role this Knight plays. For the moment it stands on the back rank, far away from the theater of action.

1	...	B–Kt2
2	Kt–B2	P–B5
3	Kt–Kt4!	

The Knight is getting there by leaps and bounds.

| 3 | ... | P–B4 |

If 3 ... PxB; 4 Kt–B6 ch, PxKt; 5 PxBP, Kt–B4; 6 RxKt, PxR; 7 Q–R6, and White forces mate.

4	PxPe.p.	Kt–B4
5	PxKtP	KtxKtP
6	QxP ch!	KxQ
7	R–R3 ch	K–Kt1

If 7 ... Kt–R4; 8 RxKt ch, K–Kt1; 9 R–R8 ch!, KtxR; 10 Kt–R6 mate!

8	Kt–R6 ch	K–R1
9	Kt–B7 ch	K–Kt1
10	R–R8 ch!	KtxR
11	Kt–R6 mate!	

picturesque mates—as in this combination of Tarrasch's.

| 1 | ... | KtxQP! |
| 2 | Q–K4 | |

With two pieces attacked and a third one threatened, (by 3 P–KR3) Black continues by sacrificing!

| 2 | ... | RxKt! |

If White replies 3 PxR, Kt–K7 ch; 4 K–R1, Kt–Kt6 ch wins the Queen by a Knight fork, or if 3 QxKt, B–QB4 wins the Queen by a pin.

3	R–B4	Kt–K7 ch
4	QxKt	B–B4 ch
5	K–R1	R–KR6!

Reminiscent of the famous Rubinstein immortal against Rotlevi, and the Lasker brilliancy against Pillsbury in 1896. The threat, brutal but simple, is 6 ... RxP mate.

| 6 | PxR | BxQ |
| 7 | RxQ | B–B6 mate! |

Black to play

248

AMATEUR-TARRASCH
Munich, 1915

White to play

249

TARRASCH-RÉTI
Vienna, 1922

One reason for the partiality many players have for retaining both Bishops is that the Bishops produce

The King himself stars in this combination which could pass off as an endgame composition!

1   R–Kt7 ch   K–R1

Naturally 1 ... K–B1 lets White swoop down on the poor Rook in the corner.

2   R–K7

The threat is 3 B–Kt7 ch, winning a piece. If Black counters this by 3 ... Kt–Kt1 attacking two pieces, he gets mated instantly.

2   ...   K–Kt1
3   P–B3!

White is not interested in taking the King Pawn at the cost of letting Black's King come out.

3	...	Kt–K1
4	K–R2!	Kt–Q3
5	R–Kt7 ch	K–R1
6	R–Q7!	Kt–Kt4
7	K–Kt3	KtxBP
8	K–B4	Kt–Kt4
9	K–K5	R–K1
10	K–B6	Resigns

If 10 ... K–Kt1 (to prevent 11 K–B7); 11 R–Kt7 ch, K–R1 (11 ... K–B1; 12 RxKtP mate); 12 R–Kt7, Kt–Q3; 13 R–Q7, Kt–Kt4; 14 K–B7, R–KKt1; 15 R–Q8!, RxR; 16 B–Kt7 mate.

13

GREAT FIGHTER
Emanuel Lasker

----

*It is remarkable, and deserves special mention, that the
great masters, such as Pillsbury, Maroczy and Janowsky play
against Lasker as though hypnotized.*

—George Marco

Lasker was the first great master to be thoroughly at home in both position and combination play. In his understanding of strategy, he was far
ahead of his time. We find such thoroughly modern concepts as exploitation
of weaknesses on the white squares, as far back as 1909, in his games
against Mieses and Tartakover at St. Petersburg. The continual switching
of attack from one weak point to another, in his game against Salwe in the
same tournament was unheard of at the time, while his use of *zugzwang* as
an endgame weapon, notably in the first match game against Marshall in
1907, shows complete familiarity with this device.

Lasker's games bristle with all sorts of combinative ideas. But where
others used their gifts for combination play to bring about sensational
climaxes, Lasker was content to strew combinations freely about in a game
that was really strategical in essence. It is no wonder that his contemporaries were bewildered by such tactics! "It is no easy matter," said Pollock
despairingly, "to reply correctly to Lasker's bad moves." Perhaps the most
appropriate summing-up of Lasker's play lies in the quote, "Lasker's style
is like limpid clear water—with a dash of poison in it!"

White to play

250

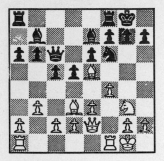

LASKER-BAUER
Amsterdam, 1899

One of the first, and most beautiful of the two-Bishop sacrifice combinations. Dufresne's comment at the time was, "From his conduct of this game one sees something of the extraordinary talent of the younger generation."

Lasker apparently started his long and glorious career *con brio*.

| 1 | Kt–R5! | KtxKt |

Forced: if 1 ... Kt–K1; 2 KtxP, KtxKt; 3 Q–Kt4 wins, or if 1 ... K–R1; 2 KtxP, KxKt; 3 Q–Kt4 ch, K–R1; 4 BxKt ch, BxB; 5 Q–R5, and mate follows.

2	BxP ch!	KxB
3	QxKt ch	K–Kt1
4	BxP!	KxB

On 4 ... P–B3 or 4 ... P–B4, White wins with 5 R–B3 and 6 R–Kt3.

| 5 | Q–Kt4 ch | K–R2 |

The penalty for 5 ... K–B3 is mate on the move.

| 6 | R–B3 | P–K4 |

Black is content to give up his Queen and remain with approximately even material, but Lasker has looked a bit further ahead.

7	R–R3 ch	Q–R3
8	RxQ ch	KxR
9	Q–Q7!	

The point of Lasker's artful combination. He wins one of the exposed Bishops.

| 9 | ... | B–KB3 |
| 10 | QxB | |

And White won easily.

Black to play

251

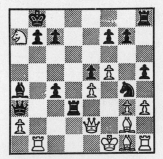

MIESES-LASKER
Berlin, 1889

Mieses, who depends only on tactics, is out-combined—beaten at his own game!

| 1 | ... | R(R1)–Q1! |

2	PxKt	P–B6!

White to play

With two powerful threats: 3 ...
R–Q7 and 3 ... P–B7.

3   Kt–B6 ch

If 3 B–K3, P–B7 attacks the Rook
and doubles the attack on the
Bishop, or if 3 Kt–Kt5, BxKt; 4 RxB,
Q–B8 ch; 5 Q–K1, R–Q8, and Black
wins the Queen.

3	...	BxKt
4	B–K3	P–B7!

Avoiding a typical Mieses trap. If
4 ... RxB; 5 QxR, P–B7; 6 RxP
ch!, BxR; 7 QxQ, and White wins.

5	QxP	RxB
6	K–B2	

If 6 QxB, Q–Q6 ch; 7 K–B2, R–
K7 ch; 8 K–Kt1, QxR ch; 9 K–R2,
RxB ch; 10 KxR, R–Q7 ch; 11 K–
B3, Q–Q6 mate.

6	...	R–QB6
7	Resigns	

There is no defense: if 7 Q–Kt2,
Q–B4 ch; 8 K–B1, R–B7, and White
must give up his Queen or be mated,
or if 7 Q–K2, Q–B4 ch; 8 K–B1 (8
K–K1, R–K6), R–B7; 9 Q–K1, R–
Q8 (the simplest, although anything
wins); 10 RxR, B–Kt4 ch, and mate
comes in a few moves.

252

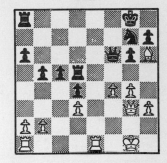

LASKER-BLACKBURNE
London, 1892

A succession of clever attacking
moves forces Black into a pin and
the loss of a piece.

1   Q–Kt2!

A threat on the exposed Rook
which is difficult to meet. If either of
Black's Rooks moves to Q1 for
mutual protection, then 2 B–Kt5
wins the exchange.

1   ...   Q–Q3

If 1 ... Q–B2; 2 R–K7 forces
2 ... QxR when 3 QxR ch gets
two Rooks for one.

2   R–K7!

Now the Knight must move—and
only one square is open.

2	...	Kt–K3
3	QR–K1	

Another thrust at the Knight
which has no good flight square. If
3 ... Kt–B2; 4 RxKt wins, while

3 ... Kt–B1 loses by 4 R–K8, a pin on the unfortunate creature. Finally, if 3 ... Kt–Q1; 4 QxR ch, QxQ; 5 R–K8 ch, K–B2; 6 R–B8 is checkmate.

3 ...	QxR
4 QxR	R–K1
5 P–B5	

White wins a piece and the game.

Black to play

253

BIRD–LASKER
Match, 1892

Sometimes a subtle, quiet move must be made to assure the success of a combination. Lasker could find those hidden moves!

| 1 ... | P–Kt6! |
| 2 RPxP | |

On 2 KtPxP, Kt–B6; 3 B–R6, R–B3; 4 B–Kt7, R–B2; 5 R–Q3, RxB; 6 RxKt, P–Kt7 wins a piece for Black.

| 2 ... | R–B8 ch! |
| 3 K–Kt2 | |

Best, as 3 Kt–Q1 blocks the defense of the last rank and allows 3

... P–R7, while 3 R–Q1 succumbs to 3 ... PxP; 4 B–K3, B–Kt5 winning the exchange.

3 ...	RxR
4 KxR	P–R7
5 R–Q1	Kt–Kt5

Threatens 6 ... Kt–B7 followed by Queening the Pawn.

| 6 R–R1 | B–B2 |
| 7 K–Kt2 | P–B3! |

A profound move whose purpose we will see later.

| 8 K–B1 | B–Kt3 |
| 9 K–Q2 | RxP! |

A surprising sacrifice when there is so little material to work with.

10 Kt–Q1

Apparently White does not like the looks of 10 KtxR, BxKt followed by 11 ... BxKtP, and White loses his Rook.

10 ...	R–Q5 ch
11 K–K2	RxKt!
12 RxR	

Obviously if 12 KxR, Kt–B7 ch; 13 K–K2, KtxR; 14 B–B4, KtxP ch; 15 BxKt, P–R8(Q) is the greater evil.

12 ...   B–K5

This could not have been played without the acute 7 ... P–B3 move as the reply would have been mate.

13 R–Q8 ch

Now it is only check.

| 13 ... | K–B2 |
| 14 R–Q1 | BxKtP |

15 B–Q8 ch   K–B1
16 B–Kt6

Still hoping that Lasker will play
hastily and fall into mate.

16 ...   B–Q4
17 P–B4   P–R8(Q)

And Black wins. (What end-game
technique!)

Black to play

254

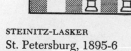

STEINITZ-LASKER
St. Petersburg, 1895-6

Steinitz was a tough man to beat,
but Lasker seems to toy with him as
he weaves a mating net around his
King.

1 ...   Kt–B4

Threatens 2 ... KtxP ch; 3 K–
R2, QxP mate. To this the defense
2 R–B3 fails, as the reply 2 ...
KtxRP is killing.

2 Kt–K4   B–K6

Cuts off White's Queen and
threatens 3 ... KtxP ch, 4 KtxKt,
QxP ch and mate next.

3 R–B3   RxB!
4 KxR   KtxRP ch
5 K–R2   KtxR ch
6 K–Kt2   Kt–R5 ch
7 K–R2

Forced, as 7 K–B1, Q–B6 ch; 8
K–K1, Kt–Kt7 means mate.

7 ...   Kt–B4
8 R–QKt1   P–R4

With a double purpose: to break
down White's Knight Pawn, and to
create a loophole for his own King.

9 R–Kt5   R–R1

Not at once 9 ... P–R5 on account of 10 RxKt.

10 P–R3   RxP!
11 Resigns

If 11 QxR, Q–K7 ch; 12 K–R3,
Q–B8 ch; 13 K–R2, Q–Kt8 ch; 14
K–R3, Q–R8 mate.

White to play

255

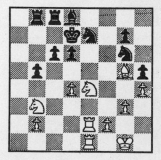

LASKER-STEINITZ
Match, 1896-7

Lasker rarely went in for direct
attack, but that he understood the

technique can be seen from the way he goes after Steinitz's King.

1   P–Kt4!   PxP
2   P–R5

It is necessary to evict the Knight so that White's Bishop can get to KB4.

2   ...   Kt–B1
3   Kt(K4)–B5 ch   PxKt
4   KtxP ch   K–Q3

On 4 ... K–K1; 5 RxKt ch, BxR; 6 RxB ch, K–Q1; 7 RxP ch leads to an easy win.

5   B–B4 ch   K–Q4
6   R–K5 ch   K–B5

If 6 ... KxP; 7 R(K1)–K4 is instant mate.

7   R–B1 ch   KxP

Now forced, as 7 ... K–Kt5 allows 8 B–Q2 mate.

8   Kt–Kt3 ch   K–Q6
9   R–K3 mate

Black to play

256

LEE-LASKER
London, 1899

The last move in the combination is a quiet step back of the Bishop. Lasker had to see the full effect of this move before setting the wheels of the combination rolling.

1   ...   RxB!
2   PxR

Capturing by 2 QxR loses the Queen by 2 ... Kt–K7 ch.

2   ...   Q–Kt5 ch
3   K–B1

Interposing by 3 Q–Kt3 also runs into the deadly 3 ... Kt–K7 ch.

3   ...   Q–Kt7 ch
4   K–K1   Q–Kt8 ch
5   K–Q2   P–B6 ch!
6   QxP

White's moves are forced: if 6 KxP, Kt–Q4 ch wins the Queen by a Knight fork.

6   ...   QxP ch
7   K–Q1

And here 7 K–B1 succumbs to the Knight fork at K7.

7   ...   P–K6
8   B–Kt3 ch   K–Kt2
9   P–Q5 ch   K–R3
10   Q–K1   B–B1!
11   Resigns

The threat is of course 11 ... B–Kt5 ch. If White plays 11 QxQ, then the recapture 11 ... PxQ leaves him helpless to stop the passed Pawn.

White to play

257

LASKER-CAPABLANCA
St. Petersburg, 1914

The decisive combination from a magnificent game won by the World's Champion against the logical contender. It was one of those occasions where Lasker won *because he had to.*

1   P–K5!

Clearance at K4 for the Knight.

1	...	QPxP
2	Kt–K4	Kt–Q4

Protecting his King Bishop Pawn. He cannot do so by 2 ... R–B2 on account of 3 Kt–Q6 ch, while 2 ... K–K2; 3 R–R7 ch, K–K1; 4 KtxP mate is even worse.

3	Kt(K6)–B5	B–B1

Black must lose the exchange: if he moves the Rook (at Q2) anywhere along the second rank, then comes 4 KtxB, RxKt; 5 Kt–Q6 ch and White wins a whole Rook.

4	KtxR	BxKt
5	R–R7	R–B1

6	R–R1	K–Q1
7	R–R8 ch	B–B1
8	Kt–B5!	Resigns

White's threats are 9 R–Q7 ch (or 9 Kt–K6 ch, or 9 Kt–Kt7 ch), K–K1; 10 RxB mate. Black's only defense is 8 ... Kt–Kt3, but after the reply 9 R–Kt8, his game falls apart.

White to play

258

LASKER-CAPABLANCA
Match, 1921

Lasker's play abounds in tactical surprises. These are not meant to be traps for the unwary. They are the hidden combinations, the manifold resources in a position which appears shaky to the uninitiate.

Here for example, Lasker offers Capablanca a Pawn, the capture of which means disaster.

1   R(K3)–K2

Capablanca's reply was 1 ... RxR, and the game was eventually drawn. But suppose he had taken the Rook Pawn? This is what would have happened:

1	...	QxRP
2	RxR	QxR
3	R–B1	Q–KB4 (or A)
4	R–B8 ch	R–Q1

If 4 ... B–Q1; 5 QxR!, PxQ;
6 RxB mate.

5	Q–B6	Q–Q6
6	Q–K8 ch	RxQ
7	RxR ch	B–B1
8	RxB mate	

Variation A

| 3 | ... | Q–Q6 |
| 4 | R–B8 ch | B–Q1 |

If 4 ... R–Q1; 5 QxQ, RxR
(unfortunately Black cannot take the
Queen); 6 Q–Q7 wins.

5   QxQ

Simpler than the flashy 5 Q–B6.

| 5 | ... | RxQ |
| 6 | B–Kt5 | |

White wins a piece and an easy
ending.

Black to play

259

MARSHALL-LASKER
Moscow, 1925

The final combination from a
game, of which an English critic
said, "Playing it over is like walking
through a beautiful garden."

Marshall has just moved 1 Q–KB3,
and threatens 2 RxR, or 2 QxBP ch
or 2 QxRP.

| 1 | ... | Kt–Kt4 |
| 2 | QxRP | |

Black must be careful: against 2
... KtxR; 3 QxP ch, K–R2; 4 Q–
R5 ch gives White a perpetual check,
while 2 ... Q–Q4; 3 QxKt, QxR;
4 QxR ch, RxQ; 5 RxQ costs a piece.

| 2 | ... | R(Q1)–Q7! |

Lasker threatens 3 ... QxP ch
followed by mate. Marshall's reply is
ingenious:

3   Kt–Q3

Guards the Bishop Pawn, attacks
the Queen and threatens a deadly
check at K8. Has Lasker prepared
for this?

3   ...   KtxR!

Lasker lets him take the Queen,
meanwhile ruining Marshall's other
schemes.

4   KtxQ

Naturally, he has no time for 4
RxR, as his own Queen is unprotected.

4	...	RxR ch
5	K–R2	KtxP
6	Q–B5	R–K1
7	KtxP	Kt–Q8

Threatens 8 ... RxP ch.

8   Q–B5   R–K3!

Guards against perpetual check and prevents White's Knight from centralizing by way of 9 Kt–Q6.

9   Q–B1   Kt–K6!

Strong (because of the threat 10 RxP ch) and pretty (because of the pleasing Knight fork that indirectly guards the Rook).

10 Q–B8 ch   K–R2

11   Q–B3   R–KKt3!

Note the mark of the master: the increase of pressure on the Knight Pawn before capturing it.

12   QxKt   R(Q7)xP ch
13   K–R1   R(Kt7)–Kt6!
14   Resigns

There is no defense to Lasker's last move which attacks the Queen while threatening 14 ... RxP mate.

In Lasker I saw, above all, the supreme tactical genius.

—Reuben Fine in *Lessons from my Games*

14

DEADLY ATTACKER
Frank J. Marshall

A masterpiece is a masterpiece though a million people say so.

—Sir Arthur Quiller-Couch

Marshall's style of attack is the nearest thing to perpetual motion on the chessboard. He keeps hammering away tirelessly and fearlessly regardless of the reputation of the man facing him. In his first big tournament Marshall tore into such giants as Lasker and Pillsbury, and brought them down to earth. His wealth of ideas can be judged by Fine's statement, "I have never met anyone, not even Alekhine, who had a keener eye for the purely combinative in chess," while his brilliance in execution may best be described in Napier's epigram, "Some of Marshall's most sparkling moves look at first like typographical errors."

White to play

260

MARSHALL-BURN
Paris, 1900
152

Marshall gives up a Bishop for two Pawns and an open position—more than enough value for his money.

1	BxP!		PxB
2	QxP!		

How shall Black defend against 3 Kt–Kt5 and 4 Q–B7 mate?

If 2 ... Q–Q2; 3 Kt–Kt5, K–B1; 4 Kt–R7 ch, K–B1; 5 Kt–B6 ch, and White wins the Queen.

If 2 ... Q–K2; 3 Kt–Kt5, K–B1; 4 R–R8 ch, BxR; 5 Kt–R7 ch, and Black must give up his Queen.

If 2 ... R–K2; 3 Kt–Kt5, K–B1; 4 Kt–R7 ch, K–Kt1; 5 Kt–B6

ch, K–B1; 6 R–R8 ch, BxR; 7 Q–Kt8
mate.

2	...	Kt–Q2
3	Kt–Kt5	Q–B3
4	R–R8 ch!	KxR
5	Q–R7 mate	

White to play

261

MARSHALL-MARCO
Monte Carlo, 1904

A combination that could qualify
as an endgame composition. From a
magnificent (but little-known) masterpiece of Marshall's.

| 1 | PxP ch | K–Kt1 |

Obviously 1 ... KxP; 2 Kt–B5
ch winning the Rook won't do.

| 2 | Kt–B5 | R–R7 ch |
| 3 | K–R3 | P–Kt7 |

Only a miracle can save White,
but Marshall has faith (and skill in
maneuvering his pieces).

| 4 | R–K7! | K–R2 |

If 4 ... P–Kt8(Q); 5 R–K8

ch, K–R2; 6 R–R8 ch, K–Kt3; 7 P–
Kt8(Q) ch, KxKt; 8 QxQ wins for
White.

| 5 | R–K8 | P–B3 |

Covers the Queening square for
White's Pawn, and makes further
resistance look hopeless.

6	R–R8 ch	K–Kt3
7	RxR	P–Kt8(Q)
8	P–Kt8(Q) ch!	BxQ
9	R–Kt2 ch!	QxR
10	Kt–R4 ch	K–Kt4
11	KtxQ	

And Marshall won the ending.

White to play

262

MARSHALL-PILLSBURY
Cambridge Springs, 1904

That Pillsbury in this position
would be mated in less than ten
moves seems incredible, but he is—
and artistically!

| 1 | Kt–K5 | |

"The great master," says Tarta-

kover, "places a Knight at K5; checkmate follows by itself."

1 ...   Q–K2
2 B–Q3

With this idea: 3 KtxBP, KtxKt;
4 BxP, R–B1; 5 RxKt, RxR; 6 R–
KB1, and White wins.

2 ...   0–0
3 R–B2

Now the threat is 4 BxP, PxB; 5
KtxP, Q–Q2 (If 5 ... RxR,
White takes the Queen with check);
6 RxR ch, K–Kt2; 7 Q–K5 ch, KxKt;
8 R–Kt8 ch and mate next move.

3 ...   K–Kt2
4 QR–KB1   B–Q2
5 R–B6!

Blockade! Marshall now has a
triple attack on the Knight Pawn
and a triple attack on the Bishop
Pawn. Black cannot evict the Rook
by 5 ... Kt–K1 as 6 RxBP ch,
RxR; 7 RxR ch loses material, while
5 ... QxR; 6 RxQ, KxR; 7 KtxB
ch followed by 8 KtxR is far too
expensive.

5 ...   R–KKt1
6 KtxKtP!   QxR

Pillsbury does not care for 6 ...
PxKt; 7 RxKtP ch, K–R1; 8 RxP ch,
K–Kt2; 9 R–R7 mate, so he gives up
his Queen for the two Rooks. But
does he see the dénouement?

7 RxQ   KxR
8 Q–K5 mate!

White to play

263

MARSHALL-WOLF
Nuremberg, 1906

Give Marshall a wide-open position and he could beat anybody. He
recognized attacking opportunities
almost by intuition, and was ready,
in positions he liked, to sacrifice
pieces without exact calculation of
all the consequences.

Typically, Marshall put question
marks after 2 KtxRP and 4 Q–R5 at
the time he played this game. Later
analysis showed his combination to
be sound, and that these brilliant
moves deserved exclamation marks
instead.

1 Kt(K4)–Kt5   P–Kt3

If 1 ... P–R3 (to save the
Pawn); 2 Q–B2, P–Kt3; 3 KtxKP
wins the exchange, 3 ... PxKt
losing instantly by 4 QxP ch.

2 KtxRP!   KxKt
3 Kt–Kt5 ch   K–Kt1

The alternative 3 ... K–R3
leads to pretty play: 3 ... K–R3;

4 Q–Kt4 (threatens mate on the
move), P–K4 (if 4 ... P–B3; 5
Q–R4 ch, K–Kt2; 6 Q–R7 mate);
5 Kt–K6! (threatens 6 Q–R4 mate
while attacking the Queen and both
Rooks), PxKt; 6 QxKtP mate.

4   Q–R5!   P–B3

The only defense. Clearly, the
punishment for 4 ... PxQ is
death.

5   BxKtP

The threats pile up: one of them
is 6 B–R7 ch, K–R1 (6 ... K–
Kt2; 7 KtxP ch costs the Queen);
7 B–B5 ch, K–Kt1; 8 BxP ch, and
White wins the Rook and then the
Queen.

5   ...   R–Q2

Obviously 5 ... PxKt allows
6 Q–R8 mate, while 5 ... Q–K2
does not prevent the reply 6 KtxP.

6   KtxP   R–R2!

A clever attempt to force a draw.
If 7 QxKt, BxP ch; 8 K–R1, B–K4
ch, and Black has a perpetual, since
9 BxR ch is answered by 9 ...
QxB ch and it's Black who does the
mating.

7	BxR ch	QxB
8	QxQ ch	KxQ
9	KtxR ch	BxKt
10	KR–Q1	Kt(B3)–K2
11	P–K4	Kt–QKt3
12	R–B7	K–Kt1
13	BxP	Kt–Kt3
14	R–Q8	Resigns

Black cannot prevent 15 R–Kt7

ch, which wins the Knight, or forces
mate if the Knight runs away.

Black to play

264

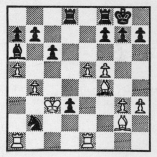

MIESES-MARSHALL
Match, 1909

From a little-known game. The
pieces are widely scattered, but Marshall summons them together
cleverly to draw a mating net around
White's King.

1	...	P–Q7
2	BxP	R–Q6 ch
3	K–B2	

The only move, 3 KxKt costing a
piece by 3 ... RxB ch.

| 3 | ... | RxP |
| 4 | R–KKt1 | |

Here too, loss of material follows
4 KxKt, RxB; 5 K–B2, R–Q1; 6 QR–
Q1, B–K7; 7 R–QR1, B–R4, and
Black wins the exchange.

4	...	Kt–B5
5	B–B4	Kt–K6 ch
6	K–Kt3	

Hoping to complicate things, as 6 BxKt, RxB; 7 QR–K1, B–Q6 ch winning a Pawn is not appetizing. But Marshall lives on complications!

6 ...   B–B5 ch
7 K–B3   Kt–Q8 ch
8 K–Q4

White sidesteps 8 KxB, R–B6 ch; 9 K–Q4, R–Q1 ch; 10 K–K4, Kt–B7 mate.

Three of Marshall's pieces are attacked but it doesn't bother him. Marshall is in his element!

8 ...   R–Q1 ch
9 K–B5   R–QB6
10 R–QB1   B–Kt4 ch
11 RxR   KtxR

Threatens 11 ... Kt–R5 mate.

12 R–QR1   Kt–Q4
13 B–Kt3   Kt–B2
14 Resigns

If 14 P–R6 (to stop 14 ... Kt–R3 mate) then 14 ... P–Kt3 mate does the trick.

Black to play

265

LEVITZKI-MARSHALL
Breslau, 1912

The winning move is a sizzler, and must have hit Levitzki like a stroke of lightning.

1 ...   BxKt
2 PxB   QxP
3 RxP   Kt–Q5
5 Q–R5

If 5 Q–K5, Kt–B6 ch; 6 PxKt (forced, as the Queen is attacked), R–Kt3 ch; 7 B–Kt2, QxKBP, and Black wins.

5 ...   QR–KB1
6 R–K5

No better is 6 R–QB5, RxP; 7 RxR, Q–K8 ch.

6 ...   R–R3
7 Q–Kt5

On 7 Q–Kt4, Kt–B6 ch; 8 PxKt, QxR (not 8 ... R–Kt3; 9 R–KKt5) wins for Black.

7 ...   RxB
8 R–QB5

White cannot play 8 PxR on account of the reply 8 ... Kt–B6 ch, so tries to gain time by attacking Black's Queen.

8 ...   Q–KKt6!!

"The most elegant move I have ever played," says Marshall himself.

Black threatens mate, and the only way to prevent it is by taking the Queen. White has three ways of capturing, and this is what happens in each case:

If 9 RPxQ, Kt–K7 mate.

If 9 BPxQ, Kt–K7 ch; 10 K–R1, RxR mate.

If 9 QxQ, Kt–K7 ch; 10 K–R1,

KtxQ ch; 11 K–Kt1, KtxR, and Black
is a piece ahead.

Not wishing to mar a brilliancy by
continuing a hopeless struggle, White
graciously resigned.

Black to play

266

JANOWSKY-MARSHALL
Match, 1912

Marshall is inspired early in the
game and brings off one of his most
attractive combinations.

1	...	KtxKt
2	PxKt	QxKt!
3	PxB	

If 3 PxQ, B–R6 ch; 4 K–Kt1, R–
K8 ch; 5 B–B1, RxB mate.

| 3 | ... | Kt–B3 |
| 4 | B–Kt2 | |

On 4 B–K3, B–R6! threatens 5 ...
RxB as well as 5 ... QxKtP ch;
6 K–K2, KtxP ch winning the Queen.

4	...	KtxKtP!
5	BxP ch	K–R1
6	PxQ	B–R6 ch
7	K–Kt1	KtxQ

| 8 | BxKt | R–K7 |
| 9 | R–QB1 | QR–K1 |

Threats: 10 ... R–K8 ch; 11
RxR, RxR mate, and 10 ... RxB;
11 RxR, R–K8 mate.

| 10 | B–B3 | R(K1)–K6 |

A brilliant continuation, but there
is a quicker win by 10 ... RxB!;
11 RxR, R–K3, and mate on the
Knight file cannot be stopped.

| 11 | B–Kt4 | |

If 11 PxR, R–Kt7 ch; 12 K–B1,
RxB ch; 13 K–Kt1, RxR ch, and
White must give up his other Rook.

11	...	R(K6)xP
12	B–Q1	R–B3!
13	Resigns	

White can delay the mate, but
not for long. If 13 B–B2, RxB; 14
RxR, R–Kt3 mate.

White to play

267

MARSHALL-BOGOLYUBOV
New York, 1924

The final combination from the
game which won a brilliancy prize
for Marshall.

| 1 | B–B5! | Kt–B7 ch |
| 2 | RxKt! | |

In keeping with Marshall's turbulent spirit. It is more to his taste than 2 K–Kt2, whether that move wins or not.

2	...	BxR
3	Q–R8 ch!	K–K2
4	QxKtP	K–Q1

Black has no time for 4 ... BxR as then 5 Q–B6 ch, K–B1; 6 QxRP ch, K–Kt1 (if 6 ... K–K2; 7 Q–Q6 mate); 7 B–R7 ch, K–R1; 8 B–Kt6 ch, K–Kt1; 9 Q–R7 ch, K–B1; 10 QxP mate.

| 5 | Q–B6 ch | R–K2 |

Obviously 5 ... K–B2; 6 QxKBP ch, K–Kt1; 7 QxR ch is not a happy alternative.

6	P–K6!	B–Q5
7	PxP!	BxQ
8	P–B8(Q) ch	K–B2
9	RxR ch	BxR
10	QxR	

Threatening to win the Queen by 11 Q–B8 ch, K–Q3; 12 Q–Q7 ch, K–B4; 13 Kt–R4 ch.

| 10 | ... | K–Q3 |

On 10 ... QxP; 11 Q–B8 ch, K–Q3; 12 Q–Q7 ch followed by 13 Kt–R4 ch wins the Queen while 10 ... Q–B7 succumbs to 11 Q–B8 ch, K–Kt3; 12 Q–Kt8 ch, K–B4; 13 Q–R7 ch, K–B5; 14 QxQ.

| 11 | Q–R8! | |

Now aiming at the Queen by way of 12 Q–K5 ch, K–B4; 13 Kt–R4 ch.

| 11 | ... | Q–Q1 |

Whereupon Marshall announced a forced mate in five moves, as follows:

| 12 | Q–K5 ch | K–B4 |
| 13 | Kt–R4 ch | K–B5 |

If 13 ... K–Kt4; 14 Q–K2 ch, KxKt; 15 B–B2 mate.

14	Q–B3 ch	K–Kt4
15	B–Q3 ch	KxKt
16	Q–B2 mate	

White to play

268

MARSHALL–FOX
New York, 1931

A great player violates principles (or seems to) now and then. Before attacking the King side, Marshall with his second move forces his opponent's Queen back where it helps defend the King!

| 1 | Kt–Kt3 | P–QKt4 |

The natural-looking 1 ... R–K1 leads to pretty play: 2 Kt–K5, B–Kt2 (develops a piece while protecting the Bishop Pawn); 3 P–QR3,

Q–K2; 4 R–Q7!, KtxR; 5 QxP ch, K–B1; 6 Q–R8 mate.

2 P–QR3!

Strange that this little move on the Queen side decides the fate of the King on the other side in only two more moves!

2 ...   Q–K2

The only other move, 2 ... QxBP is refuted by 3 R–Q4, and Black loses his Queen.

3 BxP ch!

The point: Black's Knight is pinned and may not capture.

3 ...   K–R1

On 3 ... K–B2; 4 Kt–K5 ch, K–K1; 5 B–Kt6 ch finishes Black.

4 Kt–K5   Resigns

After 4 ... P–Kt4; 5 Q–R6, QxB; 6 Kt–Kt6 ch, K–Kt1; 7 QxR is mate.

White to play

269

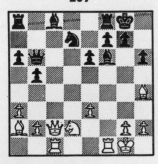

MARSHALL-GLADSTONE
New York, 1932

The tremendous leaps by Marshall's Queen in this combination, must have frightened Black's King almost to death before he was mated!

1 B–Kt1   R–Q1

Black cannot defend by 1 ... P–Kt3 as then his Bishop is loose.

2 Q–R7 ch   K–B1
3 Q–R8 ch   K–K2
4 QxKtP

Did Black miss this?

4 ...   QxP ch
5 K–R1   BxB

Practically forced: if 5 ... Q–K4; 5 Kt–K4 attacks the Bishop four times. Black could not then play 5 ... BxB on account of 6 QxP mate in reply.

6 QxP ch   K–Q3
7 Kt–K4 ch   K–Q4
8 Q–R5 ch   B–Kt4

If 8 ... P–K4; 9 Q–Q1 ch, K–K3; 10 Q–Q6 mate.

9 Q–Q1 ch!   Q–Q5
10 Q–Kt3 ch   K–K4
11 Q–Kt3 ch   K–Q4
12 Q–Q6 mate!

15

SACRIFICE SPECIALIST

Rudolf Spielmann

I warne yow wel, it is no childes pley.

—Geoffrey Chaucer

One of the reasons for Spielmann's terrific success as an attacking player was his understanding of the art of sacrifice. Spielmann gave up material with any of several objects in view: to increase the mobility of his pieces or hamper the movements of his opponent's; to break up a castled position, or to prevent castling and get the King out into the open where a King has little chance to survive; to lure enemy pieces away from important points; to present his opponent with difficult problems when time is pressing, or simply at the slight cost of a Pawn to throw him on the defense.

Spielmann himself said of these tactics, "An advantage in development is turned into a grand assault by means of a sacrifice."

Spielmann's combinations, abounding as they do in lively and unexpected sacrificial play are always a joy and delight.

Black to play

270

SCHORIES-SPIELMANN
Scheveningen, 1905

160

Spielmann has given up a Pawn. In return for this, White's Queen is out of play. Spielmann must drive home the attack before White gets a chance to recover and reorganize his forces.

    1 ...   Kt–Q5

With the immediate threat of winning a piece by 2 ... B–B7; 3 Q–R2, P–Kt6.

    2 Kt–K4

If 2 KtxKt, QxKt; 3 KtxB, QxP ch; 4 RxQ, R–K8 mate.

2 ...	KtxKt ch
3 PxKt	Q–Kt3 ch
4 K–R1	

Forced: if 4 Kt–Kt3, B–B7; 5 Q–R2, P–Kt6 wins the Queen.

4 ...	RxP!
5 R–K1	

If 5 KtxB, B–B7; 6 Q–R2, RxP; 7 R–KKt1, Q–B3 ch ends in mate.

5 ...	RxP
6 B–Kt5	Q–R4
7 Kt–B6 ch	PxKt
8 RxR ch	K–B2
9 Resigns	

White to play

271

SPIELMANN-REGGIO
Ostend, 1906

A pretty bit of play by Spielmann, who bottles up a Bishop with his Pawns.

1	P–Kt6

Threatens 2 BxP ch or 2 RxP.

1 ...	BPxP
2 PxP	P–KR3
3 RxP!	RxR

If 3 ... PxR; 4 P–Kt7, R–B1; 5 BxP wins.

4 BxR	Kt–K2

Black loses after 4 ... PxB by 5 P–Kt7, Kt–K2; 6 Kt–Q5, B–K3 (if 6 ... Kt–Kt1; 7 KtxB, RPxKt; 8 BxKt wins); 7 KtxB.

5 B–B7 ch	K–B1
6 B–Kt5	B–Kt5
7 K–Q2!	

Intending 8 R–R1 followed by 9 R–R8 ch.

7 ...	B–KR4

If Black can only remove the Knight Pawn!

8 R–KB1!	P–B3
9 P–KKt4!	

And wins. If 9 ... BxP(Kt5); 10 B–K6 discovers check and wins a piece.

White to play

272

SPIELMANN-JANOWSKY
Carlsbad, 1907

Spielmann, familiar with the technique of conducting a King side attack, strips away the Pawn obstruction to get at the King with his pieces.

1   Q–KB2!

Threatens mate on the move, and forces. . . .

1	. . .	P–KKt4
2	PxP	PxP
3	Q–Q2!	

Attacking the Knight Pawn. Black's Queen cannot protect the Pawn without abandoning the Bishop.

3   . . .   P–Kt4

To swing the Rook over by way of QR3 to the King side. If instead 3 . . . P–Kt5; 4 Q–Kt5 leaves Black helpless to meet the deadly threat of check on the Rook file.

4	QxP	R–R3
5	R–K4	

Intending 6 R–R4 ch, R–R3; 7 RxR ch, PxR; 8 QxP mate.

5	. . .	R–R3
6	Kt–B5!	

Direct attack on the Rook, discovered attack on the Queen, threat of mate on the move—White must win something!

6	. . .	Q–Kt3
7	Q–Q8 ch	

On 7 KtxR instead the reply is not 7 . . . QxQ allowing 8 Kt–B7 ch winning, but simply 7 . . . QxR.

7	. . .	K–R2
8	QxB	R–R4

9	R–Kt4	R–Kt4
10	R–R4 ch	Resigns

If 10 . . . K–Kt1; 11 Kt–K7 ch wins, or if 10 . . . R–R4; 11 RxR ch, QxR; 12 QxP mate.

White to play

273

SPIELMANN-MIESES
Match, 1910

In the midst of a winning attack, Spielmann is alert enough to watch out for surprise moves—especially from an opponent who is a combination player himself.

1   R–Q7 ch   K–Kt3

The only move: if 1 . . . K–Kt1; 2 Kt–Kt4 ch, Q–B5; 3 R–Q8 ch, (an instructive example of the exploitation of an overworked piece —Black's Rook at KB1 having the job of protecting the Queen and the other Rook) K–B2; 4 QxQ ch, RxQ; 5 RxR and White wins, or if 1 . . . K–B1; 2 Q–R3, K–Kt1; 3 RxP ch!, KxR; 4 Q–Q7 ch, K–Kt1, 5 KtxP ch, K–R1; 6 Kt–Q8!, and Black cannot survive the threats of 7 Q–B8 mate,

7 Q–Kt7 mate and 7 B–K4 ch followed by mate.

2   Kt–B4 ch   K–R3

Or 2 ... K–Kt4; 3 Q–K5 ch, P–B4 (3 ... KxKt; 4 P–Kt3 mate); 4 RxP ch, K–R3; 5 RxP ch, KxR; 6 Q–B7 ch and mate next move.

3   Q–B7!

An unexpected offer of a piece, as Black will capture the Knight with check!

3 ...   Q–B8 ch
4   K–R2!

Spielmann, who has seen all, avoids the tempting 4 R–Q1 (attacks the Queen while threatening mate), QxKt; 5 B–Q3, P–B7 ch! and Black wins.

4 ...   QxKt ch
5   P–Kt3   Q–Kt4
6   P–R4   Q–Kt3
7   B–Q3 ch   K–R4
8   Q–K5 ch   P–B4
9   RxKtP!

But this is an offer which must not be accepted.

9 ...   RxP ch
10 K–R3   R–Kt5

Black may have been too discouraged to try this trap: 10 ... P–B7; 11 Q–K1 ch, Q–Kt5 ch; 12 RxQ, P–B8(Q) ch!; 13 QxQ, PxR mate. The simple refutation of 10 ... P–B7 is 11 BxBP, RxB; 12 RxQ, PxR (12 ... KxR; 13 Q–Q6 ch costs a Rook); 13 Q–K7, R–QR1 (to pre-

vent mate); 14 Q–QKt7, R–R3; 15 Q–B6, and White forces mate.

11 RxQ   PxR
12 Q–B7   Resigns

If 12 ... R–QR1; 13 Q–B6 indicates that mate will come next move.

White to play

274

SPIELMANN-RUBINSTEIN
Carlsbad, 1911

The target is Black's King Knight Pawn. Spielmann cannot attack it with more pieces than Black can bring up to its defense. But he can pin and paralyze a couple of its defenders. Watch the technique of a combination which assures an invasion by the Rooks!

1   Q–R6!

Intending 2 B–Q6, K–R1 (if 2 ... R–K8; 3 RxP ch, K–R1; 4 Kt–Kt6 mate, or if 2 ... K–B1; 3 RxP wins); 3 Kt–Kt6 ch, K–Kt1; 4 KtxR ch winning easily.

1 ...   **K–B1**   *Black to play*

There was no relief in 1 ...
KtxB; 2 PxKt, Kt–K5; 3 P–B6.

2 Kt–Kt6 ch!   PxKt
3 Q–R8 ch   Kt–Kt1
4 B–Q6

Two black pieces are now pinned.
What defense is there? If
 (a) 4 ... QKt–B3; 5 PxP steals
a Rook (in broad daylight, as the
Continental writers say).
 (b) 4 ... PxP; 5 RxP, QKt–
B3; 6 RxKt ch, KtxR; 7 RxKt mate.
 (c) 4 ... RxP; 5 RxP, RxB; 6
QxP mate.
 (d) 4 ... R–B3; 4 RxP, RxR;
5 PxR!, QKt–B3; 6 R–K1, Kt–K5; 7
BxKt, PxB; 8 R–B1 ch, and White
mates quickly.

4 ...   **Q–Q1**
5 RxP

Object: 6 RxP, RxR; 7 QxR ch,
K–K1; 8 B–R5 ch followed by mate.

5 ...   **Kt–B3**
6 RxKt!   **RxR**

As good as anything else. It loses,
but then 6 ... Q–K1; 7 QxP
mate is not an attractive alternative.

7 RxP   Resigns

Mate cannot be postponed much
longer.

275

RUBINSTEIN-SPIELMANN
Pistyan, 1912

The star of this fine combination
is Black's King Rook Pawn. It sup-
ports the invasion of the Bishop at
Kt7, then that of the Queen, aids in
a mating possibility, and finally by
its threat of promoting to a Queen,
induces Rubinstein to resign!

1 ...   **B–B6 ch**
2 K–Kt1   **B–Kt7**
3 RxR   **BxQ!**
4 RxR   **Q–Q6!**

Crafty! Black's answer to 5 RxB is
5 ... Q–B6, forcing checkmate.

5 R–K8

To meet 5 ... BxKt with 6 R–
K3 regaining his piece.

5 ...   **Q–B6**
6 KxB   **Q–R8 ch**
7 B–Kt1   **Q–Kt7 ch**
8 K–K1   **QxB ch**
9 K–Q2   **QxRP ch**
10 Resigns

The continuation could be 10 Kt–K2 (on 10 R–K2; QxP is the brutal convincer), Q–Kt7; 11 R–KKt1, QxR; 12 KtxQ, P–R7, and the Pawn wins the game.

White to play

276

Teplitz, 1928

A sacrificial combination can have several motivations:

1. It can achieve a victory of mind over matter—the lesser force conquering the greater.
2. It can create artistic effects.
3. It can bring about mate in the most efficient, economical manner.

Spielmann's combination satisfies all three desiderata.

1	Kt–B7	Q–K1
2	Q–K5 ch	K–Kt2
3	B–KB4	

Threatens 4 Q–B7-instant mate.

3	...	P–B5
4	Q–B7 ch	K–R3
5	Kt–Q8!	

Spielmann is not concerned with such petty affairs as removing the harmless King Rook.

| 5 | ... | Kt–B3 |

If 5 ... B–B3 (to prevent 6 Q–Kt7 ch) White wins neatly by 6 Q–B8 ch, K–R4 (or 6 ... K–Kt4; 7 P–R4 ch, K–B4; 8 Kt–Kt7 mate); 7 Kt–Kt7 ch, K–Kt4; 8 P–R4 ch, K–R3; 9 Kt–B5 ch, K–R4; 10 P–Kt4 ch, PxPe.p.; 11 KtxP mate.

| 6 | Q–Kt7 ch | K–Kt4 |

On 6 ... K–R4; 7 KtxKt ch, BxKt; 8 P–Kt4 ch, PxPe.p.; 9 Q–R6 mate.

| 7 | P–R4 ch | K–B4 |

Forced, as 7 ... K–R4 runs into the mate in the previous note.

| 8 | QxKt ch! | BxQ |
| 9 | KtxP mate! | |

White to play

277

Carlsbad, 1929

One of the advantages derived in hitting the opponent with a combination is that it gives him no time to carry out his own plans, or to organize his forces properly for defense. Note how Spielmann breaks into Black's King side position by a sacrifice which cannot be ignored.

| 1 | P–R5 | Kt–K2 |
| 2 | BxKtP! | KxB |

Refusing the Bishop could lead to this: 2 ... BxP; 3 B–B6, B–R8; 4 B–Q5!, BxB; 5 Q–R6, Kt–B4; 6 Q–Kt5 ch, and White mates next move.

| 3 | Q–Kt5 ch | Kt–Kt3 |
| 4 | P–R6 ch! | |

Certainly not 4 PxKt, RPxP, and no one would ever speak to Spielmann again!

| 4 | ... | K–Kt1 |
| 5 | Q–R6 | |

And White mates next move.

White to play

278

SPIELMANN-HONLINGER
Match, 1929

A grand combination by Spielmann from one of the most brilliant games ever played.

1   Q–R5!

You would hardly suspect that so much beautiful play could evolve from this rude threat of mate!

1   ...   P–Kt3

On 1 ... P–R3, White breaks in by 2 BxP, KxB; 3 Kt(K3)–B5 ch, PxKt; 4 KtxP ch, K–Kt1; 5 QxP, B–B3; 6 Kt–K7 ch, QxKt; 7 Q–R7 mate. Against 1 ... P–B4 Spielmann had prepared 2 Kt(Kt3)xP, PxKt; 3 KtxP (threatens 4 KtxB ch, QxKt; 5 BxP ch, K–R1; 6 B–Kt6 ch, K–Kt1; 7 Q–R7 mate), Kt–KB3; 4 Q–Kt5, P–Kt3; 5 KR–K1, B–B4; 6 R–K6, Q–Q4; 7 Kt–R6 ch, K–Kt2 (if 7 ... K–R1; 8 QxKt ch); 8 RxKt!, QxQ; 9 RxKKtP check, discovered check, double check and checkmate!

2   Kt–Kt4!

Not showing off (2 ... PxQ; 3 Kt–R6 mate) but to get a grip on the squares KB6 and KR6.

2   ...   B–KB3

Blocking the diagonal. If instead 2 ... P–B3; 3 BxKtP, PxB; 4 QxP ch, K–R1; 5 Kt–R5 wins, or if 2 ... Kt–KB3; 3 Q–K5, K–Kt2 (on 3 ... Q–Q4 threatening mate, 4 QxQ, BxQ—not 4 ... KtxQ; 5 Kt–R6 mate–5 KtxKt ch wins a piece); 4 KtxKt, BxKt; 5 Kt–R5 ch!, PxKt; 6 Q–Kt5 ch, K–R1; 7 Q–R6!, and White forces mate. A beautiful

bit of play in the notes, where so
many fascinating ideas lie hidden.

| 3 | KtxB ch | KtxKt |
| 4 | Q–R6 | |

Not 4 Q–K5, as 4 ... Q–Q4
threatening mate forces White to exchange Queens.

| 4 | ... | R–B1 |
| 5 | QR–Q1 | Q–K2 |

To evade discovered attack on the
Queen.

6 KR–K1

A developing move which attacks.
The follow-up would be 7 Kt–B5
(attacks the Queen while threatening 8 Q–Kt7 mate), KtPxKt; 8 BxKt,
and this time the attack on the
Queen combined with the mate
threat is irresistible.

| 6 | ... | Kt–K1 |

From here the Knight guards
KKt2, a critical square.

7 Kt–B5!

Spielmann never runs out of ideas.

| 7 | ... | Q–B4 |

Honlinger avoids 7 ... KtPxKt;
8 BxP, P–B3; 9 BxKP ch, K–R1; 10
R–Q7, and White crashes through.

| 8 | R–K5 | B–Q4 |

Now comes a magnificent finish to
a remarkable combination!

9 Kt–K7 ch!

A Knight sacrifice which clears the
way for a Queen sacrifice!

| 9 | ... | QxKt |

Black must capture, as 9 ...
K–R1 allows 10 QxR mate.

10	QxRP ch!	KxQ
11	R–R5 ch	K–Kt1
12	R–R8 mate!	

Black to play

279

GRUNFELD-SPIELMANN
Sopron, 1934

Spielmann overwhelms his opponent with as dazzling a collection of
pins, actual and threatened, as ever
you saw on a chessboard!

| 1 | ... | BxQKtP! |

The first move of a strong attack,
for the sake of which Spielmann has
sacrificed a piece.

2 R–K1

Clearly, 2 KtxB, QxB ch; 3 K–Kt1,
QxB; 4 Kt–Q3 (he must stop 4 ...
R–K8 ch), R–K7 is ruinous for
White.

2 ...	Q–B3 ch
3 Kt–B2	

The only move, since 3 B–B3 allows a fatal pin on the Knight by 3 ... B–B5.

3 ...	B–Q5

More pressure on the pinned Knight, and a threat of mate.

4 Q–Kt3	R–K5!

Preparing to double Rooks. This, as Spielmann points out, is superior to the natural 4 ... R–K4, since it refutes the freeing attempt 5 B–Q3 by 5 ... R–Kt5.

5   P–KR4

Good moves are getting scarce: 5 Q–KB3 loses by 5 ... RxB!; 6 QxR, B–B5!, while 5 B–KB3 fails after 5 ... B–B5 ch; 6 K–Kt1 (6 B–K2, RxB; 7 RxR, R–K1), RxR ch; 7 BxR, R–K1; 8 B–Q2, BxKt ch!; 9 QxB (if 9 KxB, Q–Q5 ch; 10 B–K3, QxB mate), Q–R8 ch, and Black wins.

5 ...	QR–K1

Threatens 6 ... RxB; 7 RxR, B–B5.

6 B–QKt5	RxR ch
7 BxR	R–K6!

To drive the Queen off, where it will no longer guard the Knight.

8 Q–Kt5	RxB ch

And to destroy the Knight's other protector.

9 KxR	QxKt ch
10 K–Q1	BxKtP
11 R–K1	B–B6 ch
12 B–K2	B–B6!
13 BxB	QxB ch
14 K–B2	

Against 14 R–K2, Spielmann would win by clearing the board of pieces, thus: 14 ... Q–Q6 ch; 15 R–Q2, QxR ch; 16 QxQ, BxQ; 17 KxB, after which the most stubborn opponent would be inclined to submit.

14 ...	BxR
15 Resigns	

16

ARTIST OF THE CHESSBOARD

Akiba Rubinstein

----

*Could we look into the head of a chess player, we should
see there a whole world of feelings, images, ideas, emotion
and passion.*

— Alfred Binet

So much has been said of Rubinstein's astounding endgame technique—
from Fine's, "In the endgame Rubinstein is supreme," to Tartakover's,
"Rubinstein is the Rook ending of a game begun by the Gods thousands of
years ago,"—that we tend to overlook his accomplishments in other depart-
ments. His openings, if not so sharp and aggressive as Alekhine's, were carefully and soundly constructed. His midgames reflected profound position
judgment, and the combinations he evolved were of classic beauty.

Black to play

280

ROTLEVI-RUBINSTEIN
Lodz, 1907

The outstanding feature of almost
every combination is surprise in the
form of a brilliant move or two. In
this combination, from "Rubinstein's
Immortal Game," there is a whole
shower of brilliant surprise moves.

1	...	B–Kt3 ch
2	K–R1	Kt–Kt5
3	B–K4	

To eliminate one of Black's menacing Bishops.

The alternatives are not appeal-
ing:

(a) 4 QxKt, RxB, and Black
threatens 5 ... RxKt, as well as
6 ... R–Q7.

169

(b) 4 Kt–K4, RxB!; 5 QxR, BxKt; 6 QxB, Q–R5 (threatens mate); 7 P–R3, Q–Kt6; 8 PxKt, Q–R5 mate.

| 3 ... | Q–R5! |
| 4 | P–Kt3 |

If 4 P–R3, Black sails in with 4 ... RxKt!; 5 BxR (on 5 BxB, RxP ch; 6 PxR, QxP ch forces mate), BxB; 6 QxKt (or 6 QxB, Q–Kt6; 7 PxKt, Q–R5 mate), QxQ; 7 PxQ, R–Q6, and the threat of 8 ... R–R6 mate leaves White no time to save his Bishop.

| 4 ... | RxKt!! |
| 5 | PxQ |

Other defenses offer no solution. If 5 BxR, BxB ch leads to mate, while 5 BxB, RxKtP with the threat of 6 ... KtxRP is decisive.

| 5 ... | R–Q7!! |

"My center is giving way, my right is pushed back—excellent! I'll attack!" said Marshall Foch.

Rubinstein's Queen is gone, and three pieces are *en prise*, so he offers a fourth!

| 6 | QxR |

Let's see what else White could have done:

(a) 6 BxB, RxQ; 7 B–Kt2, R–R6!; 8 BxR, RxP mate.

(b) 6 BxR, RxQ, and White cannot prevent 7 ... RxP mate or 7 ... BxB ch followed by mate.

(c) 6 QxKt, BxB ch; 7 R–B3, RxR, and mate is unavoidable.

6 ...	BxB ch
7	Q–Kt2	R–R6!
8	Resigns

There is no way to stop the Rook from mating.

Black to play

281

SALWE–RUBINSTEIN
Lodz, 1907

Rubinstein has a couple of passed Pawns with a lust to expand. He satisfies their fierce ambition with a combination which includes giving up his Queen. His new Queen (a transformed passed Pawn) makes short work of White.

| 1 ... | P–Q7! |
| 2 | R–Q1 |

Capturing the Pawn loses: 2 QxQP, R–KR3 (threatens 3 ... QxKt ch!; 4 RxQ, P–B7 mate); 3 K–Kt1, Q–Kt6 ch; 4 K–B1, RxKt!; 5 RxR, B–Q6 ch; 6 QxB, QxR; 7 Q–B2, Q–R8 ch; 8 K–B2, Q–Kt7 ch; 9 K–K1, Q–Kt8 ch; 10 K–Q2, P–B7; 11 Q–B8, Q–K8 ch and Black wins.

| 2 ... | Q–Kt6 |
| 3 | Q–K7 |

Counter-attack on Rook and Bishop. White prefers this to 3 R(Q1)xP, R–KR3, and Black has a mighty threat in 4 ... RxKt ch.

3 ...   R–QB1
4 R(B2)xQP

Other possibilities were:
(a) 4 QxB, QxR; 5 R–KKt1, P–Q8(Q); 6 RxQ, Q–Kt7 mate.
(b) 4 R(Q1)xP, R–B8 ch; 5 R–B1, P–B7 ch; 6 QxB, Q–Kt8 ch; 7 RxQ, RxR mate.
(c) 4 R(Q1)–KB1, Q–Kt7 ch; 5 RxQ, PxR ch; 6 K–Kt1, PxR(Q) ch, and Black wins.

4 ...   Q–K8 ch!
5 RxQ   P–B7 ch
6 QxB   PxR(Q) ch
7 K–Kt2   QxR ch
8 Resigns

Black to play

282

VIDMAR-RUBINSTEIN
Prague, 1908

With very little left on the board Rubinstein manipulates the pieces skillfully to end his combination with an artistic Knight fork—a finish Vidmar does not wait to see!

1 ...   Kt–B5!
2 Kt–B6 ch

If 2 KtxKt, PxKt; 3 R–Q1, R–R7; 4 R–K1 (4 BxP, KtxP ch forfeits the Bishop), P–B6 wins for Black.

2 ...   K–B3
3 Kt–Kt8   KtxRP
4 KtxP   Kt–B7

Attacks the Knight Pawn twice, and also threatens 5 ... Kt–K8 ch winning the exchange.

5 R–Q2   Kt–K8 ch
6 K–B1

Forced, as his own Knight is attacked.

6 ...   Kt–B6!

Black covers the square Q8 so that after 7 ... KtxP ch, White's Rook cannot interpose.

7 B–Q1   KtxP
8 R–Q3

Clearly White must harass Black's Knights.

8 ...   KtxB
9 Resigns

The finish, had Vidmar continued, would have been 8 K–K2, Kt–Kt8 ch; 9 K–Q2 (if the King retreats, 9 ... Kt–Kt7 ch wins the Rook), KtxBP; 10 R–Q6 (to protect the Knight), Kt–K5 ch, and Black wins the Rook with a pretty Knight fork.

Black to play

283

BELSITZMANN-RUBINSTEIN
BELSITZMANN-RUBINSTEIN
Warsaw, 1917

Rubinstein's Queen sacrifice could
have been made by a lesser master.
But how many would have foreseen
the previous offer of a Knight which
made the Queen sacrifice possible?

| 1 | ... | Q–R5 |
| 2 | P–Kt3 | |

If 2 P–KR3, P–Kt4; 3 Kt–Kt4,
(otherwise 3 ... P–KR4 followed
by 4 ... P–KKt5 breaks through),
KtxKt; 4 QxKt, QxQ; 5 PxQ, Kt–K7
ch; 6 K–R1, P–KR4, and Black wins.

| 2 | ... | Q–R6 |
| 3 | P–QB3 | P–KR4! |

In a combination, time is of the
essence. It is more important to attack along the Rook file (and therefore open it up without delay) than
it is to waste a move by retreating
the Knight.

| 4 | PxKt | P–R5 |
| 5 | Q–K2 | |

Expecting 5 ... PxP; 6 BPxP,
BxP; 7 Kt–B5 ch followed by 8
KtxB, and his game might still hold
together. But Rubinstein's response
gives him no time at all.

5	...	QxRP ch!
6	KxQ	PxP ch
7	K–Kt1	R–R8 mate

White to play

284

RUBINSTEIN-BOGOLYUBOV
Vienna, 1922

The moves Rubinstein made in his
combination were strong enough to
defeat Bogolyubov and radiant
enough to secure the prize for brilliancy.

| 1 | R(B1)–B5! |

This fortifies White's grip on the
Queen Bishop file, since disputing it
by 1 ... KR–B1 costs a piece
after 2 RxB.

| 1 | ... | KR–Q1 |
| 2 | Kt–K5! | |

Further infiltration. Black cannot

remove the Knight as after 2 ...
BxKt; 3 PxB, QxP; 4 RxB, White
wins a piece.

2 ...   B–KB3
3 Kt–B6!

An attack on both Rooks, which
Black cannot meet by 3 ... BxKt.
The recapture by 4 R(B5)xB would
win his Queen.

3 ...   P–K3

Bogolyubov counts on 4 KtxQR,
RxKt, after which he regains the exchange by 5 ... B–Q1.

4 P–KKt3!

A quiet move in the midst of all
the excitement. White gives his King
a flight square in the event of an
unexpected check on the eighth
rank.

4 ...   R(Q1)–QB1
5 KtxR   RxKt

Apparently Black will regain the
exchange, but Rubinstein has looked
a good deal ahead.

6 BxP!   B–Q1

On 6 ... PxB; 7 Q–R7 gets the
piece back, and leaves White the
exchange ahead.

7 B–K8!   Q–B1

If 7 ... BxR; 8 QxB, QxQ; 9
RxQ, RxB; 10 RxB, and White, a
Pawn ahead, wins the ending easily.

8 RxB!

(For a Rubinstein combination,
the annotator must have a plentiful
supply of exclamation points.)

8 ...   BxQ
9 RxR

Black's Bishop is attacked, and
loss of his Queen for Rook and
Bishop is threatened by 10 BxP ch.

9 ...   Q–Q3

Counter-attack is the only hope.

10 R–Kt7   B–Kt3
11 R–B6   Q–Kt5
12 BxP ch   Resigns

White to play

285

RUBINSTEIN–HROMADKA
Mahrisch-Ostrau, 1923

Rubinstein's offer of the Queen
(which must not be accepted!) dis-
guises his real intention. The problem-like Queen move enables his
Bishop to come in victoriously at B5.
An impressive combination!

1 P–KKt3   KtxRP
2 RxP   Q–Q3

Yields the seventh rank, but if 2 ... KtxQ, 3 RxQ, R(Kt1)–B1; 4 P–R6, P–QKt3; 5 B–K6, and White has a strong threat in 6 B–Q7.

| 3 | Q–Kt6!! | R–Q2 |

The penalty for taking the Queen is mate, as follows: 3 ... PxQ; 4 PxP ch, B–R2; 5 RxB ch, K–Kt1; 6 R(B7)xP ch, K–B1; 7 B–R6, and Black will be mated.

| 4 | B–B5! | RxR |

The alternative 4 ... Q–B2 loses a Rook after 5 QxQ, RxQ; 6 RxR, BxR; 7 BxR.

5	BxQ	R–B7 ch
6	QxR!	KtxQ
7	B–B5	

Better than 7 BxR, BxB which merely wins the exchange. This move nets a whole piece. Black of course resigned.

White to play

286

RUBINSTEIN-TARTAKOVER
Marienbad, 1925

Classic endgame play by Rubin-

stein whose concluding combination takes into account a pretty stalemate try of his desperate opponent.

| 1 | R–Q7! |

White expects 1 ... P–QKt3, whereupon he intended to put pressure on with 2 B–Kt2, R–Kt3; 3 R(B1)–B7.

| 1 | ... | B–K6 |

A little trap: if White doubles Rooks by 2 R(B1)–B7, then 2 ... R–B8 ch; 3 K–R2, B–B5 ch wins the exchange. But in attacking the Rook, Black overlooks the reply—giving him choice of Rooks!

2	RxQKtP!	R–QKt3
3	RxR(Kt6)	BxR(Kt3)
4	R–B6	

Threatens to win a piece by 5 B–Q6.

4	...	P–KR4
5	B–Q6	R–Kt2
6	P–QKt4	P–R4

Giving White a passed Pawn, but otherwise he loses his Queen Rook Pawn after 7 P–R5.

7	P–Kt5	K–R2
8	P–Kt4	PxP
9	PxP	K–Kt1
10	K–Kt2	K–B2
11	K–B3	B–Q1
12	K–K4	K–K1
13	K–Q5	P–Kt4

If 13 ... K–B2 (to keep White's King from reaching K6); 14 R–B8, B–B3; 15 K–B6, R–R2; 16 B–B5 wins for White. The text is intended to leave Black short of moves, to give him a chance to try a stalemate swindle.

14	K–K6	B–Kt3
15	R–B8 ch	B–Q1
16	B–B5	R–Kt1

Hoping that White will "capture first and think later."

17	R–B6	R–Kt2
18	P–Kt6	R–Kt1
19	R–B7!	BxR

Forced, as 19 ... R–B1 is countered by 20 R–KKt7. Once the Rook swings over to the King side, all is lost.

| 20 | PxB | R–B1 |
| 21 | B–Kt6 | R–R1 |

If 21 ... K–B1; 22 K–Q7, and Black must give up his Rook for the Pawn.

| 22 | B–R7! | Resigns |

If 22 ... R–B1; 23 B–Kt8, K–B1; 24 K–Q7, and Black must concede.

White to play

287

RUBINSTEIN-JANOWSKY
Marienbad, 1925

The sacrifice of one piece opens a diagonal enabling White to sacrifice another piece! The ensuing attack is irresistible.

| 1 | Kt–Kt5! | PxKt |

The Knight had to go, as the threats (2 Kt–K6 and 2 BxP ch) were too strong.

| 2 | BxP ch | K–R1 |

Coming out into the open by 2 ... K–B2 leads to 3 Q–Kt6 ch, K–K2; 4 Q–K6 mate.

3	BxP ch	KxB
4	Q–Kt6 ch	K–R1
5	R–R3	Q–Q2

Or 5 ... B–B1; 6 B–Kt8 ch, BxR; 7 Q–R7 mate.

| 6 | B–Kt8 ch | QxR |
| 7 | PxQ | Resigns |

If Black plays 7 ... RxB to avoid 8 Q–R7 mate, then 8 Q–R6 is the mating move.

Black to play

288

MICHEL-RUBINSTEIN
Semmering, 1926

The action is all on the Queen side when suddenly Rubinstein switches his attack to the other wing. Nine checks in succession by his Queen put an end to the white King's career. A profound combination, even for a Rubinstein.

| 1 ... | P–B5! |
| 2 QxBP | Q–B4! |

Black's chief threat, besides the obvious 3 ... QxP ch, is 3 ... RxB; 4 QxR, B–Kt4; 5 Q–B8, QxP ch; 6 R–B2, Q–K8 ch, and mate next move.

3 K–B2

Certainly not 3 QxQ, BxQ, and White is still menaced with 4 ... RxB and 4 ... BxP ch.

| 3 ... | QxRP |
| 4 Kt–B8 | |

Any other move loses a piece at once.

4 ...	B–R5 ch
5 P–Kt3	RxB
6 Kt–Q6	

The only hope, since 6 PxB is refuted by 6 ... R–B3 winning the Knight.

| 6 ... | RxKt! |

Looks risky, as White gets a passed Pawn on the sixth rank, but Rubinstein has calculated the sequel carefully.

7 PxR	B–QKt4
8 Q–B7	Q–R8
9 PxB	Q–B8 ch
10 K–Kt3	Q–K8 ch
11 R–B2	Q–Kt8 ch
12 K–B3	

If 12 R–Kt2, QxKP is mate.

| 12 ... | Q–R8 ch |
| 13 R–Kt2 | |

On 13 K–Kt3, B–B3 threatening 14 ... Q–Kt8 ch is decisive.

| 13 ... | Q–Q8 ch |
| 14 K–Kt3 | |

While here 14 K–K4 allows 14 ... Q–Q4 mate.

| 14 ... | Q–Kt5 ch |
| 15 K–B2 | Q–K7 ch |

And Black mates next move.

White to play

289

RUBINSTEIN-GRUNFELD
Semmering, 1926

Just when Grunfeld has settled down to defend a difficult ending, Rubinstein sacrifices a piece and conjures up a pretty mating attack.

1 R–R7!

Intending to attack the King Pawn a third time with 2 P–B3. Black could not then advance the Pawn to

K6 on account of the reply 3 RxRP
mate.

1   ...   B–Kt2

If 1 ... B–K2; 2 B–R2, R–K4;
3 RxP ch, and White is two Pawns
ahead.

2   BxKP!

This must have made Grunfeld sit
up and take notice!

2   ...   R(Q5)xB
3   RxR   RxR
4   RxP ch   K–R4
5   P–B3!

Suddenly Black is threatened with
mate by a Pawn! He can prevent this
only by giving up his Rook, so. . . .

5   ...   Resigns

White to play

290

RUBINSTEIN-NIMZOVICH
Berlin, 1928

Two tactical threats give Rubinstein possession of the open King file.

Then comes a Knight sacrifice to
touch off the final combination.

1   R–K1

A preventive maneuver. If Black
tries 1 ... Kt–Q2 (to plant the
Knight firmly at K4) the continuation; 2 KtxQP, RxKt; 3 R–K8 ch
followed by 4 RxB wins easily for
White.

1   ...   B–Kt2
2   Q–K2

Now aiming at winning the Queen
by 3 P–R4 followed by 4 P–Kt5.

2   ...   Kt–Q2

Ready to meet 3 P–R4 with 3 ...
P–Kt3. But Rubinstein now divulges
his real plans. He will force his way
into Black's position, using the open
file as a highway.

3   KtxQP!   RxKt
4   Q–K8 ch   Kt–B1
5   R–K7

Threatens mate in two.

5   ...   P–Kt3
6   Q–B7 ch   K–R1
7   R–K8   R–Q1

In the heat of the battle White
might grab the Rook. Black could
then force a perpetual check beginning with 8 ... Q–K6 ch.

8   QxBP ch   K–Kt1
9   Q–K6 ch   K–Kt2
10 P–B6 ch   Resigns

*Rubinstein was an artist whose masterpieces are the price-
less legacy of an unhappy genius.*

—Reuben Fine

17

THE FABULOUS ORIGINAL
Aron Nimzovich

The chess master today must have courage, a killer instinct, stamina and arrogance.

—Larry Evans

Nimzovich was the most original chess player that ever lived. One has only to recall his wonderfully imaginative opening (and the subsequent combinations) against Wendel in 1921, his "Immortal Zugzwang" game against Saemisch in 1923 (where he tied poor Saemisch up hand and foot) his subtle Pawn strategy against Rosselli del Turco in 1925, his blend of originality and logic against Johner in 1926, and the demonstration of his "new philosophy of the center" against Salwe in 1911, to realize that here is an unusual sort of chess master, one who is not afraid to put his own ideas to the test. Nimzovich's games, as we shall see highlighted in the combinations below, are "witch chess, heathen and beautiful."

White to play

291

NIMZOVICH-HAKANSSON
Match, 1922
178

After relegating Black's Queen to a corner of the board, Nimzovich neatly dispatches the King with a semi-smothered mate.

1   P–B3!

To open the Bishop file for the Rook's attack on King and Queen.

1   ...   R–K1

Clearing a flight square for the King. If 1 ... QPxP; 2 R–B1 follows, and the Rook will recapture.

2   BPxP   K–Q1
3   R–QB1   Q–Kt3

| 4 | P–R5 | Q–R2 |
| 5 | P–Kt6 | Q–R1 |

"Who else but Nimzovich," says Reinfeld, "could have conjured up the position of Black's Queen?"

6	R–B7	Kt–B4
7	Kt–B3	B–K2
8	KtxQP!	KtxP

If at once 8 ... PxKt then 9 BxKt wins a Pawn for White. The text prevents loss of a Pawn—but at fearful expense.

9   KtxKt

(A strange line-up on the Queen file!)

9	...	PxKt
10	QxB ch!	KtxQ
11	Kt–K6 mate!	

White to play . . . .

292

NIMZOVICH-BERNSTEIN
Carlsbad, 1923

Nimzovich is at his characteristic best in this impressive combination.

The finish, with the Rooks threatening long-distance mates, is particularly pleasing to the eye.

1	QxKt!	RxQ
2	RxR ch	Kt–K1
3	B–Q1!	RxB

The best chance: if 3 ... R–Kt8; 4 B–R4, RxR; 5 BxKt, and White wins.

4	KxR	Q–B2 ch
5	K–Q2	K–B2
6	B–R5 ch	P–Kt3
7	R(R1)–QR1!	

Threatens to pin the Queen.

7	...	Q–Kt3
8	B–K2	K–Kt2
9	K–K1	Kt–B2
10	R(R8)–R5	K–R3
11	K–B1!	Q–Kt6
12	P–R5!	Kt–K1
13	R–R6	Q–Kt7
14	PxP	PxP
15	R(R6)–R2	Q–Kt2
16	R–R7	Q–Kt7
17	K–Kt2!	

Threatens 18 R–R1 mate! If 17 ... P–Kt4, to give the King an escape square, 18 R(R1)–R6 ch forces mate.

17	...	Kt–B3
18	R–R1 ch	Kt–R4
19	BxKt!	PxB
20	R(R1)–QR1!	

Indicating that the Rook's next stop will be R6, where it will mate or force Black to give up his Queen.

| 20 | ... | Resigns |

Black to play

293

GILG-NIMZOVICH
Semmering, 1926

Under Nimzovich's direction the Knights prance about and steal the show!

1   ...   Q–R4

Threatens 2 ... BxP; 3 PxB, Kt–B7 ch, winning the Queen (White's Knight is pinned, please note).

2   Kt–B1   B–QB4

Now the idea is: 3 ... QxKt; 4 BxQ, Kt–B7 ch; 5 K–Kt2, BxB ch; 6 K–B3, KtxQ, and Black has won a piece.

3   B–K3   BxB
4   KtxB   B–Q2
5   Q–Q4   QR–K1
6   Kt–B1   P–KKt4!

Prevents the freeing move 7 Kt–B4.

7   Kt–Kt1   Kt–K5!

With two main threats: 8 ... QxP ch!; 9 KtxQ, KtxP mate and 8

... Kt(K5)–B7 ch; 9 QxKt, KtxQ mate.

8   Kt–R3   Kt(Kt5)–B3
9   BxKt

If 9 Kt–Kt1 (to prevent loss of a piece by 9 ... BxKt), Kt–B7 ch!; 10 QxKt, Kt–Kt5; 11 Q–Q4, Kt–B7 ch, and Black wins the Queen.

9   ...   KtxB
10   Kt–Kt1   Kt–B7 ch
11   K–Kt2   B–R6 ch
12   Resigns

If 12 KtxB, Q–B6 ch; 13 K–Kt1, Q–R8 mate.

Black to play

294

LUND-NIMZOVICH
Oslo, 1921

Black's Pawns are blocked and a break-through looks difficult. Not for Nimzovich though, who evolves an artful combination to turn the trick—beginning with four sacrifices in succession!

1 ...	P–Kt5!
2 PxP	

Best, as the alternatives lose quickly:

(a) 2 K–B1, RxKt!; 3 PxR, P–KKt6 (threatening to push on); 4 PxP, KxB wins for Black.

(b) 2 Kt–Kt6, P–B6 ch; 3 PxP (retreating with the King allows mate on the move), PxRP; 4 K–B1, R–R8 ch, and the Rook Pawn will Queen.

2 ...	RxKt!
3 PxR	P–Kt6!
4 PxP	

Forced, but the Bishop loses a valuable support.

4 ...	P–B6 ch!
5 PxP	P–R6

And Black wins.

Black to play

295

SAMISCH-NIMZOVICH
Copenhagen, 1923

The position on the board, at the end of Nimzovich's combination is striking evidence of his keen imagination and originality of thought. His very last move, quiet though it is, paralyzes White's whole army! None of Samisch's pieces (and this includes King, Queen, two Rooks, two Bishops and a Knight) are able to stir without causing immediate loss of material!

1 ...	P–Kt5

Banishing the Knight to the last rank.

2 Kt–Kt1	B–QKt4

Purpose: to prevent White's King Pawn from advancing.

3 R–Kt1	B–Q3!

But now Nimzovich seems to have changed his mind. He allows White to free his game.

4 P–K4	

The Pawn advances, with threats!

4 ...	BPxP!
5 QxKt	RxP

In return for the sacrificed Knight, Black has a Rook on the seventh, two Pawns (one of them a passed Pawn) possession of the King Bishop file, and two active Bishops.

6 Q–Kt5	QR–KB1

Intending 7 ... R(B1)–B6 followed by 8 ... RxP.

7 K–R1	R(B1)–B4
8 Q–K3	B–Q6

Limits the movements of the Queen. The threat is now 9 ... R–K7 winning the Queen.

9 R(B1)–K1   P–R3!!

A remarkable winning move! it leaves White completely helpless. The proof:

(a) If the Knight moves, 10 ... PxKt wins a piece.

(b) If 10 B–B1, BxKt wins.

(c) If 10 R–QB1, R–K7 wins the Queen.

(d) If 10 R(Kt1)–B1, BxR; 11 BxB, RxB ch wins.

(e) If 10 K–R2, R(B4)–B6 wins the Queen. In this variation we see how 9 ... P–R3 prevents the Queen from escaping to Kt5.

(e) If 10 P–Kt4, R(B4)–B6!; 11 BxR, R–R7 mate!

Black to play

296

HAGE-NIMZOVICH
Arnstadt, 1926

Nimzovich's position is so manifestly superior that he is entitled to a reward for his efforts in the form of a combination. There is one, and it has the virtue of clearing away any doubts White might have had about resigning.

1 ...   KtxB
2 RxKt   Kt–Q6
3 R–Kt1   KtxKtP
4 RxKt

Forced, as his own Knight was attacked. If White tries 4 R–R1, then 4 ... Kt–Q6; 5 P–R4, RxKt; 6 RxR, P–Kt7 is decisive.

4 ...   RxKt
5 R–Kt1

King moves offer no hope: 5 K–K1, R–R8 ch; 6 K–Q2, R–KB8, or 5 K–Kt1, R–R8 ch; 6 K–R2, R–QB8.

5 ...   P–Kt7
6 Resigns

Black's reply, to any move White makes, would be 6 ... R–R8.

White to play

297

NIMZOVICH-GILG
Kecskemet, 1927

"Attack on a wing is best met by play in the center," says Nimzovich, and proceeds to prove the efficacy of his formula with a sparkling combination.

1   Q–Kt3   P–KKt3   *White to play*

Weakens his black squares, but Castling allows 2 B–R6 winning the exchange for White.

2   B–Kt3   Kt–Kt5
3   BxP ch!   K–Q1

Certainly not 3 ... KxB; 4 P–K6 ch, and Black loses his Queen.

4   B–R6   Kt–B7
5   Kt–B3   Kt–Q5

Black changes his mind about capturing the Rook, as after 5 ... KtxR; 6 Kt–Q5, Q–B3; 7 B–K3!, P–Q3; 8 B–Kt6 ch, K–Q2; 9 P–K6 is mate.

6   QxQP   QxP
7   KR–K1   Q–B3

The alternative 7 ... Q–QB4; 8 B–Kt7 is a dismal prospect.

8   RxB!   Resigns

If 8 ... KxR, the Knight fork at Q5 wins the Queen, while 8 ... QxR succumbs to 9 QxKt, after which White attacks the Rook on one wing, and menaces mate by 10 Q–Kt6 on the other!

298

NIMZOVICH–NIELSEN
Copenhagen, 1930

Before making the surprise move that wins the game instantaneously, White must pin a Bishop that might interfere with his combination, and then kill it off.

It takes a sharp eye to see this stroke, but Nimzovich has a sharp eye!

1   R–B7!

An attack on the Bishop which is hard to meet. The possibilities are:

(a) 1 ... B–B3; 2 BxB, PxB; 3 R–Kt4 ch, K–R1; 4 QxP mate.

(b) 1 ... B–Q1; 2 R–Kt4, P–Kt3; 3 QxQ, PxQ; 4 R–Q7, and White wins a Pawn.

(c) 1 ... KR–K1; 2 BxP!, KxB (if 2 ... P–B4; 3 Q–KKt3, PxR; 4 B–K5 ch, and White forces mate); 3 R–Kt4 ch, K–B1 (3 ... K–R3; 4 QxP); 4 Q–KKt3, and the check at Kt8 will be fatal.

1   ...   B–Q3
2   R–Q7   QR–Q1

3   RxB!   RxR
4   Q–B6!

A beautiful move. White threatens
5 QxKtP mate. If Black takes the
Queen then comes 5 R–Kt4 ch, K–
R1; 6 BxP mate.

4   ...   Resigns

Black to play

299

MANNHEIMER-NIMZOVICH
Frankfort, 1930

The first move of the Queen is
typical of Nimzovich's subtle strategy. Clearly, the Queen intends to
help out in a combination on the
King side. While White is busy defending that area, the Queen is off
like a shot, and demolishes the vulnerable Queen side!

1   ...   Q–Kt3!

Protects the Rook at R3 in preparation for this combination: 2 ...
PxP; 3 RxR ch, QxR; 4 KtxP, Q–R5;
5 B–K3 (any move by the King,
Queen or Rook abandons the

Knight), RxKt ch and Black wins.

2   B–K3

Now the combination would not
work as after 2 ... PxP; 3 RxR
ch, QxR; 4 KtxP, Q–R5; 5 B–Kt1,
and the Bishop oscillates between
Kt1 and R2.

2   ...   Q–R3!

Menacing the Pawn? Not if he
can play 3 ... Kt–Kt7 and win
the Queen!

3   B–B2   QxP
4   B–K1   P–R4

While Mannheimer is disentan-
gling himself, Nimzovich's passed
Pawn marches leisurely down the
board.

5   K–B1   Q–Kt8

Clears the file for the Pawn's advance, and maintains pressure on the
King side. White must guard against
loss of a piece by 6 ... Kt(B5)–
Q7 ch; 7 K–Kt2, QxB, for example.

6   Kt–Kt1

Vacates the square K2 for the
King.

6   ...   P–R5
7   K–K2   P–R6
8   R–B1   P–R7

And White yielded.

White to play

300

NIMZOVICH-JOHNER
Bern, 1931

In this combination from a little-known game, we get a sampling of Nimzovich's dexterity with the Knights.

1 KtxP!	R–Kt4
2 KtxKt	QxR

The desperado motif. If 3 RxQ, RxQ wins for Black, or if 3 QxR, Black continues the desperado idea with 3 ... QxR ch; 4 KxQ, PxQ, and wins.

3 Q–B7!

Attacks the Queen while menacing the win of the exchange by 4 QxBP.

3 ...	Q–B6
4 P–QR4!	R–Kt5
5 Kt–K5	

To follow up with 6 Q–B7 ch, K–R1; 7 QxKP, when White threatens a smothered mate finish: 8 Kt–B7 ch, K–Kt1; 9 Kt–R6 ch, K–R1; 10 Q–Kt8 ch!, RxQ; 11 Kt–B7 mate!

5 ...   R–KB1

On 5 ... K–R1, White intended to continue the attack with 6 P–B4 followed by 7 R–B3 and 8 R–Kt3.

6 KtxP!

Hidden attack on Black's Queen by 7 Kt–K7 ch.

6 ...   K–R1

If instead 6 ... Q–Q7, to keep in touch with the Rook, 7 Q–R5! wins a whole Rook by the pin.

7 Q–Q6!

A painful double attack. If Black moves either Rook to QKt1, the Knight captures at QKt8, and Black may not recapture.

Johner resigned.

18

MODERN MORPHY

Paul Keres

I now see myself (after 50 years of tournament play) compelled to change my concepts of chess strategy during the years which may still lie ahead.

—Savielly Tartakover

Keres burst on the chess scene like a bombshell. Playing first board for Estonia in the International Team tournament at Warsaw in 1935, he amazed the world with the calibre of his play. He attacked like a demon, and his combinations were spectacular. This was the beginning of a meteor-like career. In the next couple of years Keres played more brilliant games than most of his fellow masters did in their entire lives!

Keres was not a child prodigy in the usual sense of the word. He reached the age of fourteen before being recognized as one of Estonia's leading masters. But he had acquired some experience earlier when he and his older brother played several hundred games together. The brother was then seven, while Paul, our hero, was four years old.

With the exception of Alekhine, Keres is the greatest attacking and combinative genius that ever lived.

Black to play

301

KARU-KERES
Correspondence, 1931

186

Disregarding the attack on his Bishop, Keres comes back with a sharp combination. He aims at the unfortunate King, who has failed to castle in time.

1 ...	P–Q6!

With this idea: If 2 PxB, KtPxP; 3 P–K4, B–B6 ch; 4 B–Q2, BxB ch; 5 RxB, P–B6!; 6 RxP, P–B7!; 7 R–B3 (7 RxQ, QRxR wins), RxP ch; 8 B–K2, Q–Q8 mate!

2	P–K4	B–B6 ch
3	B–Q2	Q–Q5

With the terrible threat 4 ...
RxP ch.

4	BxB	QxB ch
5	R–Q2	RxP ch!
6	Resigns	

Rather than submit to 6 QxR, Q–
B8 ch; 7 R–Q1, P–Q7, and White
has been mated by a Pawn.

White to play

302

KERES-LAURENTIUS
Correspondence, 1934

A combination which involves a
sacrifice or two must be sound to
succeed in correspondence play. If
there is a flaw in the combination,
the opponent has sufficient time to
find and expose it.

Keres's combination, happily, is
sound in every variation—and pretty,
too.

1 **BxBP!**   **BxB**

Against the Pawn capture, there
is a forced mate in four, as follows:
1 ... PxB; 2 Q–R5 ch, K–Kt1;
3 Q–Kt4 ch, K–B2; 4 Q–Kt7 ch, K–
K1; 5 Kt–B7 mate.

| 2 | R–Q7 ch | Kt–K2 |

Keres shows what happens on
other moves:

(a) 2 ... K–Kt1; 3 QxB!,
PxQ; 4 R–Kt7 mate.

(b) 2 ... K–Kt3; 3 RxP ch!,
BxR; 4 Q–Kt4 ch, K–B2; 5 QxB ch,
K–K1; 6 Kt–B5 ch, K–Q1; 7 Q–Q7
mate.

(c) 2 ... K–K1; 3 RxQKtP,
Kt–K4; 4 KtxP ch!, BxKt; 5 RxB,
and Black is helpless.

3	RxKt ch!	KxR
4	QxP ch	K–Q3
5	Q–B7 ch	K–Q4
6	Q–B5 mate	

White to play

303

KERES-SCHAPIRO
Correspondence, 1935

Black's position, with his King out
in the open, indicates that combinations are in the air. This does not
detract from Keres's performance.
He sacrifices pieces with grace, ease
and abandon to carry out his objective.

| 1 | QxBP! | KtxB |
| 2 | PxP | KtxKP |

What else is there? If 2 ... Kt–
B4; 3 Kt–Q5 ch, K–K3; 4 Kt–B7 ch,
K–K2; 5 PxP ch, QxP; 6 QR–K1 ch,
K–Q1; 7 R–K8 mate, or if 2 ...
R–B1; 3 PxP ch, K–K3; 4 Q–Q5 ch,
K–Q2; 5 R–B7 ch, K–K1; 6 P–Q7
ch, QxP; 7 QxQ mate.

| 3 | Kt–Q5 ch | K–K3 |
| 4 | QR–K1 |

Threatens 5 Kt–B7 ch, K–K2 (5
... QxKt; 6 RxKt ch, KxR; 7 Q–
Q5 mate); 6 RxKt ch, PxR; 7 Q–K6
mate.

| 4 | ... | Q–B1 |

To drive White's Queen off, and
to provide a flight square at Q1 for
the King.

5	Kt–B7 ch	K–K2
6	RxKt ch!	PxR
7	Kt–Q5 ch	K–Q1
8	RxB ch!	RxR
9	Q–Q6 ch

A crushing check, as Black must
lose both his Rooks.

| 9 | ... | Q–Q2 |

On 9 ... K–K1; 10 Q–K7 is
mate.

10	QxR(Kt8) ch	Q–B1
11	Q–Q6 ch	Q–Q2
12	QxR ch	Q–K1
13	QxP	Resigns

White to play

304

KERES-FINE
Ostend, 1937

Black is a Pawn up, has a couple
of passed Pawns, and controls the
QB file. He has a won ending, except
that Keres's midgame combination
takes precedence over a theoretical
advantage in the ending.

| 1 | KtxRP! | KtxKt |
| 2 | R–R3 |

This will recover the piece and
let the Queen enter the vitals.

2	...	Q–B8
3	QxKt ch	K–B1
4	R(R3)–K3	P–Q5

A plausible advance. The Pawn
attacks a Rook (which must not
abandon the other Rook), threatens
to push on, clears a path for the
Bishop and gives the King Rook
more scope. The one drawback—and
one is all Keres needs—is that it opens
a long diagonal for White's Bishop.

| 5 | Q–R8 ch | K–K2 |
| 6 | QxP |

Indicating that the penalty for taking the Rook will be instant mate.

6 ...   R–B1

If 6 ... B–Q4 (to guard the Bishop Pawn); 7 Q–B6 ch, K–B1 (or 7 ... K–Q2; 8 BxB, PxR; 9 QxP mate); 8 P–K6!, BxKP; 9 Q–R6 ch, K–K2; 10 RxB ch, K–Q2; 11 R–K7 mate.

7 Q–B6 ch   K–K1
8 P–K6!   Resigns

If 8 ... PxR; 9 PxP ch, RxP; 10 BxR ch, K–Q2; 11 Q–K6 ch, K–B2 (11 ... K–Q1; 12 Q–Q6 mate); 12 RxQ ch, and White wins.

White to play

305

KERES–BOOK
Kemeri, 1937

Keres's Knight and Queen Bishop are attacked and far away from the scene of action. Incredible as it may seem they remain unharmed, and take active part in the mating combination!

1 B–K4

Threatens 2 QxP ch and mate next move.

1 ...   P–Kt3

If 1 ... P–R3; 2 Q–Kt6, R–K1; 3 Q–R7 ch, K–B1; 4 B–Kt6 is decisive.

2 BxKtP   PxB
3 QxP ch   K–R1

If 3 ... B–Kt2; 4 R–K7 wins at once.

4 Kt–K7!

With a threat of mate on the move!

4 ...   BxKt
5 RxB!   Resigns

Black is convinced. Clearly if 5 ... QxR; 6 BxP ch leads to utter ruin.

White to play

306

KERES–MIKENAS
Kemeri, 1937

An elegant two-part combination by Keres. First he pins a Bishop on the seventh rank, and wins the exchange. *Then he pins the same Bishop* on the file, and wins a piece.

1 P–B4! R–QB1

If 1 ... B–Q1 (to unpin the Bishop); 2 RxB ch!, RxR; 3 BxP, R(Q1)–R1; 4 BxR, RxB; 5 P–Kt5, P–QR4; 6 P–Kt6 wins. Or if 1 ... K–B1 (to drive the Rook off); 2 P–QB5!, K–K1 (not 2 ... PxP; 3 BxP ch, K–K1; 4 R–K7 ch, K–Q1; 5 R–Q1 ch, nor 2 ... P–QKt4; 3 P–B6, and White wins in either case); 3 PxP, KxR (on 3 ... BxKtP; 4 RxR, BxR; 5 RxP wins the exchange); 4 PxR, B–Q3; 5 RxP, BxKtP; 6 R–Kt6, B–Q3; 7 R–Kt7 ch, B–B2 (7 ... K–K1; 8 P–K5 wins); 8 B–Kt6, K–B3; 9 RxB ch and White wins.

2 P–Kt5 P–QR4
3 P–QB5 PxP
4 BxP R–Kt2

If 4 ... R(R2)–R1; 5 P–Kt6, B–Q1; 6 P–Kt7 impales the Rooks neatly.

5 P–Kt6

The first part: Keres exploits the pin of the Bishop to win the exchange.

5 ... BxKtP
6 RxR BxB
7 R–B1

And this is part two: the continuation 8 R–Kt5 will do away with the poor Bishop entirely.

7 ... Resigns

Mikenas has seen enough.

Black to play

307

EUWE–KERES
Match, 1940

Strange as it may seem, the most brilliant combinations are often brought off against the strongest opposition. Keres, for example, creates a magnificent specimen here, and the victim is a former Champion of the World.

1 ... P–Q6!

It hurts to give up this beautiful passed Pawn, but the King Bishop needs a long diagonal.

2 RxP QxR!
3 QxQ B–Q5 ch
4 R–B2

Interposing the Knight is fatal: 4 Kt–K3, RxB; 5 R–K1, QR–K1; 6 K–B2, RxKt and Black wins. Or if 4 K–R1, RxB followed by doubling Rooks and then moving 4 ... R–K7 is a clear-cut win.

4 ... RxB
5 K–B1 QR–K1!
6 P–B5 R–K4
7 P–B6

Black's threats were: 7 ... B–
K5 and 7 ... BxR; 8 KxB, R–K7
ch; 9 K–Kt1 (if 9 QxR, RxQ ch; 10
KxR, BxKt); BxKt, and Black follows up with 10 ... B–R6 to win.

| 7 ... | PxP |
| 8 R–Q2 | |

Of course not 8 RxP, BxKt ch; 9
KxB, R–K7 ch, with an easy win for
Black.

| 8 ... | B–B1! |

Intending 9 ... B–R6; 10 R–
Q1 (to stop 10 ... R–K8 mate),
R–B4 ch, and White must give up
his Queen.

9 Kt–B4	R–K6!
10 Q–Kt1	R–B6 ch
11 K–Kt2	RxKt!

Giving up the exchange with so
little material on the board is more
surprising than the Queen sacrifice
with which Keres started his combination.

| 12 PxR | R–Kt1 ch |
| 13 K–B3 | |

The only move, since 13 K–B1
loses the Queen by a Rook check,
while 13 K–R1 loses everything by
a Bishop check.

| 13 ... | B–Kt5 ch |
| 14 Resigns | |

For if 14 K–Kt3, B–B4 ch discovers an attack on the Queen, while
on 14 K–K4, R–K1 ch; 15 K–Q5 (or
15 K–Q3, B–B4 mate); B–B6 ch
forces mate.

White to play

308

KERES–MIKENAS
Tiflis, 1947

Three of the four moves in this
combination are made by the Knight,
who circles about and then lands
right in a cluster of hostile Pawns!

1 Kt–Kt4!

Threatens mate in three, beginning with 2 Q–B6 ch.

| 1 ... | P–R4 |
| 2 Q–B6 ch | K–Kt1 |

If 2 ... K–R2; 3 R–R3, and
White threatens 4 RxP ch, PxR; 5
Q–R6 ch, K–Kt1; 6 Kt–B6 mate.

| 3 Kt–R6 ch | K–R2 |
| 4 Kt–B5! | |

Mate on the move can only be
prevented by taking the Knight. If
4 ... QPxKt; 5 RxR forces Black
to give up his Queen, while 4 ...
KtPxKt is answered by 5 R–R3, after
which the Rook captures the Rook
Pawn and mates at R8.

| 4 ... | Resigns |

Black to play

309

EUWE-KERES
Moscow, 1948

More impressive than Keres's sacrifice, and the consequent disorder it creates as Euwe's pieces try to get out of each other's way, is the technique Keres displays in fastening on the weakened white squares of his opponent in carrying out his combination.

| 1 | ... | Kt–Kt3 |
| 2 | P–KKt3 | |

Protects the Bishop Pawn, but at the cost of weakening slightly the squares KB3 and KR3. But slightly is all Keres needs!

Other ways of defending the Pawn are not prepossessing:

(a) 2 Q–Kt3, P–R3; 3 Kt–R3, BxKt; 4 QxB, KtxP, and Black wins.

(b) 2 Kt–Kt3, KtxP; 3 RxKt, QxKt; 4 R–B2, Q–R4; 5 P–KR3, QR–K1; 6 Q–Q2, B–Kt6; 7 R–B1 (to prevent 8 ... R–K8 ch), R–K7; 8 Q–Kt5, RxP ch!, and Black mates in four more moves, as fol-

lows: 9 KxR, QxP ch; 10 K–B3, B–Kt5 ch; 11 K–K3, B–K8 ch; 12 R–B3, QxR mate.

| 2 | ... | QR–K1 |
| 3 | Q–B2 | |

The only move, since on 3 Q–B3, P–R3 attacks and wins the Knight.

| 3 | ... | B–Q6 |
| 4 | R–K1 | |

If 4 R–Q1, R–K7; 5 Q–B3, KtxP; 6 PxKt, BxP; 7 Kt–R3, Q–Kt3 ch wins for Black.

4	...	RxR ch
5	QxR	BxP!
6	PxB	

Refusing the offer allows this pretty possibility: 6 Q–K6 ch, QxQ; 7 KtxQ, B–K6 ch; 8 K–R1, R–B8 ch; 9 K–Kt2 (9 KtxR, B–K5 mate); R–B7 ch; 10 K–R1 (10 K–R3, P–KR4 wins), RxKt!; 11 BxR, 12 B–K5 mate.

| 6 | ... | KtxP |
| 7 | Kt(Q2)–B3 | |

On 7 Kt(Kt5)–B3, Q–Kt3 ch; 8 K–B2 (8 Q–Kt3, Kt–K7 ch wins the Queen), B–B7!; 9 Q–B1, Kt–Q6 ch; 10 K–K2, Q–K3 ch forces the win.

| 7 | ... | Kt–K7 ch |
| 8 | K–Kt2 | P–R3 |

Clearly demonstrating that two Knights should not depend on each other for support.

| 9 | Q–Q2 | Q–B4 |

Not merely to defend the Bishop. Black threatens 10 ... Q–Kt5 ch;

11 K–R1 (11 K–B1, Q–Kt8 mate), RxKt!

10	Q–K3	PxKt
11	B–Q2	B–K5
12	Resigns	

There was no defense: if 12 QxKt, BxKt ch wins the Queen, or if 12 R–KB1, Q–Kt5 ch; 13 K–R1, RxKt; 14 RxR, QxR ch; 15 QxQ, BxQ is mate.

Black to play

310

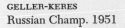

GELLER-KERES
Russian Champ. 1951

White falls into a deep Keres trap! What appears to be a desperate sacrifice of a Knight, in order to save an important Pawn, is really a scheme to lure Geller's Queen away from the King side. The rest of the combination, with Keres cleverly insinuating his Queen into the heart of White's position, is intensely interesting.

1	...	B–Q3
2	BxB	QxB
3	Q–Q2	

Double attack!

| 3 | ... | Kt–KB5 |
| 4 | QxKt(R5) | |

Geller suspects nothing!

4	...	BxKt
5	PxB	KtxP ch
6	K–Kt2	Kt–B5 ch
7	K–Kt1	Q–Q4

With two threats: 8 ... QxBP followed by 9 ... Q–Kt7 mate, and 8 ... Q–R4 followed by 9 ... Q–R6 and then mate.

| 8 | Kt–Kt3 | |

If 8 B–K4, Q–R4; 9 Q–Q2, Q–Kt4 ch; 10 Kt–Kt3 (saves the King, but unguards the Queen), Kt–R6 ch, and Black wins the Queen.

| 8 | ... | P–Q6 |

Keeps White's Bishop from reaching K4 and renews the threat of 9 ... QxBP.

| 9 | Kt–K4 | Q–KB4 |
| 10 | Q–Kt4 | |

A last hope: if 10 ... Q–R6; 11 Kt–B6 ch, after which he removes Black's Knight.

| 10 | ... | KR–K1 |

Threatens 11 ... RxKt; 12 RxR, Q–Kt4 ch; 13 K–B1, R–B8 ch; 14 R–K1, Q–Kt7 mate.

| 11 | Resigns | |

The attempt 11 Kt–Kt3 fails after 11 ... RxR ch (11 ... Q–R6 at once also wins); 12 QxR, Q–R6; 13 Q–KB1, R–B8; 14 BxP, Q–Kt7 mate.

19

SUPERB STRATEGIST

Mikhail Botvinnik

The world is not likely to tire of an amusement which never repeats itself, of a game which today presents features as novel and charms as fresh as those with which it delighted, in the morning of history, the dwellers on the banks of the Ganges and the Indus.

—Willard Fiske

Select a quartet of the greatest players that ever lived, and you would have to include Botvinnik. He is the master most qualified to join the immortal trio, Capablanca, Alekhine and Lasker.

Some idea of his style and capabilities may be gained from the comments of various critics:

Botvinnik's games show qualities of originality, force, depth and brilliancy which none of his rivals can match at present.

—Reuben Fine

He has made himself equally at home in each department of the game: opening, positional strategy, combinative tactics and endplay, so that it is impossible to say that he is stronger in one brand of play than another. His best games have the smoothness of an epic poem, rolling on grandly to their appointed end.

—William Winter

Botvinnik almost makes you feel that difficulty attracts him and stimulates him to the full unfolding of his powers. Most players feel uncomfortable in difficult positions, but Botvinnik seems to enjoy them. Where dangers threaten from every side, and the smallest slackening of attention might be fatal; in a position which requires a nerve of steel and intense concentration—Botvinnik is in his element.

—Max Euwe

194

Botvinnik is the most versatile of present-day chess masters. His play is without any weak points whatsoever, and he is equally dangerous to his adversaries in a long-drawn-out positional struggle as he is in a complicated position where the combinational possibilities are complex, and so difficult as to be almost impossible to calculate with any degree of certainty.

—Gideon Stahlberg

White to play

311

BOTVINNIK-RAGOZIN
Leningrad, 1927

Every one of Botvinnik's pieces takes part in the attack on Black's King. Nothing startling about that— except that the Queen and Bishop, who start off the combination, do so by retreating!

1 P–QB4!

A preliminary thrust at Black's center.

| 1 | ... | R–B4 |
| 2 | Q–K2 | Q–K4 |

Obviously, on 2 ... PxB, White does not recapture by 3 QxB, but replies 3 Q–Kt2 ch instead, and Black is ruined.

3 B–B1!

If now 3 ... R–R4 (to annoy White with mate threats); 4 B–Kt2 (pins the Queen), P–Q5; 5 BxQP!, QxB; 6 QxR, QxB; 7 Q–K5 ch, K–Kt1; 8 QxB ch wins easily for White.

3	...	Q–Q3
4	PxP	PxB
5	B–Kt2 ch	

This is the move that hurts!

| 5 | ... | K–Kt1 |
| 6 | Q–Kt4 ch | Kt–Kt3 |

If 6 ... K–B1; 7 Q–Kt7 ch, K–K1; 8 RxB, Q–Q2; 9 KR–K1, R–B2; 10 RxKt ch, RxR; 11 Q–Kt8 mate.

7	RxB	QxQP
8	RxKt ch!	PxR
9	QxP ch	K–B1
10	Q–Kt7 ch	K–K1
11	R–K1 ch	K–Q1
12	Q–K7 ch	K–B1
13	R–B1 ch	Resigns

Black to play

312

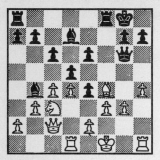

RABINOVICH-BOTVINNIK
Moscow, 1927

"The hardest thing to do is win a won game," said Marshall many a time. He knew very well the danger of having a won game. One tends to become over-confident and apt to forget that there is danger in the most placid-looking position.

The sixteen-year-old Botvinnik unfolds an impressive combination, threading his way carefully through the complications with the skill and accuracy of a seasoned master.

1 ...	P–K4!
2 QPxP	

If 2 BxP, PxKBP; 3 QxQ, PxP ch; 4 KxP, PxQ; 5 R–QB1, B–Kt5 ch; 6 K–K1, R–B6; 7 K–Q2, B–KB4, and the threat of 8 ... R–Q6 ch wins.

2 ...	RxB!
3 PxR	Q–Kt6!

With five threats:

(a) 4 ... B–QB4

(b) 4 ... P–K6
(c) 4 ... B–R6 ch
(d) 4 ... PxKBP
(e) 4 ... R–KB1

4 KtxKP

If 4 ... PxQP, B–QB4; 5 KtxP, B–R6 ch; 6 RxB, Q–Kt8 mate.

4 ...	PxKt
5 RxB	

On 5 QxP, B–QB4; 6 P–K3, B–KB4!; 7 QxB, QxBP ch, and Black wins as he pleases.

After White's actual move, it is easy for Black to play the powerful-looking 5 ... P–K6 hastily, when 6 RxP ch!, KxR (or 6 ... QxR); 7 R–Kt1 pinning the Queen, will bring him up with a shock.

5 ...	B–B4
6 P–K3	QxP ch
7 Q–B2	

Or 7 K–Kt1, BxP ch; 8 K–R2, B–B7; 9 R–KKt1, BxR ch; 10 KxB, Q–Kt5 ch, and Black picks up the other Rook.

7 ...	QxR ch
8 K–K2	Q–R6!
9 P–B5	Q–Kt5 ch
10 K–Q2	R–KB1
11 P–K6	

Second trap: if 11 ... RxP; 12 R–Q8 ch, B–B1 (12 ... R–B1; 13 Q–B7 ch forces mate); 13 QxR!, QxQ, 14 P–K7, and Black will be happy to draw by perpetual check.

11 ...	QxBP
12 QxQ	RxQ

13	RxQKtP	R–B7 ch
14	K–K1	R–B3
15	P–Kt4	BxKP
16	K–K2	B–Kt8
17	P–K7	K–B2

And White resigned after a few more moves.

White to play

313

BOTVINNIK-BATUYEV
Leningrad, 1931

Botvinnik does not gamble when he sacrifices a piece. Batuyev has several plausible defenses, and there are captures and recaptures in which the order of moves is important. No matter to Botvinnik. He takes everything into account, and works out the winning combination as precisely as though he were demonstrating a proposition in mathematics.

1	KtxP!	RxKt
2	QxP	Q–B1

If 2 ... Kt(K2)–Q4; 3 KtxKt,

KtxKt (3 ... RxR; 4 KtxKt ch, PxKt; 5 QxR ch wins, or 3 ... BxKt; 4 RxR, BxQ; 5 RxQ ch and White forces mate); 4 BxKt, BxB (on 4 ... QxB; 5 RxR ch wins); 5 RxR, BxQ; 6 RxQ ch wins for White.

Or if 2 ... B–Q4; 3 KtxB, RxR; 4 KtxKt(K7) ch (White must avoid 4 KtxKt(B6) ch, K–R1; 5 QxR, RxR ch; 6 BxR, QxP ch, and Black does the mating), K–R1; 5 RxR, QxKt (or 5 ... RxKt; 6 R–B8, RxQ; 7 BxR wins); 6 R–B8 ch, Kt–K1 (or 6 ... Kt–Kt1; 7 QxQ, RxQ; 8 RxKt mate); 7 RxKt ch, and White wins.

3   Kt–K4!

Threatens 4 QxR ch, QxQ; 5 BxQ ch, KxB; 6 Kt–Q6 ch followed by 7 KtxB.

3	...	RxR
4	RxR	Kt(B3)–Q4
5	Kt–Q6	B–R1

He cannot drive the opposing Queen off by 5 ... B–B1 as 6 KtxB, KtxKt; 7 RxKt pins his own Queen.

6	R–K1!	P–Kt3
7	KtxR	QxKt
8	QxKt(K7)!	Resigns

On 8 ... QxQ; 9 RxQ, and the pinned Knight cannot recapture, while 8 ... KtxQ; 9 RxKt leaves the pinned Queen helpless.

White to play

314

BOTVINNIK-ALATORSEV
U.S.S.R. 1931

Others before Botvinnik have sacrificed Pawns to open the Rook file for an attack. But how many have exploited its resources so ingeniously? Botvinnik uses it as a base of operations for his King Rook, followed by the Queen Rook and then the Bishop. Finally, the very threat of switching his Queen over to the file is enough to persuade Alatorsev to resign.

1 P–Kt5	PxP
2 P–KR4	B–Kt5

On 2 ... P–Kt5; 3 P–R5 will pry the file open.

3 PxP ch	Kt–R4
4 Kt(B3)–K2	Kt–K2
5 R–R4	

The attack on the Bishop gains time for doubling the Rooks.

5 ...	Q–Q2
6 R(Q1)–R1	K–Kt1
7 RxB!	QxR

8 B–R3!	Q–B6

The only move.

9 R–B1	KtxKt
10 B–K6 ch!	

An important interpolation, to compel the King's return to the Rook file.

10 ...	K–R1

Obviously 10 ... R–B2; 11 RxQ is too expensive.

11 RxQ	Resigns

After 11 ... RxR; 12 KtxKt, and Black cannot prevent the deadly 13 Q–R2 ch.

White to play

315

BOTVINNIK-BELAVIENETZ
Moscow-Leningrad, 1934

If a combination is a series of hammer blows, then this is a genuine combination. Botvinnik's forceful moves fit the description beautifully.

1   Q–Kt3

With a simple, brutal threat—2 QxP.

How shall Black defend? If 2 ... R–Kt1 (or 2 ... 0–0); 3 RxKt wins. Or if 2 ... Kt–R4; 3 Q–B7, 0–0; 4 BxKtP wins the exchange. In this variation, if Black tries 3 ... B–Kt2 (with a mate threat); then 4 Q–Kt8 ch, K–Q2; 5 RxP ch, K–B3; 6 Q–B7 mate is the penalty.

| 1 ... | R–R2 |

A desperate trap. Black hopes for the hasty 2 QxP when 2 ... R–Kt1; 3 QxKt, QxP mate swindles White out of a win.

| 2 | RxKt! |

Botvinnik has other plans!

2	...	PxR
3	Q–Kt7	R–B1
4	BxKtP	

Threatens to win a whole Rook by 5 QxR ch.

| 4 | ... | R–K2 |
| 5 | R–QB1 | B–Kt2 |

Black defends by threatening mate. Meanwhile he sidesteps such horrible deaths as might come after 5 ... B–Q2; 6 QxP(B6), or 5 ... Q–Kt2; 6 RxB ch, QxR; 7 B–Kt5 ch, R–Q2 (the alternative 7 ... K–Q1 succumbs to 8 B–R5 ch); 8 QxR mate.

| 6 | R–B5! |

Evicts the Queen from the diagonal, and prepares to continue with 9 B–Kt5 ch.

| 6 | ... | Resigns |

Black to play

316

GOGLIDZE-BOTVINNIK
Moscow, 1935

From the diagrammed position, one would not dream that there could be a combination where Black's Rooks do the mating!

Botvinnik starts his combination by driving White's Queen back to the last rank. He follows with a threat of winning a piece, which forces a series of exchanges. Just when Goglidze begins to breathe more freely, comes a sudden Queen sacrifice, and Botvinnik's Rooks swoop down for the kill.

| 1 | ... | B–B1 |
| 2 | Q–Kt5 | |

If 2 Q–Q2, Q–B7 (the occupation of this square is the key to Black's attack); 3 KR–Q1, QxQ; 4 RxQ, B–Kt5; 5 R(Q2)–Q1, R–B7, and Black wins a piece.

2	...	P–QR3
3	Q–Q3	P–K5
4	Q–Kt1	Q–B7!
5	B–R3	

On 5 B–Q1 (5 R–K1, B–Kt5), QxQ; 6 RxQ, Kt–B5 (threatens 7 ... Kt–Q7); 7 KtxKt (if 7 Kt–Kt3, QR–Kt1, and Black's pressure on the Knight file will be intolerable), BxKt; 8 R–K1, B–Kt5, and Black wins the exchange.

5 ...	BxB
6 RxB	QxB
7 QxKt	QR–Kt1

Not merely to harass the Queen, but to control both open files with his Rooks.

| 8 Q–Q6 | QxR ch! |
| 9 KxQ | R–Kt8 ch |

And Black mates next move.

White to play

317

BOTVINNIK-TARTAKOVER
Nottingham, 1936

Botvinnik is never petty. In the course of a fine combination where he can win the exchange, he gives up his own Rook instead, and finishes the game in a burst of glory.

For his conduct of the attack, Botvinnik was awarded the first brilliancy prize.

1 Kt–QB4

This Knight (who has a featured role in the drama) makes his entrance by attacking the King Pawn.

| 1 ... | Kt–Kt3 |
| 2 Kt–Q6! | B–K3 |

The Knight at Q6 cannot be touched. If 2 ... BxKt; 3 RxKt pins the unfortunate Bishop. Black's object with the text move is to strengthen his Bishop Pawn against the contemplated attack by 3 KtxB, KtxKt (3 ... RxKt; 4 Kt–B5 ch wins); 4 RxKt, KxR; 5 Q–B3 ch, K–Kt2; 6 QxP ch, and Black can concede.

Against 2 ... R–KB1, White had prepared 3 KtxB, KtxKt; 4 BxP ch, KxB; 5 RxKt ch, K–Kt4 (on 5 ... K–Kt2; 6 Kt–K8 ch wins the Queen); 6 Q–B3 (threatens 7 P–R4 ch or 7 KtxP ch), Kt–B4; 7 KtxKt!, QxR (if 7 ... KxR ; 8 Kt–Q4 ch wins the Queen); 8 Q–Kt4 mate!

3 KtxB!

Botvinnik spurns the Rook!

| 3 ... | KtxKt |

If 3 ... RxKt; 4 Kt–B5 ch, K–B1 (or 4 ... BxKt; 5 PxB, and Black must give up a piece to save his Queen); 5 BxP ch, K–K1; 6 KtxR, KxKt; 7 B–Kt5, Kt–B5; 8 RxKt, PxR; 9 P–K5, and White wins a piece and the game.

4	RxKt!	KxR
5	Q–R5	

Threatens mate in two by 6 QxRP ch, Kt–Kt3; 7 B–Kt5 mate.

5	...	Kt–Kt3

Gives the King a flight square at K2. The attempt to protect the Rook Pawn and the King Rook by 5 ... R–R1 is drastically refuted by 6 R–B1 ch, K–Kt2; 7 RxP ch, BxR; 8 QxBP mate.

Now, how does Botvinnik prevent the King from escaping?

6 Kt–B5!

"This quiet move, which was not easy to foresee," says Botvinnik, "ends the struggle."

6	...	R–KKt1

The Knight cannot be taken: if 6 ... BxKt; 7 PxB wins a piece. Defending the Rook Pawn loses neatly, as Botvinnik shows: 6 ... R–R1; 7 P–KR4 (threatens 8 B–Kt5 ch, PxB; 9 QxP mate), BxRP; 8 R–Q1, QR–Q1; 9 B–Kt5 ch, PxB; 10 QxP ch, K–K3; 11 Kt–Kt7 mate.

7 QxP

Threatens instant mate. If instead 7 R–B1, BxKt; 8 PxB, Black saves himself by a counter-combination, Reinfeld points out, with 8 ... QxB ch!; 9 KxQ, Kt–B5 dble. ch, and Black regains the Queen and wins.

7	...	BxP

Not for the sake of winning a Pawn, but to clear a square for the King.

8	R–Q1	QR–Q1
9	Q–Kt5 ch	K–K3
10	RxR	P–B3
11	RxR!	

Simplest, since 11 ... PxQ; 12 RxKt ch is hopeless for Black.

11	...	Kt–B5
12	Q–Kt7	Resigns

White to play

318

BOTVINNIK-RESHEVSKY
Avro, 1938

A beautiful combination with psychological overtones. Botvinnik is a Pawn ahead in a difficult, colorless position. Instead of trying to squeeze out a win with his extra material, Botvinnik prefers to sacrifice, and complicate matters for Reshevsky, who was in time trouble. The combination, it turned out, would have succeeded even if Reshevsky had taken as much time as Paulsen was supposed to have consumed in his game against Morphy.

1	KtxQP	B–K3

On 1 ... PxKt, Botvinnik expected to continue with 2 P–B7, QxP; 3 BxR, BxP; 4 B–KR1, and his passed Pawn should assure the win.

Botvinnik could now play 2 Kt–B4, but this would offer Reshevsky no immediate problems.

2 RxB!

But this combination will!

2 ...   PxR
3 Kt–B5!

Botvinnik avoids 3 QxP ch, K–R2, and his pinned Knight is lost.

3 ...   Q–K1

The alternative 3 ... QxR ch; 4 QxQ, KPxKt prolongs the game, but does not save it.

4 KtxB   KxKt
5 R–Q7 ch!   R–B2

Black tries to hold on to the Bishop Pawn.

6 B–K5!

Attacks the Pawn once more, and also threatens to win a piece by 7 Q–KB3 and 8 QxKt ch. The order of moves, you will note, is important. If at once 6 Q–KB3, P–K4 shuts off White's Bishop.

Clearly, 6 ... RxR; 7 PxR, Q–Q1; 8 BxR, QxB; 9 Q–QB3, Q–Q1; 10 BxKt ch, QxB; 11 QxQ ch is ruinous.

6 ...   K–Kt1
7 RxP   RxR
8 BxR   R–R8 ch
9 K–R2   R–R2

10 B–K5   R–KB2
11 P–B7   Kt–Q2
12 Q–B2!   R–B1
13 P–B8(Q)!   Resigns

For 13 ... QxQ allows mate on the move.

"A triumph for the two Bishops," says Botvinnik.

White to play

319

BOTVINNIK-CAPABLANCA
Avro, 1938

Botvinnik, a Pawn down, starts a combination. The combination, a blazing brilliant, is flawless. Had it not been so, Botvinnik would have been torn to shreds by his opponent, the toughest defensive player in the world.

1 R–K6!   RxR

Black must exchange. If instead 1 ... Kt–K5; 2 KtxKt, PxKt; 3 PxP! wins at once. Or if 1 ... K–B2; 2 RxKt ch!, KxR; 3 PxP ch, and now there are these possibilities:

(a) 3 ... K–K2; 4 Q–B7 ch, K–Q1; 5 P–Kt7, and White wins.

(b) 3 ... K–K3; 4 Q–B7 ch, K–Q3; 5 Kt–B5 ch, K–B3; 6 QxR ch followed by 7 QxQ.

(c) 3 ... KxP; 4 Q–B5 ch, K–Kt2; 5 Kt–R5 ch, K–R3 (or 5 ... K–Kt1; 6 Q–Kt5 ch, K–B2; 7 Q–B6 ch and mate at Kt7); 6 P–R4!, R–KKt1; 7 P–Kt4 (threatens 8 Q–B4 ch, K–Kt3; 9 Q–B6 mate), Q–B3; 8 B–R3!, and the threat of 9 B–B8 ch is decisive.

| 2 | PxR | K–Kt2 |

Forced, since a Knight move allows a fatal check at B7.

3 Q–B4!

Threatens to win at once by 4 Kt–B5 ch!, PxKt; 5 Q–Kt5 ch, K–B1; 6 QxKt ch, K–K1; 7 Q–B7 ch, K–Q1; 8 P–K7 ch.

| 3 | ... | Q–K1 |
| 4 | Q–K5 | Q–K2 |

He must blockade the Pawn. If instead 4 ... Kt–QR4; 5 B–B1! forces 5 ... Q–K2, to prevent these two winning threats:

(a) 6 Q–B7 ch, K–Kt1; 7 B–R6.

(b) 6 B–R6 ch, KxB; 7 QxKt, and Black is helpless to ward off the threat: 8 Kt–B5 ch, K–R4; 9 Q–R4 mate.

5 B–R3!

The first of two sacrifices which had to be calculated with the utmost accuracy to assure the win.

| 5 | ... | QxB |

Black must take the Bishop. If instead 5 ... Q–K1 (5 ... Q–

Q1; 6 Kt–R5 ch, PxKt; 7 Q–Kt5 ch, K–R1; 8 P–K7 wins at once); 6 Q–B7 ch, K–Kt1; 7 B–K7, Kt–Kt5 (7 ... K–Kt2; 8 B–Q8 ch); 8 Q–Q7!, Q–R1 (8 ... Q–Kt1, 9 B–Q6); 9 B–Q8, and White wins.

6 Kt–R5 ch!   PxKt

And he must take the Knight! After 6 ... K–R3; 7 KtxKt, Q–B8 ch; 8 K–B2, Q–Q7 ch; 9 K–Kt3, QxBP ch; 10 K–R4, QxP ch; 11 Kt–Kt4 ch! (a clever interposition which had to be foreseen) and White wins.

| 7 | Q–Kt5 ch | K–B1 |
| 8 | QxKt ch | K–Kt1 |

If 8 ... K–K1; 9 Q–B7 ch, K–Q1; 10 Q–Q7 mate.

9 P–K7!

Beautiful play! Botvinnik avoids the tempting 9 Q–B7 ch, K–R1; 10 P–K7 which looks overwhelming. Black, with the knife at his throat, would effect a last-minute escape by 10 ... Q–B8 ch; 11 K–B2, Q–Q7 ch; 12 K–Kt3, QxBP ch; 13 K–R4, QxP ch; 14 KxP, Q–K4 ch, and draws by perpetual check.

The move actually made keeps the Queen Pawn protected, and prevents perpetual check.

9	...	Q–B8 ch
10	K–B2	Q–B7 ch
11	K–Kt3	Q–Q6 ch
12	K–R4	Q–K5 ch
13	KxP	Q–K7 ch

Clearly, if 13 ... Q–Kt3 ch; 14 QxQ ch, PxQ ch; 15 KxP, and White mates next move.

14	K–R4	Q–K5 ch
15	P–Kt4	

Destroying the last hope. If 15 K–R3, P–KR4, and the threat of 16 ... Q–Kt5 mate will compel White to take the draw.

15	...	Q–K8 ch
16	K–R5	Resigns

Black to play

320

SMYSLOV-BOTVINNIK
Leningrad, 1941

An attractive combination, with some pleasing long-range Rook moves.

1	...	R(Kt1)–QR1

With this pretty idea: 2 ... R–R8; 3 Q–Kt4, R(R1)–R5; 4 Q–Kt2, KtxB; 5 PxKt, Q–K8 mate.

2	Q–KR1	R–R8
3	Q–R3	

To pin the Knight. Now if 3 ... KtxB; 4 QxQ squelches any attempts at mate.

3	...	R–KKt8
4	PxP	R(R1)–R8!

Prepared to penalize 5 RxKt with 5 ... R(Kt8)–K8 followed by mate at Q8 with the other Rook.

5	R–K3

Vacating the square KB3 for the King's use.

5	...	R(R8)–Q8 ch
6	K–K2	KtxP ch!

Very neat! After 7 RxKt (or 7 PxKt); R(Kt8)–K8 ch forces 8 K–B3. The King now cuts off the Queen's protection by the Rook, and enables Black to snap up the Queen!

7	Resigns

Black to play

321

MAKAGONOV-BOTVINNIK
Sverdlovsk, 1943

How easy it is to lose a won game! Right at the very end, when his advanced passed Pawns make resistance seem futile, Botvinnik can still make a misstep which will wreck everything!

1 ...   KtxP

Ready to meet the attack on his Queen by 2 R–KKt7 ch, with 2 ... KtxB; 3 RxQ, KtxR, and Black is a piece ahead.

2 B–B4

Now how does Black save his Queen?

2 ...   Kt–K4!

A clever resource!

3 R–K7

Naturally, 3 BxKt, Q–R4 ch followed by 4 ... QxB is hopeless.

3 ...	Q–B7 ch
4 K–K1	K–B1
5 BxKt	QxP
6 R–B7 ch	K–Q1
7 R–B1	P–R4
8 B–Q4	

White loses after 8 B–B7 ch, K–Q2; 9 BxP, Q–Kt7; 10 R–B7 ch, K–Q3; 11 R–Kt7, K–B3; 12 R–Kt8, P–R5 (12 ... QxB also wins); 13 B–R7, P–R6.

8 ...	P–Kt4
9 R–R1	Q–Kt6
10 K–B2	

White can win a Pawn by 10 B–Kt6 ch, K–Q2; 11 RxP, but he must return it after 11 ... K–B3, 12 B–Q8 (12 R–R6, K–Kt2 costs a piece); QxP ch.

| 10 ... | P–R5 |
| 11 K–B3 | Q–B7 |

12 K–B4	K–Q2
13 K–K5	Q–K5 ch
14 K–B6	Q–K2 ch
15 K–Kt6	P–R6
16 R–KB1	P–Kt5!

Botvinnik gives his opponent a thrill. He lets him pin the Queen.

17 R–B7

At this point Botvinnik can commit chessic suicide by making the natural move 17 ... P–Kt6. The continuation—and it would come in a split-second—would be 18 RxQ ch, KxR; 19 B–B5 ch, K–K3; 20 BxP, and White wins!

17 ...   QxR ch!

But this is the way to win it!

18 KxQ   P–Kt6

And White resigns, as 19 ... P–Kt7 cannot be stopped.

White to play

322

BOTVINNIK–EUWE
The Hague, 1948

Botvinnik's elegant finishing combination owes its existence to an earlier combination—a brilliancy that appears only in the notes!

1   P–B3!

Threatens 2 PxP, opening the King Bishop file.

1 ...   Kt–Q4

Black offers an exchange of Queens to relieve the pressure. Taking the Pawn instead would plunge him into this pretty loss: 1 ... PxP; 2 B–Kt1 (threatens 3 BxKt, QxB; 4 QxP mate), P–R3; 3 RxP, Kt–Q4; 4 R–Kt3!, QxQ; 5 RxP ch, K–R1; 6 R–R7 dble. ch, K–Kt1; 7 R–R8 mate.

2   QxQ   KtxQ
3   PxP   P–QKt3
4   R–Q1

Threatens 5 RxP, RxR; 6 R–Q8 mate.

4 ...   Kt–Kt3
5   R–Q6   B–R3
6   R–B2   B–Kt4
7   P–K5!

Preparing to break in by 8 P–K6, PxP; 9 R–Q7.

Black cannot prevent the Pawn's advance by 7 ... QR–K1, when 8 P–K6!, PxP; 9 BxP ch, K–R1; 10 R–Q7, RxB; 11 RxP!, RxR; 12 RxKt ch, R(B7)–B3; 13 BxR ch wins for White.

7 ...   Kt–K2
8   P–K4

Prevents 8 ... Kt–Q4, blocking the Bishop,

8 ...   P–QB4

Opposing Rooks by 8 ... QR–Q1 loses on the spot by 9 RxKBP, so Black tries other means of counterplay.

9   P–K6!

Botvinnik is not interested in the prospects arising from 9 RxKtP, B–B3. He sticks to plan—the demolition of Black's King side.

9 ...   P–B3

The position is tricky: if 9 ... PxP; 10 RxKP, RxR; 11 KxR, K–B1; 12 BxP ch, KxB; 13 RxKt ch, and White wins. But suppose in this, White tries 11 RxKt dis. ch (instead of 11 KxR) then 11 ... K–B1; 12 RxP (attacks one Rook and threatens the other), R–B8 mate!

10   RxKtP   B–B3
11   RxB!   KtxR
12   P–K7 ch   R–B2
13   B–Q5!   Resigns

For after 13 ... R–QB1; 14 P–K8(Q) ch, RxQ; 15 BxKt, R–Q1; 16 B–Q5, and White wins the exchange, and remains a piece ahead.

White to play

323

BOTVINNIK–KERES
Moscow, 1952

Scintillating maneuvers on the King side, with Botvinnik outplaying Keres in the combinative style for which Keres himself is famous.

1 Kt–Q6

Threatens (aside from 2 Kt–B8) 2 KtxBP, KxKt (if 2 ... RxKt; 3 B–K6, KtxB; 4 QxR ch); 3 B–K6 dble. ch, K–Kt3 (3 ... KxB; 4 Q–B5 mate); 4 Q–Kt3 ch, K–R3; 5 Q–R4 ch, K–Kt3; 6 R–B3, KtxB; 7 Q–K4 ch!, K–R3; 8 R–R3 ch, K–Kt4; 9 R–Kt3 ch, and White mates next move.

1 ...	Q–B2
2 B–K4	Kt–K3
3 Q–R4	

To weaken the castled position by forcing one of the King side Pawns to advance.

3 ...	P–KKt3

This will provide possibilities for White's pieces to station themselves in the holes at KB6 and KR6, but the alternative 3 ... P–KR3 is worse: 3 ... P–KR3; 4 Kt–B5, R(K2)–K1; 5 KtxP ch, PxKt; 6 QxP, Kt–B1; 7 R–B3, and Black is through.

4 BxKt!	PxB
5 R–B1	

Before swinging over to the King side, the Rook drives Black's Queen off the open file.

5 ...	Q–Q2
6 R–QB3	R–KB1
7 Kt–B5!	

A powerful move, which allows little choice of reply. If 7 ... PxKt; 8 R–Kt3 ch, Kt–Kt2; 9 Q–B6, and White mates next move. Or if 7 ... R(K2)–K1; 8 Kt–R6 ch, K–R1 (8 ... K–Kt2; 9 Q–B6 ch, KxKt; 10 R–R3 mate); 9 Q–B6 ch, Kt–Kt2; 10 KtxP ch, K–Kt1; 11 Kt–R6 ch, K–R1; 12 QxR ch, RxQ; 13 RxR mate.

7 ...	R(B1)–K1
8 Kt–R6 ch	K–B1

Other King moves allow 9 Q–B6 ch, with the win in the previous note.

9 Q–B6	Kt–Kt2
10 R(B3)–KB3	

Still threatening mate, this time by 11 QxBP ch, RxQ; 12 RxR ch, QxR; 13 RxQ mate.

10 ...	R–B1
11 KtxP	R–K3
12 Q–Kt5	Kt–B4

The King must stay where he is, as 12 ... K–Kt1; 13 Kt–R6 ch is fatal, while on 12 ... K–K1; 13 Kt–Q6 ch forces Black to give up his Queen.

13 Kt–R6	Q–Kt2

There was one last mating possibility in 13 ... K–K1; 14 RxKt, PxR; 15 Q–Kt8 ch, K–K2; 16 KtxP mate.

14 P–KKt4	Resigns

20

CHESSBOARD MAGICIAN

Alexander Alekhine

----

*In the next world, if there is no chess, I would rather
complete extinction—check and checkmate!*

—John Paris

ALEKHINE'S achievements are enormous:

Alekhine has won more first prizes in international tournaments than any
other master; he was Champion of the World for eighteen years, until his
death; he was an annotator who had few equals and no superior; he was
one of the truly great blindfold players in history; his contributions to chess
theory are of such importance as to justify saying, "The openings consist of
Alekhine's games with a few variations."

Alekhine's games can be described in a word—wonderful! They form a
collection of masterpieces imbued with artistry, originality, imagination and
brilliance. In the field of combination play, Alekhine is unsurpassed. His
creations, rich in variety and color, are always of absorbing interest. At his
best, and that was often, Alekhine astounded the world with a wealth of
inspired combinations dazzling in their beauty and splendour.

Black to play

324

VYGODCHIKOV-ALEKHINE
Correspondence, 1908

208

An early combinative gem, as
evidence of Alekhine's youthful pro-
ficiency.

1 ...   Q–Kt3

Superior to the plausible 1 ...
Q–R6, upon which would follow 2
B–B3, R–Kt1; 3 Q–K5, Kt–B5
(threatens mate); 4 Q–Kt5, B–Kt5
(renews the threat); 5 BxP ch!, RxB;
6 Q–Q8 ch, and Black must submit
to a draw by perpetual check.

2 B–B2

If 2 K–R1 (to get out of the line of fire) Kt–K8 cuts off the Rook and forces mate, and if 2 K–B1, B–R6 again embarrasses the King.

2	...	QxB
3	K–R1	Q–Kt3
4	R–KKt1	B–R6

Strengthens the bind, and meanwhile discloses an attack on the Knight.

5	Kt–Kt6	Kt–B5!
6	RxQ	B–Kt7 ch
7	RxB	

If 7 K–Kt1, Kt–R6 mate.

7	...	PxR ch
8	K–Kt1	Kt–K7 ch
9	KxP	KtxQ
10	Resigns	

White to play

325

ALEKHINE–FELDT
Tarnopol, 1916

From a blindfold exhibition, a fascinating specimen of Alekhine alertness. In the very act of complet-ing his development, Alekhine spies an opportunity for a combination, and startles his seeing opponent with a sudden sacrifice of a Knight followed by a spectacular offer of the Queen!

1   Q–K2

Ostensibly a quiet developing move. It brings the Queen into play, and lets the Rooks come into the game.

| 1 | ... | P–B4. |

Suspecting no danger, Black attacks the center, while opening a diagonal for his Queen Bishop.

2   Kt–B7!

Attacks the Queen, and threatens (if 2 ... Q–B1) 3 QxP followed by 4 Kt–R6 dble. ch, K–R1; 5 Q–Kt8 ch!, RxQ, 6 Kt–B7 mate.

| 2 | ... | KxKt |
| 3 | QxP ch! | |

But this piece cannot be taken! If 3 ... KxQ; 4 Kt–Kt5 mate is the beautiful reply.

| 3 | ... | K–Kt3 |

On 3 ... K–Kt1; 4 Kt–Kt5 forces Black to give up several pieces to avoid immediate mate.

| 4 | P–KKt4! | Resigns |

There are two mate threats, one by the Bishop, and one by the Knight. Black cannot escape both.

Black to play

326

Odessa, 1918

From a blindfold exhibition on six boards. A lot of Queen sacrifices in this combination, most of them by Alekhine. Devilish ingenious, this young man!

| 1 | ... | B–Kt7 ch |
| 2 | **K–Kt1** | Kt–Q4! |

An offer—of a sort. Accepting the Queen means checkmate for White.

| 3 | **RxR** ch | QxR |
| 4 | **Kt–K4** | QxKt! |

Once again daring White to take the Queen.

| 5 | **B–Q2** | Q–K6! |

A pretty move, but now it's White's turn.

6   R–K1!

And he replies by offering his Queen!

| 6 | ... | B–B4 |

Obviously, White would mate on 6 ... QxQ.

| 7 | **RxQ** | PxR |
| 8 | **Q–B1** | |

Whereupon Alekhine announced a forced mate in three by 8 ... PxB; 9 B–Q1 (to give the King a flight square), Kt(B3)–Kt5 (to take it away); 10 Any, Kt–B6 mate.

Black to play

327

Moscow, 1920

Alekhine's first combination opens the King Bishop file and prepares the second combination. This consists of clever interaction by a Rook, Queen and Knight who take turns in utilizing the last rank to assail White's King.

| 1 | ... | P–K4! |
| 2 | **P–B4** | |

If 2 BxP, P–Q4; 3 R–B4, QxR wins a piece.

| 2 | ... | P–Q3 |

White cannot try to win the Pawn as after 3 PxP, PxP; 4 BxP, KtxB; 5 RxKt, RxR; 6 QxR, Q–B7 ch; 7 K–R1, Q–B8 ch is followed by mate.

3	P--R3	R–K3!
4	PxP	PxP
5	B--B5!	

The best chance. Clearly, 5 BxP, R(B1)–K1 will lead to loss of material.

| 5 | ... | R–B2! |
| 6 | R–Kt1 | |

To this Black cannot reply with the tempting 6 ... Kt–Q7, as 7 QxKt, QxR; 8 Q–Q8 ch and mate next would follow. So he gives his King some air.

| 6 | ... | P–R3 |
| 7 | RxKtP | Kt–Q7! |

But now the move is as effective as it is unexpected!

If White defends by 8 R–K3, the continuation 8 ... R–KKt3; 9 R–Kt8 ch, K–R2; 10 R–Kt2 (on 10 QxKt, Q–B8 ch; 11 K–R2, R–B7 wins), Kt–B6 ch; 11 K–R1 (11 RxKt, QxR wins the exchange, or 11 K–B1, Kt–Q5 ch; 12 Q–B2, Q–Q2, and White must either give up the exchange, or his Queen for a Rook and Knight), QxP ch!; 12 PxQ, R–Kt8 mates neatly.

| 8 | RxRP | Q–B7! |

This prevents White's Rooks from returning to his first rank to help defend the King.

| 9 | R–R8 ch | K–R2 |
| 10 | K–R1 | |

White is helpless to stop a check on his vulnerable first rank, but hopes to get some protection by interposing the Bishop.

| 10 | ... | R–B8 ch |
| 11 | B–Kt1 | RxB ch! |

Nothing prevails against the Alekhine fury.

| 12 | KxR | Q–B8 ch |
| 13 | K–B2 | |

On 13 K–R2, Kt–B8 ch (drives the King back); 14 K–Kt1, Kt–Kt6 ch, and Black wins the Queen.

| 13 | ... | R–B3 ch |
| 14 | K–K3 | |

If 14 K–Kt3, Kt–B8 ch; 15 K–Kt4, Q–Kt4 mate.

| 14 | ... | Kt–Kt8 ch! |
| 15 | Resigns | |

Otherwise he must choose between 16 K–K4, KtxP—a family check, or 16 K–Q3, QxP ch; 17 K–K4, Q–Q5 mate.

White to play

328

ALEKHINE-STERK
Budapest, 1921

Alekhine is famous for surprise moves. In the midst of some skillful fencing on the Queen side (the scene of all the activity) comes a sudden move by a Bishop—and in a flash, Alekhine is attacking the King side!

1	B–Q3	BxKt
2	KR–B1!	KtxP
3	BxKt	BxB
4	QxB	Kt–B4
5	Q–K2!	

Superior to 5 Q–Kt1 (preparing to reply to 5 ... B–R4 with 6 P–QKt4) as then 5 ... B–Kt5; 6 P–QR3, Q–Kt2; 7 PxB, Kt–Kt6 gives Black good chances.

5 ...   B–R4
6 QR–Kt1

Threatens 7 P–QKt4, winning a piece.

6 ...   Q–R3

Ingeniously unpinning his Knight.

7 R–B4

Renews the threat of 8 P–QKt4.

7 ...   Kt–R5!

Clever play. He intends to meet 8 P–QKt4 with 8 ... Kt–B6, where the Knight immune to capture attacks Queen and Rook.

8 B–B6!

What a move! Believe-it-or-not, White threatens mate! He intends 9 R–KKt4 (discovering an attack on Black's Queen), QxQ; 10 RxP ch, K–R1; 11 R–Kt6 mate.

8 ...   KR–B1

The best defense. If instead 8 ... P–KR4; 9 R–KKt4!, QxQ; 10 RxP ch, K–R1; 11 Kt–Kt5!, and Black cannot prevent 12 R–R7 dble. ch, K–Kt1; 13 R–R8 mate.

9 Q–K5!

And this move, leaving the Rook and Bishop *en prise*, must have been even more of a shock than the previous move.

9 ...   R–B4

Alekhine planned these wins against other defenses:
9 ... QxR; 10 Q–KKt5, K–B1; 11 QxP ch, K–K1; 12 Q–Kt8 ch, K–Q2; 13 Kt–K5 ch, K–B2; 14 QxP ch, K–Kt1; 15 KtxQ.
9 ... RxR; 10 Q–KKt5, K–B1 (10 ... R–KKt5; 11 QxR, P–Kt3; 12 QxKt); 11 QxP ch, K–K1; 12 Kt–K5!, and the Queen mates at Kt8 next move.

9 ... PxB; 10 R–Kt4 ch, K–B1; 11 Q–Q6 ch, K–K1; 12 R–Kt8 mate.

| 10 | Q–Kt3! | P–Kt3 |
| 11 | RxKt | |

Despite the complications on the King side, one of the points of this combination is the capture of the stranded Knight on the Queen side.

11	...	Q–Q6
12	R–KB1	Q–B4
13	Q–B4	Q–B7
14	Q–R6	

And Black yields.

Black to play

329

TORRES-ALEKHINE
Seville, 1922

Alekhine visualizes mating possibilities on the long diagonal. The famous Alekhine touch clears away all the obstructions as if by magic!

1	...	P–Q5!
2	PxP	PxP
3	BxP	BxB

4	RxB	RxR
5	KtxR	QxKt!
6	PxQ	Kt–B7 dble. ch
7	K–Kt1	KtxP mate

White to play

330

ALEKHINE-YATES
London, 1922

Steinitz used to say, "I play my King all over the board; I make him fight!" How Steinitz would have loved this Alekhine combination! In the very midgame Alekhine's King takes a walk to the middle of the board and attacks a Rook. The Rook can retreat, or stay to be defended, but either way the result is mate!

1	K–B2!	K–R2
2	P–R4!	R–KB1
3	K–Kt3	R(KB1)–QKt1
4	R–B7	B–Kt4

Black can do very little. A general exchange of pieces leaves Black with an untenable ending, for example: 4 ... R–QB1; 5 RxR, RxR; 6 RxR, BxR; 7 Kt–Q3 followed by 8

Kt–B5 and White picks off the Pawns.

5   R(B1)–B5!

Threatens 6 R–K7, R–K1; 7 R–KB7, and the attack on the Bishop gives White the tempo he needs to play 8 R(B5)–B7, doubling Rooks on the seventh rank.

5	...	B–R3
6	R(B5)–B6	R–K1
7	K–B4	K–Kt1
8	P–R5	

Further restraint on Black's King, as will be seen.

8	...	B–B8
9	P–Kt3	B–R3
10	R–B7	

Preparing to double Rooks. Black cannot oppose this by playing either Rook to B1, as one Rook must protect the Bishop, and the other the King Pawn.

10	...	K–R2
11	R(B6)–B7	R–KKt1
12	Kt–Q7!	

Threatens 13 Kt–B6 ch winning the exchange. Note how White's 8 P–R5 keeps Black's King fenced in.

12	...	K–R1
13	Kt–B6!	

An attack on the Rook which forces it away from the Knight Pawn. The Knight of course must not be captured.

13	...	R(Kt1)–KB1

Expecting White to exchange Rooks.

14	RxP!	RxKt
15	K–K5!	

The kick in many an Alekhine combination is at the tail-end of it!

Black cannot move the Rook nor defend it with the other Rook on account of the reply 16 R–R7 ch, K–Kt1; 17 R(B7)–Kt7 mate!

15	...	Resigns

Black to play

331

RÉTI-ALEKHINE
Baden-Baden, 1925

Spectacular combination play from a game which Alekhine himself considered one of the most brilliant he ever played.

CHESS WORLD said of this game that it was "the gem of gems" and that "Alekhine's chess is like a god's."

1	...	R–K6!

An astonishing beginning! White must not take the Rook as after 2 PxR, QxP ch; 3 B–Kt2 (3 K–B1, KtxP mate), KtxP, and White cannot prevent mate, to say nothing of saving his Queen.

Meanwhile, Black threatens 2 ... RxP ch.

2	Kt–B3	PxP
3	QxP	Kt–B6!
4	QxP	QxQ
5	KtxQ	KtxP ch
6	K–R2	

If 6 K–B1, KtxP ch; 7 PxKt, BxKt; 8 BxB, RxB ch; 9 K–Kt2, R(R1)–R6; 10 R–Q8 ch, K–R2; 11 R–R1 ch, K–Kt3; 12 R–R3, R(B6)–Kt6, and White must give up the Knight or be mated in two moves by the Rooks.

6	...	Kt–K5!

With three Rooks *en prise*, Black begins a new combination which ends a dozen moves later in winning the Knight at White's QKt7, a piece far away from the scene of the fighting!

7 R–B4

White loses after 7 PxR, Kt(K5)xR; 8 R–B2 (or 8 KtxKt, KtxR), KtxKt ch; 9 BxKt (9 K–Kt2, Kt–K8 ch is even worse), BxB, and Black is a piece ahead.

7	...	KtxBP

Alekhine does not fall into 7 ... BxKt; 8 R(B4)xKt, RxR; 9 BxB, Kt–B6; 10 BxR, KtxB, and White is out of the woods.

8	B–Kt2	B–K3
9	R(B4)–B2	Kt–Kt5 ch!
10	K–R3	

Obviously 10 K–R1 allowing 10 ... R–R8 ch is fatal.

10	...	Kt–K4 ch
11	K–R2	RxKt!
12	RxKt	

Taking the Rook loses a piece at once: 12 BxR, KtxB ch; 13 K–Kt2, KtxR.

12	...	Kt–Kt5 ch!
13	K–R3	Kt–K6 ch
14	K–R2	KtxR
15	BxR	Kt–Q5!

Once again the sting at the end of the combination! If 16 R–K3, KtxB; 17 RxKt, B–Q4, and Black wins the Knight, which unfortunately cannot be protected by the Rook.

16 Resigns

A wonderful combination, marked by fantastic maneuvering of the minor pieces.

Black to play

332

DAVIDSON–ALEKHINE
Semmering, 1926

It is astonishing how quickly Alekhine works his way into the enemy position. Once there, he gives away a couple of pieces, but exacts heavy payment in return. The decisive combination in a brilliancy prize game.

| 1 ... | Kt–K4 |

The threat of 2 ... KtxKt ch; 3 PxKt, QxB forces White to exchange Knights, and part with the best defender of the King side castled position.

2	KtxKt	QxKt(K4)
3	B–K3	B–B2
4	Kt–K2	Q–R7 ch
5	K–B1	BxP!
6	PxB	QxRP ch
7	K–Kt1	B–R7 ch
8	K–R1	Kt–B5!
9	KtxKt	

If 9 BxKt, B–Kt6 ch; 10 K–Kt1, Q–R7 ch; 11 K–B1, QxP mate.

9 ...	BxKt dis. ch
10	K–Kt1	B–R7 ch
11	K–B1	Q–B6 ch!
12	KxB	R–K4

Intending mate in two by 12 ... R–R4 ch and 13 ... R–R8 mate.

| 13 | Q–B5 | RxQ |
| 14 | BxR | |

Black can now play 14 ... QxB, but prefers to remove the more active Bishop.

| 14 ... | Q–R4 ch |
| 15 | K–Kt2 | QxB |

And Black won.

Black to play

333

STOLTZ-ALEKHINE
Bled, 1931

Just when Stoltz seems to have recovered from the effects of Alekhine's combination, comes a quiet move by the King, who bestows the good old *coup-de-grâce*.

| 1 ... | R–Q4! |

This is not mere playing to the gallery. Alekhine explains that the more natural 1 ... R–Q7 or 1 ... R–Q3 allows White to counterattack by 2 Q–B5, a move which the text prevents.

Black's threat is 2 ... Q–Q2 ch; 3 K–R4 (3 K–Kt2, R–Q7 wins a piece), R–R4 ch!; 4 KxR, Q–R6 mate.

| 2 | Kt–B4 | Q–Q2 ch |
| 3 | P–Kt4 | |

What else is there? If 3 K–Kt2, R–Q7 ch wins the Queen, or if 3 K–R4, R–Q7; 4 Q–K4, RxP ch; 5 K–Kt5, P–R3 mate.

| 3 ... | R–Q5! |

Attacks the Knight and the pinned Pawn behind it.

4   Q–Kt2

Indirectly defending the Knight: if 4 ... BxKt; 5 RxB, RxR; 6 Q–R8 ch and mate next move.

4 ...   P–QB3

Black's threat, once the Knight moves away, is further attack on the Pawn by 5 ... P–KR4. This explains White's next blocking move.

5   Kt–R5   B–Kt4

A necessary preliminary to ... P–Kt3, evicting the Knight. If at once 5 ... P–Kt3 (a horrible mistake) 6 Kt–B6 ch would come like a shot.

6   Q–K2   P–KKt3
7   Kt–Kt3   P–KR4
8   Kt–K4   QxP ch!

A simplification, apparently designed to leave Black a Pawn up in a Rook ending.

9   QxQ   PxQ ch
10   KxP   RxKt ch
11   KxB   K–Kt2!

A fiendish move! White's King is held tight while Black implies that he will proceed by 12 ... P–B3 ch; 13 RxP, R–K4 ch; 14 K–B4, KxR, to win a Rook.

12   Resigns

White to play

334

London, 1926

A scintillating combination from a game played in a blindfold exhibition. White sacrifices a Rook in order to Queen two Pawns—both of which are immediately captured! It's all part of the plot though, in this impressive ending, which Alekhine himself considers one of his best achievements in blindfold chess.

1   P–B5!   KtPxP
2   P–Kt6   R–B1
3   Q–B3   KR–K1

Capturing the Queen is clearly disastrous: 3 ... BxQ; 4 RxQ ch, K–Kt3; 5 P–R5 ch, KxP (or 5 ... K–B3; 6 R–K6 ch, K–Kt2; 7 BxRP ch) 6 R–K6, K–Kt5; 7 B–B3 mate.

4   BxB   PxB
5   QxKP!

This continuation, involving a Rook sacrifice, had to be seen earlier, or else the previous moves would have had no meaning.

5	...	QxQ
6	RxQ	RxR
7	RxP ch	RxR
8	PxR	R–K1
9	PxKt(Q)	RxQ
10	B–K6!	

And this, the star move, certainly had to be anticipated.

10	...	K–Kt3
11	P–B7	R–KB1
12	P–B8(Q)	RxQ
13	BxR	P–QB5
14	B–R6	P–B6
15	B–Q3	K–B3
16	K–B3	K–K4
17	K–K3	P–R4
18	B–B2	K–B3
19	K–B4	K–Kt2
20	KxP	K–R3

Does he think that Alekhine, even with his eyes closed, will play 21 K–B6 allowing a stalemate?

21	K–B4!	Resigns

Black to play

335

MACKENZIE-ALEKHINE
Birmingham, 1926

At the point where the combination seems to be dying out, Alekhine, always alert, finds a Pawn move that gives it new life. Apparently he knew how to apply Pillsbury's dictum, "So set up your attacks that when the fire is out, it isn't out!"

1	...	PxP
2	RxP	Q–Q4 ch
3	K–B1	

Interposing either Rook costs the exchange after 3 ... Kt–B3, while 3 K–Kt1 might let Black capture the Queen Pawn later with check.

3	...	Kt–B4!
4	R–K7	Kt–Q6
5	R(K1)–K4	

White holds on to the valuable center Pawn.

5	...	R–Q2!
6	Q–K2	

The alternative 6 RxR was not attractive: 6 RxR, QxR(K5); RxBP, R–K1, and Black threatens 8 ... Q–B6 ch followed by 9 ... R–K8 ch, as well as 8 ... Q–R8 ch; 9 Kt–Kt1, R–K8 ch, winning easily in either case.

6	...	RxR
7	RxR	Q–R8 ch
8	Kt–Kt1	KtxBP!

Attacks the Queen directly and the Rook indirectly. The Knight cannot be taken, as after 9 PxKt, RxP ch; 10 K–K1, QxKt ch; 11 K–Q2, R–B7, and White's Queen is pinned.

9	QxP ch	Q–Q4!

What can White do? Exchanging Queens loses a Rook at once, while 10 Q–B2 (to prevent 10 ... Q–Kt7 ch) allows a painful discovered check.

10   **RxBP!**

An ingenious move. White expects 10 ... Kt–K3 ch; 11 K–K1, KtxR; 12 QxKt, and he can still cause trouble. But Alekhine has an even more ingenious reply!

10   ...   **P–QKt4!**
11   **Q–B6**

Not 11 QxQ ch, KtxQ ch, which nets Black a whole Rook.

11   ...   **Kt–K3 ch**
12 · **K–K1**   **KtxR**
13   **QxKt**   **Q–K5 ch**

If 14 Kt–K2 (King moves are met by 14 ... QxQP ch winning the Knight); R–K1, and White cannot defend the Knight with his Queen, thanks to Alekhine's cute 10 ... P–QKt4 move.

14   Resigns

Black to play

336

YATES-ALEKHINE
Kecskemet, 1927

Under-promotion is a pleasing device, but rare in practical play. Alekhine, who never misses a trick, tops off a neat combination with checkmate, by transforming his Pawn into a Knight, instead of a Queen!

1   ...   **R–Q4!**
2   **Q–B8 ch**

If instead 2 QxP, R–Q7 ch; 3 K–Kt3, Kt–K5 ch; 4 K–R4, P–R7; 5 QxP ch, R–Q3; 6 Q–Kt3 ch, K–B3; 7 Q–Kt1, P–R8(Q)!; 8 QxQ, R–Q1, and White must give up his Queen or be mated.

2   ...   **K–B2**
3   **K–Kt3**   **K–Kt3**
4   **Q–B6**   **R–Q7!**

Intending to follow with 5 ... K–R4 (threat: 6 ... Kt–K5 ch); 6 QxKt, R–Kt7 mate.

5   **K–R4**   **P–R7**
6   **K–Kt3**

Otherwise Black plays 6 ... R–Q4, cutting off the Queen so that his Pawn may advance, or 6 ... R–Q6, with a mate threat by the Rook.

6   ...   **K–R4!**

Beautiful! If White replies 7 QxKt (to avoid 7 ... Kt–K5 ch), then 7 ... P–R8(Kt)! is checkmate.

White resigned, rather than subject his King to this fate.

Black to play

337

KEVITZ
PINKUS -ALEKHINE
New York, 1929

A combination from a séance of three games played simultaneously against teams of consulting masters.

Who but an Alekhine would have seen the necessity for moving the King over to the opposite end of the board before starting the decisive action? The combination that this piece of strategy initiated is one of the most attractive in the Alekhine repertoire.

1 ...	K–B2
2 B–Kt1	K–K1
3 B–B2	K–Q1
4 B–Kt1	K–B1
5 B–B2	K–Kt2
6 B–Kt1	K–R3
7 B–B2	Q–R4

Another bit of strategy: the Queen and Bishop must change places.

8 B–Kt1	B–Kt5
9 K–Kt2	Q–R6 ch

10 K–R1	P–Kt3
11 B–B2	

The preparations are complete, so Alekhine starts the wheels of the combination going.

11 ...	P–B4!
12 PxP	PxP
13 RxR	

On 13 B–Kt1, Kt–K5, threatening 14 ... KtxKt; 15 QxKt, B–B6 ch forces the win. If White (after 13 ... Kt–K5) tries 14 KtxKt then 14 ... RxKt; 15 RxR, B–B6 is mate, or if 14 Kt–B1, P–B5, and Black pauses for a reply.

13 ...	PxR

And now if White takes the King Pawn, he loses by this fascinating combination: 14 RxP, RxR; 15 QxR, B–B6 ch!; 16 KtxB, Q–B8 ch; 17 Kt–Kt1 (or 17 B–Kt1, QxKt mate!), Kt–Q6!, and the Knight's attack on the Queen together with the threat of 18 ... KtxB mate will exact a resignation.

14 Q–K3	P–K5
15 P–Q6!	

This gives Black a chance to go wrong. The alternative 15 QxKtP loses after 15 ... R–R2; 16 B–Kt1, Kt–Q6 (threatens 17 ... Kt–B7 ch; 18 BxKt, QxRP mate); 17 R–KB1, QxR!; 18 KtxQ, B–B6 mate.

15 ...	PxP
16 B–Kt1!	

Very ingenious! If Black wins a

Rook by force, he gets mated! After 16 ... B–B6 ch; 17 KtxB, PxKt; 18 QxBP, RxR; 19 Q–R8 mate!

16 ...   P–B5!

But Alekhine is not caught so easily!

17 Resigns

After 17 PxP, B–B6 ch; 18 KtxB, PxKt (now the Pawn is protected); 19 Q–B2, RxR, and White must submit.

White to play

338

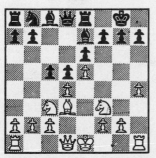

ALEKHINE-ASGEIRSSON
Reykjavik, 1931

Alekhine starts off with a stereotyped sacrificial combination—the kind that Tarrasch called, "the BxP ch, followed by Kt–Kt5 ch, Q–R5 ch and mate, hooray! attack." But being Alekhine, he takes a banal idea and turns it into a thing of beauty, as the subsequent attractive play shows.

1   BxP ch   KxB
2   Kt–Kt5 ch   K–Kt1

Naturally, Black could not last long after 2 ... K–Kt3; 3 Q–Q3 ch.

3   Q–R5   BxKt
4   PxB   K–B1

The King seems to be escaping.

5   P–Kt6!   K–K2

Black must not capture, as after 5 ... PxP; 6 QxKtP, White's Rook will come in decisively at R8.

6   PxP   R–B1
7   0–0–0   P–R3

To prevent 8 Kt–Kt5.

8   PxP

Opens a file for the Rook, and also threatens 9 Kt–K4 followed by 10 Kt–Q6.

8   ...   Kt–Q2
9   RxP!

Offering a Rook which must not be taken, viz.: 9 ... PxR; 10 KtxP ch, K–K3; 11 Kt–B4 ch, K–K2; 12 P–K6, Kt–B3; 13 Q–K5 (threatens mate on the move), RxP; 14 Kt–Kt6 ch, K–K1; 15 R–R8 ch, and White forces mate.

9   ...   Q–R4
10 Q–Kt5 ch   KxP
11 R–R7   R–KKt1
12 R–Q4!   QxBP
13 RxKt ch!   BxR
14 Kt–K4   Q–Kt5
15 Kt–Q6 ch   K–B1
16 Q–B6 ch!   PxQ
17. R–B7 mate

White to play

339

ALEKHINE-JUNGE
Cracow, 1942

The Alekhine alertness is legendary. In placid positions that seem thoroughly devoid of promise, he finds exciting opportunities for brilliant lightning-like strokes. The combination that follows illustrates that facet of his genius.

1   Q–K3

Immediate threat: 2 KtxKt, RxKt; 3 RxR, QxR; 4 QxKt, winning a piece.

| 1 ... | KtxKt |
| 2 PxKt | P–QB4 |

To prevent 3 Q–B5, fearfully cramping Black's game.

3   P–B6!

This menaces Black with 4 Q–Kt5, P–Kt3; 5 Q–R6, and mate at Kt7.

| 3 ... | PxP |
| 4 Q–R6 | |

Now intending 5 B–B2 with new terrors.

| 4 ... | P–B4 |
| 5 BxP ch! | |

The typical Alekhine bolt from the blue. The Bishop can be taken three ways, none of them satisfactory to Black:

(a) 5 ... KxB; 6 QxP ch, and Black loses his Queen.

(b) 5 ... RxB; 6 Q–Kt5 ch, R–Kt2; 7 RxR ch, K–B2; 8 QxP ch, K–K2; 9 Q–B8 ch, K–K3; 10 QR–Q1, and Black cannot survive long.

| 5 ... | QxB |

Black must take the Bishop, since 5 ... K–R1 allows 6 Q–B6, mate on the move.

6   RxR

And now Black canot capture the troublesome Rook, as after 6 ... RxR; 7 Q–Kt5 ch, Q–Kt2; 8 QxR ch, he loses his Knight. So he tries to block off White's other Rook.

| 6 ... | Kt–R5 |
| 7 P–QKt3 | Resigns |

White to play

340

ALEKHINE-PRAT
Paris, 1913

An elegant combination from a simultaneous exhibition. Even in playing twenty games at once, Alekhine did not avoid complications, but relied on his genius for combination play to bring about magnificent victories.

1 KtxKBP!

Réti had this sort of stroke in mind when he said, "The scheme of a game is played on positional lines; the decision of it, as a rule, is effected by combinations."

1 ...	KxKt
2 P–K5	Kt(K2)–Kt1

The other Knight must stay put. The plausible 2 ... Kt(B3)–Q4 is refuted by 3 PxP ch, KxP; 4 B(R3)xKt!, KxB; 5 Q–Kt6, R–KB1; 6 QxKtP ch, K–K3; 7 R–B6 ch, RxR; 8 QxR mate. Or if 2 ... Kt(B3)–Kt1; 3 PxKP dble. ch and mate.

3	B–Q6	Q–B1
4	Q–K2	P–QKt4
5	B–Kt3	P–QR4
6	QR–K1!	P–R5

Hoping to drive the terrible Bishop away from the diagonal leading to his King.

Instead of retreating compliantly, Alekhine announced a forced mate in ten moves, as follows:

7	Q–R5 ch!	KtxQ
8	PxP dble. ch	K–Kt3
9	B–B2 ch	K–Kt4
10	R–B5 ch	K–Kt3!

This holds out longest. If 10 ... K–Kt5; 11 P–R3 ch, K–Kt6; 12 R–

K4 (threatens 13 R–Kt4 mate), Kt(Kt1)–B3; 13 R–B3 mate.

11	R–B6 dble. ch	K–Kt4
12	R–Kt6 ch	K–R5
13	R–K4 ch	Kt–B5
14	RxKt ch	K–R4
15	P–Kt3	Any
16	R–R4 mate	

White to play

341

ALEKHINE–MOLINA
Buenos Aires, 1926

Alekhine could unearth exquisite combinations, though the conditions were difficult. Here is one from an exhibition arranged against eight strong players, where a tournament time-limit prevailed.

1 P–KR3   KtxKtP

Tempting, as it seems to win the exchange.

2 QxRP!

This must have come as a surprise to Black—in every variation!

2 ...   RxQ

Black had other replies, against which Alekhine had prepared these combinations:

(a) 2 ... RxR; 3 RxR, RxR; 4 KtxR, and White's passed Pawn assures the win.

(b) 2 ... KtxR; 3 RxR, ktxB (threatens mate); 4 PxKt, RxR; 5 QxR, B–B1; 6 Kt–K5.

(c) 2 ... B–Q3; 3 QxR!, RxQ; 4 RxKt, Q–K3; 5 R(Kt2)–Q2, and Black's pieces are held fast by the pin.

3	RxR ch	B–B1
4	BxP	P–R3
5	RxB ch	K–R2
6	R(Q1)–Q8	Q–Kt8 ch
7	K–R2	R–Kt2

Black has managed to hold on to his material advantage, but now comes a crushing move.

8   Kt–R4!

The threat is mate on the move. If Black gives his King a flight square by 8 ... P–Kt3, the continuation 9 B–Q4, P–B3; 10 BxP is fatal, or if 8 ... P–Kt4; 9 R–R8 ch, K–Kt2; 10 R(Q8)–Kt8 ch, K–B3; 11 RxRP ch, K–K4; 12 R–K8 ch, K–B5; 13 B–Q6 mates him.

8   ...   Resigns

Black to play

342

GRUNFELD-ALEKHINE
Carlsbad, 1923

This splendid combination is the climax of a game considered by Yates and Winter the finest ever played. "For in the perfect chess combination (they say) as in a first rate short story, the whole plot and counter-plot should lead up to a striking finale, the interest not being allayed until the very last moment."

1   ...   Kt–K4

Intending to occupy the outpost Q6. "The plausible 2 R–B2 (to answer 2 ... Kt–Q6 by 3 KtxKP) would lead to some remarkable combinations," say Yates and Winter, and give this beautiful analysis:

2 R–B2, Kt–Q6!; 3 KtxKP, QxKt; 4 RxKt (if 4 QxKt, QxQ followed by 5 ... RxR), RxR; 5 QxR, RxKt (not 5 ... BxKt because of 6 Q–Q1). An impressive win of a piece. If in this 4 RxR, RxR; 5 RxKt, BxKt; 6 RxB, Q–Kt8 ch; 7 R–Q1, R–B8;

8 RxR, QxR ch; 9 Q–B1, QxKtP, and Black has a winning ending.

2	Kt–R2	Kt–Q6
3	RxR	QxR!
4	P–B3	RxKt!
5	PxP	

Capturing the Rook loses nicely: 5 PxR, BxP ch; 6 K–B1, Kt–B5; 7 QxP (or 7 Q–Q2, Q–B5 ch; 8 K–K1, P–K6!; 9 QxB, Q–K7 mate), Q–B5 ch; 8 K–K1, KtxP ch; 9 K–Q2, B–K6 ch, and White must give up his Queen.

Grunfeld saw this combination, but expected to win back his piece with the text move.

5 ...　　　　　　Kt–B5!

But this move and the next, must have given him a jolt!

6 PxKt　　　　　Q–B5!

Attacks two loose pieces, the Queen and the Knight. If now 7 Kt–B3 (attempting to protect both pieces), QxQ; 8 KtxQ, RxR ch wins for Black.

7 QxQ

Grunfeld lets himself be mated, but there was no defense.

7	...	RxR ch
8	Q–B1	B–Q5 ch

And Black mates next move.

White to play

343

ALEKHINE-VERLINSKI
Odessa, 1918

From a game I recently discovered an exciting combination played by Alekhine in his youth.

After leaving Black with only to-and-fro moves by his Rook, our hero polishes him off with an exquisite checkmate.

1 Kt(Q2)–K4 ch　　BxKt

On 1 ... K–Q4; 2 P–B4 ch, PxP; 3 KtPxP is mate.

2 KtxB ch　　　　K–K3

Black cannot save the Bishop Pawn. If 2 ... K–Q4; 3 P–B4 ch, PxP; 4 KtPxP ch forces the King to abandon the Pawn.

3 KtxP ch　　　　K–Q4

The King must step gingerly. If 3 ... K–B3; 4 Kt–Q7 ch catches the Rook, while 3 ... K–B4 allows 4 R(R1)–B1, with mate on the move.

4	RxR	KtxR
5	P–Kt4!	Kt–B3
6	P–K4 ch	K–Q3

Obviously, not 6 ... K–Q5 when White can either win the Rook at once or play 7 R–K1 followed by mate next move.

7   R–R7!

This holds the King fast, and pre-vents Black's Knight from moving. (A Knight move would of course be penalized by 8 R–Q7 mate.)

7	...	R–KKt1
8	R–KB7	R–Kt3
9	P–R4	R–R3
10	P–B4	R–Kt3
11	Kt–Kt7 ch	K–K3
12	Kt–Q8 ch	K–Q3
13	P–B5 mate!	

21

MASTER OF MASTERS

José R. Capablanca

> Some of Capablanca's finest games remind me of the compositions of DeFalla in their blend of intricacy, elusiveness, dignity and basic simplicity.
>
> —Gilbert Highet

The greatest compliment one can pay a master is to compare his play to Capablanca.

Of a Morphy game against Boden, Konig says, "Morphy's endgame play recalls Capablanca's easy, elegant style."

Commenting on a Smyslov ending, Liepnieks and Spence say, "An ending reminiscent of Capablanca at his best."

The Botvinnik win against Alekhine at Avro in 1938 has this concluding note by Reinfeld, "Botvinnik's masterly treatment bears comparison with Capablanca's finest efforts in this field."

Winter pays tribute to Alekhine's outstanding positional play against Bogolyubov in the fifth game of their 1929 match, thus: "A very fine positional game by Alekhine. It might have been played by Capablanca, the highest praise that can be given to this sort of game."

O'Kelly annotating the fifth game in the Botvinnik-Smyslov match in 1957, says of the former's win, "*Toute la partie est du reste admirablement menée par Botvinnik qui joue ici dans un style logique et clair qui rappelle Capablanca.*"

Capablanca handled every phase of the game with equal facility. He was superb in the opening, marvelous in the midgame and wonderful in the ending. He could see complicated combinations in a flash, and work out the details with amazing speed and accuracy. "What others could not see in a month's study, he saw at a glance," says Fine. His technique was flawless, and his style so graceful and elegant as to make chess look easy. No player in all the world's history has equalled in artistry, logic and crystalline clarity the masterpieces produced by Capablanca.

Capablanca was a genius, the greatest ever produced by chess.

Black to play

344

CORZO-CAPABLANCA
Havana, 1900

From an opening which Corzo expected would bewilder a twelve-year-old opponent. How was Corzo to know that no one would ever beat Capablanca with a King's Gambit?

The concluding combination is bright, sparkling and satisfyingly accurate.

1	...	KtxP!
2	QxKt	Q–B4!
3	Kt–K2	

Of course not 3 QxQ, when 3 ... BxQ ch in reply forces mate.

| 3 | ... | Q–Kt3 |

Menacing White with 4 ... B–QB4.

4	QxQ	RPxQ
5	Kt–Q4	B–QB4
6	P–B3	R–R5!

With the threat of 7 ... RxKt; 8 PxR, BxP ch and mate next.

7	B–K2	BxKt ch
8	PxB	RxQP
9	P–Kt3	Kt–B3
10	B–Kt2	R–Q7
11	B–R5 ch	KtxB!
12	BxR	P–B6
13	PxP	

To prevent loss of the Rook by 13 ... PxP, or the King by 13 ... P–B7 ch; 14 K–B1, B–B4, and 15 ... B–Q6 mate.

| 13 | ... | Kt–B5 |
| 14 | B–K5 | |

On 14 R–K1, B–R6; 15 B–K5 (if 15 RxB, KtxR ch and mate next move), R–Q8; 16 B–B3, Kt–K7 is mate.

14	...	R–Kt7 ch
15	K–B1	R–B7 ch
16	K–K1	Kt–Q6 ch

Black wins the Bishop and the game.

White to play

345

CAPABLANCA-CORZO
Havana, 1900

This magnificent combination, played by Capablanca when he was twelve years old far surpasses any attempts by any other child prodigy —and this goes for Paul Morphy, Sammy Reshevsky, Paul Keres, Arturito Pomar and Bobby Fischer.

It has a scope and grandeur of concept that is breath-taking. The Queen sacrifice is brilliant, the complications that arise are handled with consummate ease, and the ensuing ending is played by Capablanca with flawless accuracy.

1 P–B4!

To eliminate Black's Queen Pawn, and give himself two connected passed Pawns.

1	...	Q–K3
2	PxP	QxP (Q4)
3	P–K6	

Forces Black to attack the Queen, since 3 ... BxP, 4 RxB wins a piece for White.

3	...	B–Kt4
4	QxB!	QxQ
5	P–Q5 ch	R–Kt2
6	PxKt	

White's immediate threat is 7 KtxP followed by 8 Kt–K6.

6	...	P–KR3

If Black tries to counter-attack by 6 ... QxQP or 6 ... QxKtP, 7 R–K8 ch forces mate, while on 6 ... R–KB1 Capablanca intended 7 Kt–Q4 (attacks the Queen and threatens 8 Kt–K6), QxQP; 8 R–K8, QxBP (or 8 ... R(Kt2)xP; 9

KtxP ch, K–Kt1; 10 Kt–R6 mate!); 9 RxR ch, QxR; 10 KtxP and White wins.

7	Kt–Q4	QxR

Against 7 ... Q–Q2, Capablanca had prepared a beautiful win. His analysis goes: 7 ... Q–Q2; 8 KtxP, QxBP; 9 BxR ch, K–R2 (9 ... K–Kt1; 10 KtxP ch wins the Queen); 10 R–K7 winning the Queen as 10 ... QxP (clearly 10 Q–R4; 11 B–K5 ch, K–Kt1; 12 R–Kt7 ch, K–B1; 13 Kt–Q6 ch leads to mate); 11 B–K5 ch, K–Kt3; 12 R–Kt7 ch, K–R4; 13 Kt–Kt3 ch, K–R5; 14 R–B4 ch, PxR; 15 R–Kt4 is mate!

8	RxQ	RxP
9	RxP	RxR
10	KtxR ch	K–R2
11	Kt–K7!	

Cuts the King off and prevents him from approaching the precious passed Pawn.

11	...	R–KB1
12	K–Kt2	P–KR4
13	P–Q6	P–Kt5
14	PxP	PxP
15	B–K5	K–R3
16	P–Q7	R–Q1

Otherwise 17 B–B7 followed by 18 P–Q8(Q), RxQ; 19 BxR leaves White two pieces ahead.

17	Kt–Kt8 ch!	RxKt

On 17 ... K–Kt3; 18 Kt–B6, K–B2; 19 B–B7 wins for White.

18	B–B6	K–Kt3
19	P–B8(Q)	RxQ

20	BxR	P–Kt4
21	K–B2	K–B4
22	K–K3	K–K4
23	K–Q3	K–Q4
24	K–B3	P–Kt6
25	B–R4	P–Kt7
26	B–B2	P–R4
27	P–Kt4	K–K5
28	B–Kt6	

But not 28 PxP, which allows a draw, since the Bishop does not control the Rook Pawn's Queening square.

28	...	K–Q4
29	K–Q3	K–B3
30	B–Kt1	K–Q4
31	B–R2	K–B3
32	K–Q4	P–R5
33	K–K5	K–Kt3
34	K–Q5	K–R3
35	K–B5!	

Carefully avoiding the little trap 35 K–B6, P–Kt8(Q); 36 BxQ, and Black draws by stalemate!

35	...	Resigns

White to play

346

CAPABLANCA-MARSHALL
Match, 1909

The concluding combination from a game which Capablanca himself considered one of his best.

1   Q–B3!

A powerful move, with an immediate threat on the Queen Pawn. Black can parry this with 1 ... PxP, but at the cost of giving White's Bishop more scope. The move he plays permits his Rook to reach Q3, protecting the center.

1	...	BxKt
2	KtPxB	R–Q3
3	Q–R5	R–R2
4	Q–Kt6	

Intending 5 R–Kt4 followed by 6 R–R7.

4	...	Kt(B2)–R3

Capablanca had this pretty win prepared against 4 ... Kt–K2: 5 R–R8 ch, KtxR; 6 RxKt ch, Kt–Kt1; 7 Q–R7, K–B2; 8 BxKtP!, and Black is ruined, e.g. If 8 ... QxB; 9 QxKt ch, K–K2; QxP mate, or if 8 ... Q–Kt1; 9 BxR, and the Queen must not touch either Bishop.

5	RxKt!	PxR

On 5 ... KtxR; 6 BxKt, PxB; 7 RxP, and the check at R8 will win Black's Queen.

6	BxP ch	K–K2

Or 6 ... KtxB, 7 RxKt, and White wins as in the previous note. If Black then tries 7 ... R–KKt2, White breaks the pin by 8 R–R8 ch, mating in two more moves.

7	Q–Kt7 ch	K–K1
8	QxKt ch	K–Q2
9	Q–R7 ch!	

Played with Capablanca's customary accuracy. It is important that the Bishop's path be free, and that the Queen be protected one move later.

9	...	Q–K2
10	B–B8!	

Attacks the pinned Queen, forces an exchange, and wins a Rook for a Bishop.

10	...	QxQ
11	RxQ ch	K–K1
12	RxR	Resigns

White to play

347

CAPABLANCA-FONAROFF
New York, 1918

An exquisite combination, this is one of my favorites. I like the way pressure is brought on Black's one weak spot, the Queen Pawn; I like the way the Pawn is suddenly captured; I like the move 6 ... R–

Q8, which Black must have thought Capablanca overlooked; and I like the witty reply it elicited—an elegant pin and Knight fork combination.

1	Kt–B5	

The Knight combines a threat of mate on the move with an attack on the Queen Pawn.

1	...	B–B3
2	Q–KKt3	Kt–K4
3	B–B4	Q–B2
4	QR–Q1	QR–Q1

The Queen Pawn is attacked by two pieces and protected by two pieces. An electronic chess-playing machine would consider it safe from capture.

5	RxP!	RxR
6	BxKt	

Attacks the Rook three times. If Black now plays 5 ... BxB, then 6 QxB threatening mate and simultaneously attacking the pinned Rook wins a piece at once.

6	...	R–Q8

But now Black threatens mate (by 7 ... RxR) and attacks the Bishop with two pieces. Has Capablanca overlooked this?

7	RxR	BxB
8	Kt–R6 ch!	K–R1
9	QxB!	QxQ
10	KtxP ch	

A pretty Knight fork which regains the Queen, and leaves White a piece ahead.

10	...	Resigns

White to play

348

CAPABLANCA-AMATEUR
Havana, 1912

In their book CAPABLANCA, THE
CHESS PHENOMENON, Euwe and
Prins say, "It is astonishing how carefully Capablanca's combinations are
calculated. Turn and twist as you
will, search the variations in every
way possible, you come to the inevitable conclusion that the moves
all fit in with the utmost precision."

1   Kt–B4!

A surprising sacrifice, whose object
is to provide play for the Bishops on
the long diagonals.

1 ...   PxKt

Refusing to take the Knight might
lead to one of these possibilities:
(a) 1 ... KtxB ch; 2 QxKt,
Q–K2; 3 KtxB, QxKt; 4 Q–Q4 and
White wins.
(b) 1 ... Kt(R3)–B2; 2 Kt-
(B3)xKt, KtxKt; 3 P–B4!, PxKt; 4
BxP ch, K–R1 (if 4 ... B–K3;

5 RxB wins); 5 RxB! and White's
next capture 6 BxKt is fatal.

2	BxP ch	Kt(R3)–B2
3	RxB!	QxR
4	KtxKt	B–K3

Black has no choice.

| 5 | R–Q1 | Q–K2 |
| 6 | R–Q7! | |

This surprise offer is the point of
the earlier Knight sacrifice.

6 ...   BxR

Refusing the Rook loses: 6 ...
Q–K1; 7 KtxKt (threatens 8 Kt–R6
mate), RxKt; 8 Q–B3!, RxR; 9 Q–
R8 ch, K–B2; 10 Q–Kt7 mate.

7   KtxB

The threat is 8 Kt–B6 ch, K–Kt2;
9 Kt–Kt4 ch, K–Kt1; 10 Kt–R6 mate.

7 ...   KR–B1

On 7 ... QxKt; 8 Q–B3! is
immediately conclusive.

| 8 | Q–B3 | RxB |
| 9 | PxR | Resigns |

Black must move the Knight to
avoid mate. If 9 ... Kt–Q1; 10
Q–R8 ch, K–B2; 11 Q–Kt7 ch, K–K3
(11 ... K–K1; 12 Kt–B6 ch);
12 Kt–B8 ch, K–Q3; 13 B–R3 ch
and White wins the Queen. Or if
9 ... Kt–Q3; 10 Q–R8 ch, K–B2;
11 Kt–K5 ch, K–K3; 12 QxR, and
White has won a piece.
The play on the long diagonal is
impressive.

Black to play

349

JANOWSKY-CAPABLANCA
New York, 1916

A favorite technique of Capablanca's, beautifully illustrated in this ending, is to increase a positional advantage by a series of little combinations.

1 ...   P–Kt5!

A sacrifice to give his white-squared Bishop more mobility.

2 PxP

If 2 BxP; BxB, 3 PxB and Black can either regain the Pawn by 4 ... R–Kt1 or advance 4 ... P–R4 with threats against the pinned Knight.

2 ...   B–QR5

Intending to get to the Knight by way of 3 ... B–B7 and 4 ... B–K5 ch. If White stops this by 3 R–QB1; then 3 ... RxP ch!, 4 KxR; B–Kt4 ch, 5 K–B3; BxR wins for Black.

3 R–QR1   B–B7
4 B–Kt3

Black was threatening to win the Knight by 5 ... B–K5 ch; this cuts off the pressure of the Rooks.

4 ...   B–K5 ch
5 K–B2   P–R4!

There is no relief for White in 5 Kt–K3, the continuation 5 ... P–R5; 6 KtxR, PxB ch followed by 7 ... RxKt winning two pieces for a Rook.

6 R–R7   BxKt

Makes it possible for the Pawn to advance and attack the pinned piece.

7 RxB   P–R5
8 BxP

The best chance, as otherwise he loses a piece without compensation.

8 ...   RxR ch
9 K–B3   RxRP
10 BxB

Against 10 RxB ch Capablanca had prepared this pretty win: 10 ... K–B1; 11 B–B6, R(Kt1)–R1, and to prevent mate White must simplify into a lost position by 12 BxR; KxR.

10 ...   R–R6 ch
11 K–B2   R–QKt6
12 B–Kt5 ch

To shut out one of the deadly Rooks.

12 ...   K–Kt3
13 R–K7   RxP ch

14	K–B3	R–QR1
15	RxP ch	

Does he really hope to swindle Capablanca by 15 ... K–R4; 16 R–R6 mate?

15	...	K–R2
16	Resigns	

If 16 K–Kt3 (to escape mate in one), R–R6 ch; 17 K–R4, R–R7 effects the mate in two.

White to play

350

CAPABLANCA-RIBERA
Barcelona, 1935

From a ten-game simultaneous exhibition against picked opponents, at a time limit of 30 moves an hour. In effect, Capablanca was playing men of tournament strength at a rate (for him) of 300 moves an hour!

The following delightful affair must have been enacted at breath-taking speed, but then Capablanca always had the faculty of calculat-ing combinations with lightning rapidity. In fact, as a youngster, Capablanca won most of the games of a ten-game match at rapid transit chess against Lasker himself, and elicited this comment from the then Champion of the World, "Young man, you play remarkable chess! You never make a mistake!"

1	P–Q5!	KtxP
2	BxB	KtxB
3	BxP ch!	

Appearances to the contrary, this is not the usual Bishop-sacrifice combination which the master player perpetrates so often against the unsuspecting. It is only the beginning of the real combination!

3	...	KxB
4	Kt–Kt5 ch	K–Kt1

The penalty for 4 ... K–Kt3 is swift: 5 Q–R5 ch, K–B3; 6 Kt–R7 mate.

5	RxKt!	QxR

On the alternative capture 5 ... BxR, White forces the play by 6 Q–R5, KR–K1; 7 QxP ch, K–R1; 8 R–K1, and the threats cannot be parried.

6	Q–R5	R–Q1
7	QxP ch	K–R1
8	P–KR4	

Preparing for 9 Kt–R5, which if played at once lets Black swoop down with a mate.

8	...	Q–K1
9	Kt–R5!	

Since Black loses a Rook if he exchanges Queens, White can go about his business. The threat is 10 QxP—mate on the move.

9	...	Q–B1
10	Kt–B6!	

Poses a problem: if Black takes the Queen, the Knight mates; if he takes the Knight, the Queen mates.

10	...	Kt–Kt1
11	Q–R5 ch	Resigns

After 11 ... Kt–R3; 12 Q–Kt6 removes any lingering doubts.

Black to play

351

BERNSTEIN-CAPABLANCA
Moscow, 1914

In answer to a query of Marshall's as to the game Capablanca himself considered the best he ever played, Capablanca said, "I think my most finished and artistic game was the one I played against Dr. Bernstein at Moscow, on February 4th, 1914."

This is the beautiful final combination from the game:

1	...	BxKt
2	RxB	Kt–Q4

To drive off the blockader, and then advance the Pawn.

White must not now play 3 RxP, since the pretty reply 3 ... Kt–B6 wins the exchange.

3	R–B2	P–B6
4	KR–QB1	R–B4

Now comes some maneuvering by White's Knight as Bernstein tries to win the weak-looking Bishop Pawn.

5	Kt–Kt3	R–B3
6	Kt–Q4	R–B2
7	Kt–Kt5	

Looks good, since the Knight's threat against the Rook gains a tempo for the attack on the Pawn.

7	...	R–B4

Apparently White can now win the Pawn. It is attacked three times, and protected only twice. So Bernstein, not suspecting the stunning surprise that awaits him, takes the Pawn.

8	KtxBP	KtxKt
9	RxKt	RxR
10	RxR	Q–Kt7!

An astounding move, which offers White these choices:

(a) 11 QxQ, R–Q8 mate.

(b) 11 R–Q3, Q–B8 ch; 12 Q–Q1, QxQ ch; 13 RxQ, RxR mate.

(c) 11 R–B8, Q–Kt8 ch; 12 Q–

B1, QxQ ch, followed by 13 ... RxR, winning.

(d) 11 Q–K1, QxR; 12 QxQ, R–Q8 ch and mate next.

(e) 11 R–B2, Q–Kt8 ch; 12 Q–B1, QxR and Black wins.

Not relishing any of these prospects, White resigned.

White to play

352

CAPABLANCA-SUBAREV
Moscow, 1925

The decisive combination from the game which was awarded first brilliancy prize.

1   **RxR** ch   **KxR**

Recapturing with the Queen or the Rook loses immediately by the discovered check.

2   **QxP**

Threatens immediate disaster by 3 R–K1 ch, B–K4 (3 ... K–Q3; 4 Q–Kt6 ch forces mate); 4 P–Q6 ch, K–Q1; 5 Q–Kt6 ch, K–B1; 6 R–B1 ch and quick mate.

2   ...   **BxKt**

Black's idea is to disrupt White's Pawn position before the anticipated exchange of Queens.

3   **R–K1 ch!**

But this interpolation upsets all his plans.

3   ...   **B–K4**

The only move: if 3 ... K–Q3; 4 Q–Kt6 ch, KxP; 5 R–Q1 ch wins, or if 3 ... K–Q1; 4 Q–R8 ch, K–B2; 5 RxR, and Black threatened with mate, cannot even save his Bishop.

4   **P–Q6 ch!**   **K–K3**

Best, since 4 ... KxP loses the Queen after 5 R–Q1 ch, while 4 ... K–Q1 succumbs to 5 Q–Kt6 ch, K–B1; 6 R–B1 ch.

5   **Q–Kt3 ch**   **K–B4**
6   **Q–Q3 ch**   **K–Kt4**
7   **Q–K3 ch**   **K–B4**

Or 7 ... K–R4; 8 P–Kt4 ch, K–R5; 9 Q–R6 mate.

8   **Q–K4 ch!**   **K–K3**

On 8 ... K–Kt4; 9 Q–R4 ch, K–B4; 10 Q–Kt4 is mate.

9   **Q–B4 ch**   **KxP**
10 **R–Q1 ch**

Wins the Queen and the game.

White to play

353

CAPABLANCA-ALEKHINE
Match, 1927

A combination, powerful and elegant, against the greatest combination player of all time. It was said that you had to beat Alekhine three times in one game to defeat him—once in the opening, once in the midgame, and once in the ending.

1   Q–Kt2

Threatens 2 Q–R3 ch, K–Kt1 (interposing a piece at K2 allows 3 R–R8 mate); 3 B–R7 ch, K–R1; 4 R(Q4)–R4, P–Kt4; 5 Q–Kt2 ch, P–B3; 6 QxP ch, Q–Kt2; 7 B–B5 ch, PxR; 8 RxP ch, K–Kt1; 9 BxB ch, RxB; 10 QxR ch, Q–B2; 11 R–R8 ch, and White wins the Queen.

1   ...   Q–B4
2   B–Q5!

An intimation of further terrors in store. The immediate threat is 3 BxB, PxB (3 ... RxB; 4 R–R8 ch wins a Rook); 4 R–Q7 (now menacing two mates on the move), R–K2;

5 R–R8 ch, K–B2; 6 RxR ch, QxR; 7 RxR, and White wins a Rook.

2   ...   R–R3
3   R–K4

Clearance for the Queen's attack on the Knight Pawn.

If Black defends by 3 ... P–KKt3, White's reply is 4 Q–B6 followed by 5 R–R8 mate. If Black tries instead 3 ... P–B3; 4 R–R8 ch, K–B2 (4 ... B–Kt1; 5 RxB mate); 5 RxR wins a piece.

3   ...   R–Q3
4   R–R7!   K–K2

The King must flee. The attempt 4 ... Q–Kt5 ch; 5 K–B1, RxB fails after 6 QxP ch, K–K2; 7 QxP ch, K–Q3; 8 Q–B7 mate.

5   QxP   K–Q1
6   BxB   PxB

If 6 ... R(K1)xB; 7 Q–B8 ch, K–B2; 8 QxP ch (8 RxR does not win a Rook, the refutation being 8 ... R–Q8 ch, with an attack on the unprotected Queen), K–B1; 9 QxP ch, and mate in two more moves.

7   QxP   Q–Kt5 ch

Menaced with loss by 8 Q–Kt8 ch, Q–B1; 9 QxR ch, Black is compelled to exchange Queens. The alternative 7 ... R–Q6 (the Rook must stay on the Queen file) allows mate in three.

8   QxQ   PxQ
9   P–B5   R–B3
10 RxKtP   RxP
11 R–R7!

Intending to remove all the Rooks by 12 R–Kt8 ch, R–B1; 13 RxR ch, KxR; 14 R–R8 ch followed by 15 RxR.

If Black prevents this by 11 ... R–QB1, White mates by 12 R–Q4!, a beautiful specimen of long-range epaulette mate.

11 ...   Resigns

Black to play

354

BOGOLYUBOV-CAPABLANCA
Bad Kissingen, 1928

"This is an ending to thrill every chess player," say Euwe and Prins of this combination, "and one that must be included with the supreme achievements of Capablanca."

For Capablanca this victory must have been especially gratifying. It proved once again that Bogolyubov had been deluding himself when he made the statement, "There is nothing more to fear from the Capablanca technique."

1 ...   Kt–Q3!

Indicating that he plans 2 ... Kt–K5 followed by 3 ... R–B7 and mate at Q7.

2	Kt–B3	P–Kt5
3	PxP	PxP
4	Kt–Q1	

If 4 Kt–R2, Kt–K5!; 5 KtxP, R–B5; 6 Kt–R2, R–B7; 7 R–Q1, RxP; 8 Kt–B1, R–B6 mate.

4	...	R–B7
5	R–B2	P–Kt6!
6	R–R1	Kt–K5
7	R–K2	R(B1)–B3

White must wait to see what happens to him. If he disturbs the position by 7 RxR, then 7 ... RxR is the reply, followed by 8 ... R–Q7 mate, or if 7 Kt–B3, R(B3)xKt ch; 8 PxR, RxP is mate.

8 R–Kt1   P–K4!

In a position where the defender's pieces are fully occupied in holding off those of the attacker, the extra pressure that even a Pawn can bring to bear may be enough to cause a position to collapse.

9 R–R1

On 9 PxP, Black plays 9 ... R(B3)–B5 and then 10 ... Kt–B4 mate.

9	...	R(B3)–B5!
10	R–R5	Kt–B4 ch!
11	Resigns	

After 11 PxKt (or 11 RxKt) Black mates by 11 ... P–K5.
A pleasing finish.

White to play

355

CAPABLANCA-STEINER
Los Angeles, 1933

A delightful combination with an air of casual elegance about it. It is as though Capablanca were simply toying with his opponent!

1	Q–R5 ch	K–Kt2
2	PxP	QPxP

Naturally, if 2 ... BPxP; 3 R–B7 ch is fatal.

3	RxP!	KxR
4	R–B1 ch	Kt–B4
5	KtxKt!	PxKt
6	RxP ch	K–K2
7	Q–B7 ch	K–Q3
8	R–B6 ch	K–B4

Black cannot save himself by 8 ... QxR as after 9 QxQ ch, K–Q2; 10 QxKP, White's extra Pawns assure him an easy win.

9   QxKtP

With two major threats: 10 Q–Kt4 mate and 10 QxBP mate.

9   ...   Q–Kt3

Black's reply seems to guard against both threats, but now comes the second surprise sacrifice.

10	RxP ch!	QxR
11	Q–Kt4 mate	

White to play

356

CAPABLANCA-LEVENFISH
Moscow, 1935

The rare times that Capablanca ventured on a King side attack were the times when a King side attack was the quickest way to win. The combinations that went into these attacks were sharp, energetic and accurate. Victory was Capablanca's aim, but it had to be achieved logically. The combinations, to be truly brilliant, must be sound beyond question. They must prevail against the best play possible on the other side of the board.

1   Q–R3!

With threats on both sides of the

board. If Black plays 1 ... Q–Kt3 (to prevent 2 Kt–B6), then 2 Kt–Kt4 menaces him with 3 KtxKt eh followed by 4 QxP mate, as well as 3 B–B7, winning the exchange.

1 ...	R–B4
2 RxR	BxR
3 B–KKt5	

Clearly intending 4 BxKt and 5 QxRP mate.

| 3 ... | P–R3 |

The alternative 3 ... P–Kt3 loses by 4 Kt–B6, Q–B2; 5 BxKt, QxKt; 6 Q–R6.

4 Kt–Kt4!

Threatens a quick win by 5 KtxP ch, PxKt; 6 QxRP.

| 4 ... | B–K2 |

Obviously not 4 ... PxB, when 5 KtxKt ch forces mate.

| 5 BxKt | PxB |

On 5 ... BxB, White wins by 6 KtxP ch, PxKt; 7 QxRP, R–K1; 8 B–R7 ch, K–R1; 9 B–Kt6 ch, and mate in two more moves.

| 6 KtxRP ch | K–Kt2 |
| 7 Q–Kt4 ch! | K–R1 |

If 7 ... KxKt; 8 Q–R4 ch, K–Kt2; 9 Q–R7 mate.

| 8 Q–R5 | K–Kt2 |
| 9 KtxP! | |

Very neat! Black, though threatened with mate on the move (to say nothing of loss of the Queen) must not touch the Knight, as after 9 ... RxKt; 10 Q–R7 ch, K–B1; 11 Q–R8 mate is the penalty.

| 9 ... | R–R1 |
| 10 Q–Kt6 ch | Resigns |

I have known many chess players, but only one chess genius, Capablanca.

—Emanuel Lasker

INDEX

(The numbers refer to the diagrams.)

Adeler-Amateur	27	Amateur-Steinitz	221
Ahues-Amateur	89	Amateur-Steinitz	224
Alatorsev-Riumin	132	Amateur-Tarrasch	248
Alekhine-Asgeirsson	338	Amateur-Tartakover	104
Alekhine-Bogolyubov	168	Anderssen-Alexander	199
Alekhine-Capablanca	186	Anderssen-Amateur	194
Alekhine-Cohn	170	Anderssen-De Rivière	193
Alekhine-Feldt	325	Anderssen-Dufresne	190
Alekhine-Fletcher	29	Anderssen-Dufresne	192
Alekhine-Johner	136	Anderssen-Kieseritzky	191
Alekhine-Junge	339	Anderssen-Mayet	197
Alekhine-Levenfish	180	Anderssen-Morphy	144
Alekhine-Molina	341	Anderssen-Paulsen	200
Alekhine-Pomar	127	Anderssen-Zukertort	198
Alekhine-Prat	340	Augustin-Bongrantz	4
Alekhine-Reshevsky	148		
Alekhine-Rosselli	135	Barda-Keller	114
Alekhine-Selesniev	118	Barnes-Morphy	205
Alekhine-Schwartz	334	Batuyev-Simagin	6
Alekhine-Sterk	171	Belsitzmann-Rubinstein	283
Alekhine-Sterk	328	Berger	37
Alekhine-Verlinski	343	Bernhardt	71
Alekhine-West	146	Bernstein-Capablanca	351
Alekhine-Yates	330	Bernstein-Cohn	85
Amateur-Andresen	51	Beyer-Wade	99
Amateur-Capablanca	58	Bird-Lasker	253
Amateur-Soultanbeieff	46	Bird-Morphy	212
Amateur-Soultanbeieff	47	Black-Bigelow	179

Blackburne-Amateur	110	Davidson-Alekhine	332
Blasej-Mikulka	31	Denker-Dake	79
Blumich-Ahues	178	Denker-Feit	77
Bogolyubov-Amateur	42	Denker-Schwartz	78
Bogolyubov-Capablanca	354	Duras-Cohn	83
Boleslavsky-Bisguier	123	Duras-Tchigorin	189
Boleslavsky-Kasparyan	134		
Botvinnik-Alatorsev	314	Ernst-Loose	10
Botvinnik-Batuyev	313	Euwe-Alekhine	141
Botvinnik-Belavienetz	315	Euwe-Alekhine	163
Botvinnik-Boleslavsky	158	Euwe-Fischer	113
Botvinnik-Bronstein	164	Euwe-Keres	307
Botvinnik-Capablanca	319	Euwe-Keres	309
Botvinnik-Euwe	322	Euwe-Smyslov	142
Botvinnik-Keres	323		
Botvinnik-Ragozin	311	Fine-Yudovich	177
Botvinnik-Reshevsky	318	Fisher-Steinitz	223
Botvinnik-Smyslov	137	Flohr-Botvinnik	161
Botvinnik-Tartakover	317	Flohr-Romanovsky	185
Bron	74	Fox-Capablanca	162
Bronstein-Mikenas	91	Fox-Casper	105
Canal-Amateur	86	Geller-Keres	310
Capablanca-Alekhine	353	Geller-Najdorf	150
Capablanca-Amateur	348	Gerasimov-Smyslov	90
Capablanca-Bogolyubov	151	Gerbec-Amateur	95
Capablanca-Corzo	345	Gereben-Troianescu	101
Capablanca-Fonaroff	347	Gilg-Nimzovich	293
Capablanca-Illa	139	Goglidze-Botvinnik	316
Capablanca-Levenfish	356	Gonssiorovski-Alekhine	326
Capablanca-Marshall	346	Grunfeld-Alekhine	342
Capablanca-Nimzovich	155	Grunfeld-Eliskases	66
Capablanca-Ribera	350	Grunfeld-Spielmann	279
Capablanca-Schroeder	116	Gygli-Henneberger	43
Capablanca-Spielmann	20		
Capablanca-Steiner	355	Hage-Nimzovich	296
Capablanca-Subarev	352	Haller-Pollock	112
Casas-Piazzini	53	Halosar-Poschauko	13
Chatard-Amateur	12	Hart-Enders	96
Christoffel-Staehelin	108	Hartlaub-Amateur	175
Corzo-Capablanca	344	Hoit-Amateur	72

Horwitz and Kling	75	Lasker-Tarrasch	165
Horwitz-Popert	172	Lee-Lasker	256
Hromadka-Opocensky	107	Levenfish-Freymann	49
		Levitzki-Marshall	265
Janny-Kardhodo	28	Lexandrovich-Krumhauser	69
Janowsky-Amateur	59	Lund-Nimzovich	294
Janowsky-Capablanca	349		
Janowsky-Marshall	266	Mackenzie-Alekhine	335
Janowsky-Pillsbury	234	Makagonov-Botvinnik	321
Johner-Nimzovich	119	Mannheimer-Nimzovich	299
Johner-Nimzovich	138	Marache-Morphy	201
		Marco-Salter	52
Kakovin	106	Maroczy-Mieses	122
Karu-Keres	301	Marshall-Bogolyubov	267
Kashdan-Tenner	55	Marshall-Burn	260
Kasparyan-Amateur	98	Marshall-Fox	268
Keres-Book	305	Marshall-Gladstone	269
Keres-Fine	304	Marshall-Janowsky	124
Keres-Laurentius	302	Marshall-Lasker	120
Keres-Mikenas	306	Marshall-Lasker	157
Keres-Mikenas	308	Marshall-Lasker	259
Keres-Schapiro	303	Marshall-Marco	261
Keres-Smyslov	143	Marshall-Pillsbury	262
Kevitz and Pinkus-Alekhine	337	Marshall-Swiderski	169
Kholmov-Isakov	67	Marshall-Wolf	263
Kohler-Graf	103	McConnell-Pillsbury	233
Komke-Mai	182	Michel-Rubinstein	288
Kretschmar-Vasica	8	Mieses-Amateur	87
Kubart-Blechschmidt	173	Mieses-Lasker	251
Kubbel	15	Mieses-Marshall	264
		Mikenas-Aronin	97
Lamparter-Green	24	Mikenas-Lebedev	76
Landstatter-Amateur	26	Moravec	48
Lasker-Bauer	250	Morphy-Amateur	207
Lasker-Blackburne	252	Morphy-Amateur	209
Lasker-Capablanca	159	Morphy-Amateur	210
Lasker-Capablanca	257	Morphy-Amateur	211
Lasker-Capablanca	258	Morphy-Baucher	213
Lasker-Ragozin	184	Morphy-Duke of Brunswick	
Lasker-Steinitz	9	and Count Isouard	214
Lasker-Steinitz	255	Morphy-Forde	208

Morphy-Harrwitz	215	Rabinovich-Nimzovich	187
Morphy-Lewis	217	Ragozin-Romanovsky	111
Morphy-Mongredien	21	Ragozin-Veresov	94
Morphy-Thompson	216	Rasmusson-Niemi	188
Morrison-Capablanca	140	Rauzer-Botvinnik	121
Munk-Amateur	19	Reshevsky-Bronstein	145
		Réti-Alekhine	152
Najdorf-Amateur	34	Réti-Alekhine	331
Nedelkovic-Udovcic	7	Réti-Tartakover	117
Nielsen-Amateur	176	Richardson-Delmar	40
Nimzovich-Alekhine	153	Richter	5
Nimzovich-Alekhine	154	Richter-Amateur	174
Nimzovich-Bernstein	292	Rinck	62
Nimzovich-Gilg	297	Rinck	65
Nimzovich-Hakansson	291	Rinck	73
Nimzovich-Johner	300	Rosanes-Anderssen	195
Nimzovich-Nielsen	298	Rosanes-Anderssen	196
Nimzovich-Tarrasch	246	Rossolimo-Amateur	92
		Rossolimo-Amateur	183
Olsen-Jacobsen	11	Rotlevi-Rubinstein	280
		Rubinstein-Bogolyubov	284
Panov-Botvinnik	130	Rubinstein-Grunfeld	289
Paulsen-Morphy	204	Rubinstein-Hromadka	285
Pavelchik-Amateur	41	Rubinstein-Janowsky	287
Pillsbury-Gunsberg	231	Rubinstein-Nimzovich	290
Pillsbury-Gunsberg	237	Rubinstein-Spielmann	275
Pillsbury-Judd	236	Rubinstein-Tarrasch	181
Pillsbury-Marco	235	Rubinstein-Tartakover	286
Pillsbury-Pollock	230		
Pillsbury-Swiderski	238	Saint-Amant and F. de l'A.-	
Pillsbury-Tarrasch	229	Morphy	206
Pillsbury-Walbrodt	228	Salvioli-Amateur	23
Pillsbury-Winawer	232	Salwe-Rubinstein	281
Pillsbury-Wolf	239	Samisch-Nimzovich	295
Place-Amateur	109	Schlechter-Perlis	128
Platov	56	Schories-Spielmann	270
Pollock-Allies	50	Schulten-Morphy	202
Popov-Riumin	22	Schulten-Morphy	203
		Selesniev	3
Rabinovich-Alekhine	327	Selesniev	61
Rabinovich-Botvinnik	129	Seletsky	35
Rabinovich-Botvinnik	312	Sepp-Sundberg	32

Sereda-Gambarashvilli	100	Tarrasch-Alapin	240
Smyslov-Botvinnik	131	Tarrasch-Alekhine	115
Smyslov-Botvinnik	320	Tarrasch-Amateur	57
Smyslov-Euwe	133	Tarrasch-Gottschall	156
Somov-Nasimovich	93	Tarrasch-Janowsky	244
Soultanbeieff-Borodin	80	Tarrasch-Réti	249
Soultanbeieff-Courtens	45	Tarrasch-Romberg	241
Soultanbeieff-Defosse	82	Tarrasch-Satzinger	247
Soultanbeieff-Liubarski	39	Tarrasch-Scheve	243
Soultanbeieff-Liubarski	44	Tarrasch-Schlechter	166
Soultanbeieff-Mendlewitz	38	Tarrasch-Schlechter	167
Soultanbeieff-Wery	81	Tarrasch-Tchigorin	242
Spielmann-Capablanca	125	Tavernier-Grodner	25
Spielmann-Eliskases	160	Tchigorin-Znosko-Borovsky	36
Spielmann-Grunfeld	277	Tietz-Ramisch	88
Spielmann-Honlinger	278	Torre-Lasker	30
Spielmann-Janowsky	272	Torre-Shapiro	102
Spielmann-Mieses	273	Torres-Alekhine	329
Spielmann-Reggio	271	Troitzky	14
Spielmann-Rubinstein	274	Trultsch-Heidenreich	54
Spielmann-Tarrasch	245	Tylor-Winter	68
Spielmann-Walter	276		
Steinitz-Bardeleben	227	Vidmar-Rubinstein	282
Steinitz-Lasker	254	Vidmar-Teichmann	126
Steinitz-Mongredien	218	Vollmer	60
Steinitz-Mongredien	219	Votruba	18
Steinitz-Rock	220	Vygodchikov-Alekhine	324
Steinitz-Sellman	225		
Steinitz-Tchigorin	226	Wade-Bennett	64
Steinitz-Van der Meden	222		
Sterk-Marshall	84	Yates-Alekhine	336
Stoltz-Alekhine	333	Yates-Sultan Khan	149
Szabo-Boleslavsky	147	Young-Doré	33
		Znosko-Borovsky-Price	17
Taimanov-Kusminich	2	Zukertort-Englisch	63
Tal-Klaman	1	Zuraliev-Romanov	70

A CATALOGUE OF SELECTED DOVER BOOKS
IN ALL FIELDS OF INTEREST

A CATALOGUE OF SELECTED DOVER BOOKS
IN ALL FIELDS OF INTEREST

THE NOTEBOOKS OF LEONARDO DA VINCI, edited by J.P. Richter. Extracts from manuscripts reveal great genius; on painting, sculpture, anatomy, sciences, geography, etc. Both Italian and English. 186 ms. pages reproduced, plus 500 additional drawings, including studies for Last Supper, Sforza monument, etc. 860pp. 7⅞ x 10¾. USO 22572-0, 22573-9 Pa., Two vol. set $15.90

ART NOUVEAU DESIGNS IN COLOR, Alphonse Mucha, Maurice Verneuil, Georges Auriol. Full-color reproduction of Combinaisons ornamentales (c. 1900) by Art Nouveau masters. Floral, animal, geometric, interlacings, swashes — borders, frames, spots — all incredibly beautiful. 60 plates, hundreds of designs. 9⅜ x 8¹/₁₆. 22885-1 Pa. $4.00

GRAPHIC WORKS OF ODILON REDON. All great fantastic lithographs, etchings, engravings, drawings, 209 in all. Monsters, Huysmans, still life work, etc. Introduction by Alfred Werner. 209pp. 9⅛ x 12¼. 21996-8 Pa. $6.00

EXOTIC FLORAL PATTERNS IN COLOR, E.-A. Seguy. Incredibly beautiful full-color pochoir work by great French designer of 20's. Complete Bouquets et frondaisons, Suggestions pour étoffes. Richness must be seen to be believed. 40 plates containing 120 patterns. 80pp. 9⅜ x 12¼. 23041-4 Pa. $6.00

SELECTED ETCHINGS OF JAMES A. McN. WHISTLER, James A. McN. Whistler. 149 outstanding etchings by the great American artist, including selections from the Thames set and two Venice sets, the complete French set, and many individual prints. Introduction and explanatory note on each print by Maria Naylor. 157pp. 9⅜ x 12¼. 23194-1 Pa. $5.00

VISUAL ILLUSIONS: THEIR CAUSES, CHARACTERISTICS, AND APPLICATIONS, Matthew Luckiesh. Thorough description, discussion; shape and size, color, motion; natural illusion. Uses in art and industry. 100 illustrations. 252pp.
21530-X Pa. $3.00

TEN BOOKS ON ARCHITECTURE, Vitruvius. The most important book ever written on architecture. Early Roman aesthetics, technology, classical orders, site selection, all other aspects. Stands behind everything since. Morgan translation. 331pp.
20645-9 Pa. $3.75

THE CODEX NUTTALL. A PICTURE MANUSCRIPT FROM ANCIENT MEXICO, as first edited by Zelia Nuttall. Only inexpensive edition, in full color, of a pre-Columbian Mexican (Mixtec) book. 88 color plates show kings, gods, heroes, temples, sacrifices. New explanatory, historical introduction by Arthur G. Miller. 96pp. 11⅜ x 8½. 23168-2 Pa. $7.50

CATALOGUE OF DOVER BOOKS

CREATIVE LITHOGRAPHY AND HOW TO DO IT, Grant Arnold. Lithography as art form: working directly on stone, transfer of drawings, lithotint, mezzotint, color printing; also metal plates. Detailed, thorough. 27 illustrations. 214pp.
21208-4 Pa. $3.50

DESIGN MOTIFS OF ANCIENT MEXICO, Jorge Enciso. Vigorous, powerful ceramic stamp impressions — Maya, Aztec, Toltec, Olmec. Serpents, gods, priests, dancers, etc. 153pp. 6⅛ x 9¼.
20084-1 Pa. $2.50

AMERICAN INDIAN DESIGN AND DECORATION, Leroy Appleton. Full text, plus more than 700 precise drawings of Inca, Maya, Aztec, Pueblo, Plains, NW Coast basketry, sculpture, painting, pottery, sand paintings, metal, etc. 4 plates in color. 279pp. 8⅜ x 11¼.
22704-9 Pa.$5.00

CHINESE LATTICE DESIGNS, Daniel S. Dye. Incredibly beautiful geometric designs: circles, voluted, simple dissections, etc. Inexhaustible source of ideas, motifs. 1239 illustrations. 469pp. 6⅛ x 9¼.
23096-1 Pa. $5.00

JAPANESE DESIGN MOTIFS, Matsuya Co. Mon, or heraldic designs. Over 4000 typical, beautiful designs: birds, animals, flowers, swords, fans, geometric; all beautifully stylized. 213pp. 11⅜ x 8¼.
22874-6 Pa. $5.00

PERSPECTIVE, Jan Vredeman de Vries. 73 perspective plates from 1604 edition; buildings, townscapes, stairways, fantastic scenes. Remarkable for beauty, surrealistic atmosphere; real eye-catchers. Introduction by Adolf Placzek. 74pp. 11⅜ x 8¼.
20186-4 Pa. $3.00

EARLY AMERICAN DESIGN MOTIFS, Suzanne E. Chapman. 497 motifs, designs, from painting on wood, ceramics, appliqué, glassware, samplers, metal work, etc. Florals, landscapes, birds and animals, geometrics, letters, etc. Inexhaustible. Enlarged edition. 138pp. 8⅜ x 11¼.
22985-8 Pa. $3.50
23084-8 Clothbd. $7.95

VICTORIAN STENCILS FOR DESIGN AND DECORATION, edited by E.V. Gillon, Jr. 113 wonderful ornate Victorian pieces from German sources; florals, geometrics; borders, corner pieces; bird motifs, etc. 64pp. 9⅜ x 12¼.
21995-X Pa. $3.00

ART NOUVEAU: AN ANTHOLOGY OF DESIGN AND ILLUSTRATION FROM THE STUDIO, edited by E.V. Gillon, Jr. Graphic arts: book jackets, posters, engravings, illustrations, decorations; Crane, Beardsley, Bradley and many others. Inexhaustible. 92pp. 8⅛ x 11.
22388-4 Pa. $2.50

ORIGINAL ART DECO DESIGNS, William Rowe. First-rate, highly imaginative modern Art Deco frames, borders, compositions, alphabets, florals, insectals, Wurlitzer-types, etc. Much finest modern Art Deco. 80 plates, 8 in color. 8⅜ x 11¼.
22567-4 Pa. $3.50

HANDBOOK OF DESIGNS AND DEVICES, Clarence P. Hornung. Over 1800 basic geometric designs based on circle, triangle, square, scroll, cross, etc. Largest such collection in existence. 261pp.
20125-2 Pa. $2.75

CATALOGUE OF DOVER BOOKS

150 MASTERPIECES OF DRAWING, edited by Anthony Toney. 150 plates, early 15th century to end of 18th century; Rembrandt, Michelangelo, Dürer, Fragonard, Watteau, Wouwerman, many others. 150pp. 8⅜ x 11¼.   21032-4 Pa. $4.00

THE GOLDEN AGE OF THE POSTER, Hayward and Blanche Cirker. 70 extraordinary posters in full colors, from Maîtres de l'Affiche, Mucha, Lautrec, Bradley, Cheret, Beardsley, many others. 9⅜ x 12¼.   22753-7 Pa. $5.95

SIMPLICISSIMUS, selection, translations and text by Stanley Appelbaum. 180 satirical drawings, 16 in full color, from the famous German weekly magazine in the years 1896 to 1926. 24 artists included: Grosz, Kley, Pascin, Kubin, Kollwitz, plus Heine, Thöny, Bruno Paul, others. 172pp. 8½ x 12¼.   23098-8 Pa. $5.00
23099-6 Clothbd. $10.00

THE EARLY WORK OF AUBREY BEARDSLEY, Aubrey Beardsley. 157 plates, 2 in color: Manon Lescaut, Madame Bovary, Morte d'Arthur, Salome, other. Introduction by H. Marillier. 175pp. 8½ x 11.   21816-3 Pa. $4.00

THE LATER WORK OF AUBREY BEARDSLEY, Aubrey Beardsley. Exotic masterpieces of full maturity: Venus and Tannhäuser, Lysistrata, Rape of the Lock, Volpone, Savoy material, etc. 174 plates, 2 in color. 176pp. 8½ x 11.   21817-1 Pa. $4.50

DRAWINGS OF WILLIAM BLAKE, William Blake. 92 plates from Book of Job, Divine Comedy, Paradise Lost, visionary heads, mythological figures, Laocoön, etc. Selection, introduction, commentary by Sir Geoffrey Keynes. 178pp. 8½ x 11.   22303-5 Pa. $4.00

LONDON: A PILGRIMAGE, Gustave Doré, Blanchard Jerrold. Squalor, riches, misery, beauty of mid-Victorian metropolis; 55 wonderful plates, 125 other illustrations, full social, cultural text by Jerrold. 191pp. of text. 8⅛ x 11.   22306-X Pa. $6.00

THE COMPLETE WOODCUTS OF ALBRECHT DÜRER, edited by Dr. W. Kurth. 346 in all: Old Testament, St. Jerome, Passion, Life of Virgin, Apocalypse, many others. Introduction by Campbell Dodgson. 285pp. 8½ x 12¼.   21097-9 Pa. $6.00

THE DISASTERS OF WAR, Francisco Goya. 83 etchings record horrors of Napoleonic wars in Spain and war in general. Reprint of 1st edition, plus 3 additional plates. Introduction by Philip Hofer. 97pp. 9⅜ x 8¼.   21872-4 Pa. $3.50

ENGRAVINGS OF HOGARTH, William Hogarth. 101 of Hogarth's greatest works: Rake's Progress, Harlot's Progress, Illustrations for Hudibras, Midnight Modern Conversation, Before and After, Beer Street and Gin Lane, many more. Full commentary. 256pp. 11 x 14.   22479-1 Pa. $7.95

PRIMITIVE ART, Franz Boas. Great anthropologist on ceramics, textiles, wood, stone, metal, etc.; patterns, technology, symbols, styles. All areas, but fullest on Northwest Coast Indians. 350 illustrations. 378pp.   20025-6 Pa. $3.75

MOTHER GOOSE'S MELODIES. Facsimile of fabulously rare Munroe and Francis "copyright 1833" Boston edition. Familiar and unusual rhymes, wonderful old woodcut illustrations. Edited by E.F. Bleiler. 128pp. 4½ x 6⅜. 22577-1 Pa. $1.50

MOTHER GOOSE IN HIEROGLYPHICS. Favorite nursery rhymes presented in rebus form for children. Fascinating 1849 edition reproduced in toto, with key. Introduction by E.F. Bleiler. About 400 woodcuts. 64pp. 6⅞ x 5¼. 20745-5 Pa. $1.50

PETER PIPER'S PRACTICAL PRINCIPLES OF PLAIN & PERFECT PRONUNCIATION. Alliterative jingles and tongue-twisters. Reproduction in full of 1830 first American edition. 25 spirited woodcuts. 32pp. 4½ x 6⅜. 22560-7 Pa. $1.25

MARMADUKE MULTIPLY'S MERRY METHOD OF MAKING MINOR MATHEMATICIANS. Fellow to Peter Piper, it teaches multiplication table by catchy rhymes and woodcuts. 1841 Munroe & Francis edition. Edited by E.F. Bleiler. 103pp. 4⅝ x 6. 22773-1 Pa. $1.25

THE NIGHT BEFORE CHRISTMAS, Clement Moore. Full text, and woodcuts from original 1848 book. Also critical, historical material. 19 illustrations. 40pp. 4⅝ x 6. 22797-9 Pa. $1.35

THE KING OF THE GOLDEN RIVER, John Ruskin. Victorian children's classic of three brothers, their attempts to reach the Golden River, what becomes of them. Facsimile of original 1889 edition. 22 illustrations. 56pp. 4⅝ x 6⅜. 20066-3 Pa. $1.50

DREAMS OF THE RAREBIT FIEND, Winsor McCay. Pioneer cartoon strip, unexcelled for beauty, imagination, in 60 full sequences. Incredible technical virtuosity, wonderful visual wit. Historical introduction. 62pp. 8⅜ x 11¼. 21347-1 Pa. $2.50

THE KATZENJAMMER KIDS, Rudolf Dirks. In full color, 14 strips from 1906-7; full of imagination, characteristic humor. Classic of great historical importance. Introduction by August Derleth. 32pp. 9¼ x 12¼. 23005-8 Pa. $2.00

LITTLE ORPHAN ANNIE AND LITTLE ORPHAN ANNIE IN COSMIC CITY, Harold Gray. Two great sequences from the early strips: our curly-haired heroine defends the Warbucks' financial empire and, then, takes on meanie Phineas P. Pinchpenny. Leapin' lizards! 178pp. 6⅛ x 8⅜. 23107-0 Pa. $2.00

ABSOLUTELY MAD INVENTIONS, A.E. Brown, H.A. Jeffcott. Hilarious, useless, or merely absurd inventions all granted patents by the U.S. Patent Office. Edible tie pin, mechanical hat tipper, etc. 57 illustrations. 125pp. 22596-8 Pa. $1.50

THE DEVIL'S DICTIONARY, Ambrose Bierce. Barbed, bitter, brilliant witticisms in the form of a dictionary. Best, most ferocious satire America has produced. 145pp. 20487-1 Pa. $1.75

THE BEST DR. THORNDYKE DETECTIVE STORIES, R. Austin Freeman. The Case of Oscar Brodski, The Moabite Cipher, and 5 other favorites featuring the great scientific detective, plus his long-believed-lost first adventure — 31 New Inn — reprinted here for the first time. Edited by E.F. Bleiler. USO 20388-3 Pa. $3.00

BEST "THINKING MACHINE" DETECTIVE STORIES, Jacques Futrelle. The Problem of Cell 13 and 11 other stories about Prof. Augustus S.F.X. Van Dusen, including two "lost" stories. First reprinting of several. Edited by E.F. Bleiler. 241pp.
20537-1 Pa. $3.00

UNCLE SILAS, J. Sheridan LeFanu. Victorian Gothic mystery novel, considered by many best of period, even better than Collins or Dickens. Wonderful psychological terror. Introduction by Frederick Shroyer. 436pp. 21715-9 Pa. $4.50

BEST DR. POGGIOLI DETECTIVE STORIES, T.S. Stribling. 15 best stories from EQMM and The Saint offer new adventures in Mexico, Florida, Tennessee hills as Poggioli unravels mysteries and combats Count Jalacki. 217pp. 23227-1 Pa. $3.00

EIGHT DIME NOVELS, selected with an introduction by E.F. Bleiler. Adventures of Old King Brady, Frank James, Nick Carter, Deadwood Dick, Buffalo Bill, The Steam Man, Frank Merriwell, and Horatio Alger — 1877 to 1905. Important, entertaining popular literature in facsimile reprint, with original covers. 190pp. 9 x 12. 22975-0 Pa. $3.50

ALICE'S ADVENTURES UNDER GROUND, Lewis Carroll. Facsimile of ms. Carroll gave Alice Liddell in 1864. Different in many ways from final Alice. Handlettered, illustrated by Carroll. Introduction by Martin Gardner. 128pp. 21482-6 Pa. $2.00

ALICE IN WONDERLAND COLORING BOOK, Lewis Carroll. Pictures by John Tenniel. Large-size versions of the famous illustrations of Alice, Cheshire Cat, Mad Hatter and all the others, waiting for your crayons. Abridged text. 36 illustrations. 64pp. 8¼ x 11. 22853-3 Pa. $1.50

AVENTURES D'ALICE AU PAYS DES MERVEILLES, Lewis Carroll. Bué's translation of "Alice" into French, supervised by Carroll himself. Novel way to learn language. (No English text.) 42 Tenniel illustrations. 196pp. 22836-3 Pa. $3.00

MYTHS AND FOLK TALES OF IRELAND, Jeremiah Curtin. 11 stories that are Irish versions of European fairy tales and 9 stories from the Fenian cycle — 20 tales of legend and magic that comprise an essential work in the history of folklore. 256pp. 22430-9 Pa. $3.00

EAST O' THE SUN AND WEST O' THE MOON, George W. Dasent. Only full edition of favorite, wonderful Norwegian fairytales — Why the Sea is Salt, Boots and the Troll, etc. — with 77 illustrations by Kittelsen & Werenskiöld. 418pp.
22521-6 Pa. $4.50

PERRAULT'S FAIRY TALES, Charles Perrault and Gustave Doré. Original versions of Cinderella, Sleeping Beauty, Little Red Riding Hood, etc. in best translation, with 34 wonderful illustrations by Gustave Doré. 117pp. 8⅛ x 11. 22311-6 Pa. $2.50

EARLY NEW ENGLAND GRAVESTONE RUBBINGS, Edmund V. Gillon, Jr. 43 photographs, 226 rubbings show heavily symbolic, macabre, sometimes humorous primitive American art. Up to early 19th century. 207pp. 8⅜ x 11¼.
21380-3 Pa. $4.00

L.J.M. DAGUERRE: THE HISTORY OF THE DIORAMA AND THE DAGUERREOTYPE, Helmut and Alison Gernsheim. Definitive account. Early history, life and work of Daguerre; discovery of daguerreotype process; diffusion abroad; other early photography. 124 illustrations. 226pp. 6⅙ x 9¼.
22290-X Pa. $4.00

PHOTOGRAPHY AND THE AMERICAN SCENE, Robert Taft. The basic book on American photography as art, recording form, 1839-1889. Development, influence on society, great photographers, types (portraits, war, frontier, etc.), whatever else needed. Inexhaustible. Illustrated with 322 early photos, daguerreotypes, tintypes, stereo slides, etc. 546pp. 6⅛ x 9¼.
21201-7 Pa. $6.00

PHOTOGRAPHIC SKETCHBOOK OF THE CIVIL WAR, Alexander Gardner. Reproduction of 1866 volume with 100 on-the-field photographs: Manassas, Lincoln on battlefield, slave pens, etc. Introduction by E.F. Bleiler. 224pp. 10¾ x 9.
22731-6 Pa. $6.00

THE MOVIES: A PICTURE QUIZ BOOK, Stanley Appelbaum & Hayward Cirker. Match stars with their movies, name actors and actresses, test your movie skill with 241 stills from 236 great movies, 1902-1959. Indexes of performers and films. 128pp. 8⅜ x 9¼.
20222-4 Pa. $3.00

THE TALKIES, Richard Griffith. Anthology of features, articles from Photoplay, 1928-1940, reproduced complete. Stars, famous movies, technical features, fabulous ads, etc.; Garbo, Chaplin, King Kong, Lubitsch, etc. 4 color plates, scores of illustrations. 327pp. 8⅜ x 11¼.
22762-6 Pa. $6.95

THE MOVIE MUSICAL FROM VITAPHONE TO "42ND STREET," edited by Miles Kreuger. Relive the rise of the movie musical as reported in the pages of Photoplay magazine (1926-1933): every movie review, cast list, ad, and record review; every significant feature article, production still, biography, forecast, and gossip story. Profusely illustrated. 367pp. 8⅜ x 11¼.
23154-2 Pa. $7.95

JOHANN SEBASTIAN BACH, Philipp Spitta. Great classic of biography, musical commentary, with hundreds of pieces analyzed. Also good for Bach's contemporaries. 450 musical examples. Total of 1799pp.
EUK 22278-0, 22279-9 Clothbd., Two vol. set $25.00

BEETHOVEN AND HIS NINE SYMPHONIES, Sir George Grove. Thorough history, analysis, commentary on symphonies and some related pieces. For either beginner or advanced student. 436 musical passages. 407pp.
20334-4 Pa. $4.00

MOZART AND HIS PIANO CONCERTOS, Cuthbert Girdlestone. The only full-length study. Detailed analyses of all 21 concertos, sources; 417 musical examples. 509pp.
21271-8 Pa. $6.00

THE FITZWILLIAM VIRGINAL BOOK, edited by J. Fuller Maitland, W.B. Squire. Famous early 17th century collection of keyboard music, 300 works by Morley, Byrd, Bull, Gibbons, etc. Modern notation. Total of 938pp. 8⅜ x 11.
ECE 21068-5, 21069-3 Pa., Two vol. set $15.00

COMPLETE STRING QUARTETS, Wolfgang A. Mozart. Breitkopf and Härtel edition. All 23 string quartets plus alternate slow movement to K156. Study score. 277pp. 9⅜ x 12¼.
22372-8 Pa. $6.00

COMPLETE SONG CYCLES, Franz Schubert. Complete piano, vocal music of Die Schöne Müllerin, Die Winterreise, Schwanengesang. Also Drinker English singing translations. Breitkopf and Härtel edition. 217pp. 9⅜ x 12¼.
22649-2 Pa. $5.00

THE COMPLETE PRELUDES AND ETUDES FOR PIANOFORTE SOLO, Alexander Scriabin. All the preludes and etudes including many perfectly spun miniatures. Edited by K.N. Igumnov and Y.I. Mil'shteyn. 250pp. 9 x 12.
22919-X Pa. $6.00

TRISTAN UND ISOLDE, Richard Wagner. Full orchestral score with complete instrumentation. Do not confuse with piano reduction. Commentary by Felix Mottl, great Wagnerian conductor and scholar. Study score. 655pp. 8⅛ x 11.
22915-7 Pa. $11.95

FAVORITE SONGS OF THE NINETIES, ed. Robert Fremont. Full reproduction, including covers, of 88 favorites: Ta-Ra-Ra-Boom-De-Aye, The Band Played On, Bird in a Gilded Cage, Under the Bamboo Tree, After the Ball, etc. 401pp. 9 x 12.
EBE 21536-9 Pa. $6.95

SOUSA'S GREAT MARCHES IN PIANO TRANSCRIPTION: ORIGINAL SHEET MUSIC OF 23 WORKS, John Philip Sousa. Selected by Lester S. Levy. Playing edition includes: The Stars and Stripes Forever, The Thunderer, The Gladiator, King Cotton, Washington Post, much more. 24 illustrations. 111pp. 9 x 12.
USO 23132-1 Pa. $3.50

CLASSIC PIANO RAGS, selected with an introduction by Rudi Blesh. Best ragtime music (1897-1922) by Scott Joplin, James Scott, Joseph F. Lamb, Tom Turpin, 9 others. Printed from best original sheet music, plus covers. 364pp. 9 x 12.
EBE 20469-3 Pa. $7.50

ANALYSIS OF CHINESE CHARACTERS, C.D. Wilder, J.H. Ingram. 1000 most important characters analyzed according to primitives, phonetics, historical development. Traditional method offers mnemonic aid to beginner, intermediate student of Chinese, Japanese. 365pp.
23045-7 Pa. $4.00

MODERN CHINESE: A BASIC COURSE, Faculty of Peking University. Self study, classroom course in modern Mandarin. Records contain phonetics, vocabulary, sentences, lessons. 249 page book contains all recorded text, translations, grammar, vocabulary, exercises. Best course on market. 3 12" 33⅓ monaural records, book, album.
98832-5 Set $12.50

MANUAL OF THE TREES OF NORTH AMERICA, Charles S. Sargent. The basic survey of every native tree and tree-like shrub, 717 species in all. Extremely full descriptions, information on habitat, growth, locales, economics, etc. Necessary to every serious tree lover. Over 100 finding keys. 783 illustrations. Total of 986pp.
20277-1, 20278-X Pa., Two vol. set $9.00

BIRDS OF THE NEW YORK AREA, John Bull. Indispensable guide to more than 400 species within a hundred-mile radius of Manhattan. Information on range, status, breeding, migration, distribution trends, etc. Foreword by Roger Tory Peterson. 17 drawings; maps. 540pp.
23222-0 Pa. $6.00

THE SEA-BEACH AT EBB-TIDE, Augusta Foote Arnold. Identify hundreds of marine plants and animals: algae, seaweeds, squids, crabs, corals, etc. Descriptions cover food, life cycle, size, shape, habitat. Over 600 drawings. 490pp.
21949-6 Pa.$5.00

THE MOTH BOOK, William J. Holland. Identify more than 2,000 moths of North America. General information, precise species descriptions. 623 illustrations plus 48 color plates show almost all species, full size. 1968 edition. Still the basic book. Total of 551pp. 6½ x 9¼.
21948-8 Pa. $6.00

HOW INDIANS USE WILD PLANTS FOR FOOD, MEDICINE & CRAFTS, Frances Densmore. Smithsonian, Bureau of American Ethnology report presents wealth of material on nearly 200 plants used by Chippewas of Minnesota and Wisconsin. 33 plates plus 122pp. of text. 6⅛ x 9¼.
23019-8 Pa. $2.50

OLD NEW YORK IN EARLY PHOTOGRAPHS, edited by Mary Black. Your only chance to see New York City as it was 1853-1906, through 196 wonderful photographs from N.Y. Historical Society. Great Blizzard, Lincoln's funeral procession, great buildings. 228pp. 9 x 12.
22907-6 Pa. $6.95

THE AMERICAN REVOLUTION, A PICTURE SOURCEBOOK, John Grafton. Wonderful Bicentennial picture source, with 411 illustrations (contemporary and 19th century) showing battles, personalities, maps, events, flags, posters, soldier's life, ships, etc. all captioned and explained. A wonderful browsing book, supplement to other historical reading. 160pp. 9 x 12.
23226-3 Pa. $4.00

PERSONAL NARRATIVE OF A PILGRIMAGE TO AL-MADINAH AND MECCAH, Richard Burton. Great travel classic by remarkably colorful personality. Burton, disguised as a Moroccan, visited sacred shrines of Islam, narrowly escaping death. Wonderful observations of Islamic life, customs, personalities. 47 illustrations. Total of 959pp.
21217-3, 21218-1 Pa., Two vol. set$10.00

INCIDENTS OF TRAVEL IN CENTRAL AMERICA, CHIAPAS, AND YUCATAN, John L. Stephens. Almost single-handed discovery of Maya culture; exploration of ruined cities, monuments, temples; customs of Indians. 115 drawings. 892pp.
22404-X, 22405-8 Pa., Two vol. set $9.00

CONSTRUCTION OF AMERICAN FURNITURE TREASURES, Lester Margon. 344 detail drawings, complete text on constructing exact reproductions of 38 early American masterpieces: Hepplewhite sideboard, Duncan Phyfe drop-leaf table, mantel clock, gate-leg dining table, Pa. German cupboard, more. 38 plates. 54 photographs. 168pp. 8⅜ x 11¼. 23056-2 Pa. $4.00

JEWELRY MAKING AND DESIGN, Augustus F. Rose, Antonio Cirino. Professional secrets revealed in thorough, practical guide: tools, materials, processes; rings, brooches, chains, cast pieces, enamelling, setting stones, etc. Do not confuse with skimpy introductions: beginner can use, professional can learn from it. Over 200 illustrations. 306pp. 21750-7 Pa. $3.00

METALWORK AND ENAMELLING, Herbert Maryon. Generally conceded best all-around book. Countless trade secrets: materials, tools, soldering, filigree, setting, inlay, niello, repoussé, casting, polishing, etc. For beginner or expert. Author was foremost British expert. 330 illustrations. 335pp. 22702-2 Pa. $4.00

WEAVING WITH FOOT-POWER LOOMS, Edward F. Worst. Setting up a loom, beginning to weave, constructing equipment, using dyes, more, plus over 285 drafts of traditional patterns including Colonial and Swedish weaves. More than 200 other figures. For beginning and advanced. 275pp. 8¾ x 6⅜. 23064-3 Pa. $4.50

WEAVING A NAVAJO BLANKET, Gladys A. Reichard. Foremost anthropologist studied under Navajo women, reveals every step in process from wool, dyeing, spinning, setting up loom, designing, weaving. Much history, symbolism. With this book you could make one yourself. 97 illustrations. 222pp. 22992-0 Pa. $3.00

NATURAL DYES AND HOME DYEING, Rita J. Adrosko. Use natural ingredients: bark, flowers, leaves, lichens, insects etc. Over 135 specific recipes from historical sources for cotton, wool, other fabrics. Genuine premodern handicrafts. 12 illustrations. 160pp. 22688-3 Pa. $2.00

DRIED FLOWERS, Sarah Whitlock and Martha Rankin. Concise, clear, practical guide to dehydration, glycerinizing, pressing plant material, and more. Covers use of silica gel. 12 drawings. Originally titled "New Techniques with Dried Flowers." 32pp. 21802-3 Pa. $1.00

THOMAS NAST: CARTOONS AND ILLUSTRATIONS, with text by· Thomas Nast St. Hill. Father of American political cartooning. Cartoons that destroyed Tweed Ring; inflation, free love, church and state; original Republican elephant and Democratic donkey; Santa Claus; more. 117 illustrations. 146pp. 9 x 12.
22983-1 Pa. $4.00
23067-8 Clothbd. $8.50

FREDERIC REMINGTON: 173 DRAWINGS AND ILLUSTRATIONS. Most famous of the Western artists, most responsible for our myths about the American West in its untamed days. Complete reprinting of Drawings of Frederic Remington (1897), plus other selections. 4 additional drawings in color on covers. 140pp. 9 x 12.
20714-5 Pa. $5.00'

How to Solve Chess Problems, Kenneth S. Howard. Practical suggestions on problem solving for very beginners. 58 two-move problems, 46 3-movers, 8 4-movers for practice, plus hints. 171pp. 20748-X Pa. $3.00

A Guide to Fairy Chess, Anthony Dickins. 3-D chess, 4-D chess, chess on a cylindrical board, reflecting pieces that bounce off edges, cooperative chess, retrograde chess, maximummers, much more. Most based on work of great Dawson. Full handbook, 100 problems. 66pp. 7⅞ x 10¾. 22687-5 Pa. $2.00

Win at Backgammon, Millard Hopper. Best opening moves, running game, blocking game, back game, tables of odds, etc. Hopper makes the game clear enough for anyone to play, and win. 43 diagrams. 111pp. 22894-0 Pa. $1.50

Bidding a Bridge Hand, Terence Reese. Master player "thinks out loud" the binding of 75 hands that defy point count systems. Organized by bidding problem—no-fit situations, overbidding, underbidding, cueing your defense, etc. 254pp. EBE 22830-4 Pa. $3.00

The Precision Bidding System in Bridge, C.C. Wei, edited by Alan Truscott. Inventor of precision bidding presents average hands and hands from actual play, including games from 1969 Bermuda Bowl where system emerged. 114 exercises. 116pp. 21171-1 Pa. $2.25

Learn Magic, Henry Hay. 20 simple, easy-to-follow lessons on magic for the new magician: illusions, card tricks, silks, sleights of hand, coin manipulations, escapes, and more —all with a minimum amount of equipment. Final chapter explains the great stage illusions. 92 illustrations. 285pp. 21238-6 Pa. $2.95

The New Magician's Manual, Walter B. Gibson. Step-by-step instructions and clear illustrations guide the novice in mastering 36 tricks; much equipment supplied on 16 pages of cut-out materials. 36 additional tricks. 64 illustrations. 159pp. 6⅝ x 10. 23113-5 Pa. $3.00

Professional Magic for Amateurs, Walter B. Gibson. 50 easy, effective tricks used by professionals —cards, string, tumblers, handkerchiefs, mental magic, etc. 63 illustrations. 223pp. 23012-0 Pa. $2.50

Card Manipulations, Jean Hugard. Very rich collection of manipulations; has taught thousands of fine magicians tricks that are really workable, eye-catching. Easily followed, serious work. Over 200 illustrations. 163pp. 20539-8 Pa. $2.00

Abbott's Encyclopedia of Rope Tricks for Magicians, Stewart James. Complete reference book for amateur and professional magicians containing more than 150 tricks involving knots, penetrations, cut and restored rope, etc. 510 illustrations. Reprint of 3rd edition. 400pp. 23206-9 Pa. $3.50

The Secrets of Houdini, J.C. Cannell. Classic study of Houdini's incredible magic, exposing closely-kept professional secrets and revealing, in general terms, the whole art of stage magic. 67 illustrations. 279pp. 22913-0 Pa. $3.00

THE MAGIC MOVING PICTURE BOOK, Bliss, Sands & Co. The pictures in this book move! Volcanoes erupt, a house burns, a serpentine dancer wiggles her way through a number. By using a specially ruled acetate screen provided, you can obtain these and 15 other startling effects. Originally "The Motograph Moving Picture Book." 32pp. 8¼ x 11. 23224-7 Pa. $1.75

STRING FIGURES AND HOW TO MAKE THEM, Caroline F. Jayne. Fullest, clearest instructions on string figures from around world: Eskimo, Navajo, Lapp, Europe, more. Cats cradle, moving spear, lightning, stars. Introduction by A.C. Haddon. 950 illustrations. 407pp. 20152-X Pa. $3.50

PAPER FOLDING FOR BEGINNERS, William D. Murray and Francis J. Rigney. Clearest book on market for making origami sail boats, roosters, frogs that move legs, cups, bonbon boxes. 40 projects. More than 275 illustrations. Photographs. 94pp. 20713-7 Pa $1.50

INDIAN SIGN LANGUAGE, William Tomkins. Over 525 signs developed by Sioux, Blackfoot, Cheyenne, Arapahoe and other tribes. Written instructions and diagrams: how to make words, construct sentences. Also 290 pictographs of Sioux and Ojibway tribes. 111pp. 6⅛ x 9¼. 22029-X Pa. $1.75

BOOMERANGS: HOW TO MAKE AND THROW THEM, Bernard S. Mason. Easy to make and throw, dozens of designs: cross-stick, pinwheel, boomabird, tumblestick, Australian curved stick boomerang. Complete throwing instructions. All safe. 99pp. 23028-7 Pa. $1.75

25 KITES THAT FLY, Leslie Hunt. Full, easy to follow instructions for kites made from inexpensive materials. Many novelties. Reeling, raising, designing your own. 70 illustrations. 110pp. 22550-X Pa. $1.50

TRICKS AND GAMES ON THE POOL TABLE, Fred Herrmann. 79 tricks and games, some solitaires, some for 2 or more players, some competitive; mystifying shots and throws, unusual carom, tricks involving cork, coins, a hat, more. 77 figures. 95pp. 21814-7 Pa. $1.50

WOODCRAFT AND CAMPING, Bernard S. Mason. How to make a quick emergency shelter, select woods that will burn immediately, make do with limited supplies, etc. Also making many things out of wood, rawhide, bark, at camp. Formerly titled Woodcraft. 295 illustrations. 580pp. 21951-8 Pa. $4.00

AN INTRODUCTION TO CHESS MOVES AND TACTICS SIMPLY EXPLAINED, Leonard Barden. Informal intermediate introduction: reasons for moves, tactics, openings, traps, positional play, endgame. Isolates patterns. 102pp. USO 21210-6 Pa. $1.35

LASKER'S MANUAL OF CHESS, Dr. Emanuel Lasker. Great world champion offers very thorough coverage of all aspects of chess. Combinations, position play, openings, endgame, aesthetics of chess, philosophy of struggle, much more. Filled with analyzed games. 390pp. 20640-8 Pa. $4.00

SLEEPING BEAUTY, illustrated by Arthur Rackham. Perhaps the fullest, most delightful version ever, told by C.S. Evans. Rackham's best work. 49 illustrations. 110pp. 7⅞ x 10¾.   22756-1 Pa. $2.00

THE WONDERFUL WIZARD OF OZ, L. Frank Baum. Facsimile in full color of America's finest children's classic. Introduction by Martin Gardner. 143 illustrations by W.W. Denslow. 267pp.   20691-2 Pa. $3.50

GOOPS AND HOW TO BE THEM, Gelett Burgess. Classic tongue-in-cheek masquerading as etiquette book. 87 verses, 170 cartoons as Goops demonstrate virtues of table manners, neatness, courtesy, more. 88pp. 6½ x 9¼.
                                                                         22233-0 Pa. $2.00

THE BROWNIES, THEIR BOOK, Palmer Cox. Small as mice, cunning as foxes, exuberant, mischievous, Brownies go to zoo, toy shop, seashore, circus, more. 24 verse adventures. 266 illustrations. 144pp. 6⅝ x 9¼.   21265-3 Pa. $2.50

BILLY WHISKERS: THE AUTOBIOGRAPHY OF A GOAT, Frances Trego Montgomery. Escapades of that rambunctious goat. Favorite from turn of the century America. 24 illustrations. 259pp.   22345-0 Pa. $2.75

THE ROCKET BOOK, Peter Newell. Fritz, janitor's kid, sets off rocket in basement of apartment house; an ingenious hole punched through every page traces course of rocket. 22 duotone drawings, verses. 48pp. 6⅞ x 8⅜.   22044-3 Pa. $1.50

CUT AND COLOR PAPER MASKS, Michael Grater. Clowns, animals, funny faces . . . simply color them in, cut them out, and put them together, and you have 9 paper masks to play with and enjoy. Complete instructions. Assembled masks shown in full color on the covers. 32pp. 8¼ x 11.   23171-2 Pa. $1.50

THE TALE OF PETER RABBIT, Beatrix Potter. The inimitable Peter's terrifying adventure in Mr. McGregor's garden, with all 27 wonderful, full-color Potter illustrations. 55pp. 4¼ x 5½.   USO 22827-4 Pa. $1.00

THE TALE OF MRS. TIGGY-WINKLE, Beatrix Potter. Your child will love this story about a very special hedgehog and all 27 wonderful, full-color Potter illustrations. 57pp. 4¼ x 5½.   USO 20546-0 Pa. $1.00

THE TALE OF BENJAMIN BUNNY, Beatrix Potter. Peter Rabbit's cousin coaxes him back into Mr. McGregor's garden for a whole new set of adventures. A favorite with children. All 27 full-color illustrations. 59pp. 4¼ x 5½.
                                                                     USO 21102-9 Pa. $1.00

THE MERRY ADVENTURES OF ROBIN HOOD, Howard Pyle. Facsimile of original (1883) edition, finest modern version of English outlaw's adventures. 23 illustrations by Pyle. 296pp. 6½ x 9¼.   22043-5 Pa. $4.00

TWO LITTLE SAVAGES, Ernest Thompson Seton. Adventures of two boys who lived as Indians; explaining Indian ways, woodlore, pioneer methods. 293 illustrations. 286pp.   20985-7 Pa. $3.50

HOUDINI ON MAGIC, Harold Houdini. Edited by Walter Gibson, Morris N. Young. How he escaped; exposés of fake spiritualists; instructions for eye-catching tricks; other fascinating material by and about greatest magician. 155 illustrations. 280pp. 20384-0 Pa. $2.75

HANDBOOK OF THE NUTRITIONAL CONTENTS OF FOOD, U.S. Dept. of Agriculture. Largest, most detailed source of food nutrition information ever prepared. Two mammoth tables: one measuring nutrients in 100 grams of edible portion; the other, in edible portion of 1 pound as purchased. Originally titled Composition of Foods. 190pp. 9 x 12. 21342-0 Pa. $4.00

COMPLETE GUIDE TO HOME CANNING, PRESERVING AND FREEZING, U.S. Dept. of Agriculture. Seven basic manuals with full instructions for jams and jellies; pickles and relishes; canning fruits, vegetables, meat; freezing anything. Really good recipes, exact instructions for optimal results. Save a fortune in food. 156 illustrations. 214pp. 6⅛ x 9¼. 22911-4 Pa. $2.50

THE BREAD TRAY, Louis P. De Gouy. Nearly every bread the cook could buy or make: bread sticks of Italy, fruit breads of Greece, glazed rolls of Vienna, everything from corn pone to croissants. Over 500 recipes altogether. including buns, rolls, muffins, scones, and more. 463pp. 23000-7 Pa. $4.00

CREATIVE HAMBURGER COOKERY, Louis P. De Gouy. 182 unusual recipes for casseroles, meat loaves and hamburgers that turn inexpensive ground meat into memorable main dishes: Arizona chili burgers, burger tamale pie, burger stew, burger corn loaf, burger wine loaf, and more. 120pp. 23001-5 Pa. $1.75

LONG ISLAND SEAFOOD COOKBOOK, J. George Frederick and Jean Joyce. Probably the best American seafood cookbook. Hundreds of recipes. 40 gourmet sauces, 123 recipes using oysters alone! All varieties of fish and seafood amply represented. 324pp. 22677-8 Pa. $3.50

THE EPICUREAN: A COMPLETE TREATISE OF ANALYTICAL AND PRACTICAL STUDIES IN THE CULINARY ART, Charles Ranhofer. Great modern classic. 3,500 recipes from master chef of Delmonico's, turn-of-the-century America's best restaurant. Also explained, many techniques known only to professional chefs. 775 illustrations. 1183pp. 6⅝ x 10. 22680-8 Clothbd. $22.50

THE AMERICAN WINE COOK BOOK, Ted Hatch. Over 700 recipes: old favorites livened up with wine plus many more: Czech fish soup, quince soup, sauce Perigueux, shrimp shortcake, filets Stroganoff, cordon bleu goulash, jambonneau, wine fruit cake, more. 314pp. 22796-0 Pa. $2.50

DELICIOUS VEGETARIAN COOKING, Ivan Baker. Close to 500 delicious and varied recipes: soups, main course dishes (pea, bean, lentil, cheese, vegetable, pasta, and egg dishes), savories, stews, whole-wheat breads and cakes, more. 168pp. USO 22834-7 Pa. $2.00

COOKIES FROM MANY LANDS, Josephine Perry. Crullers, oatmeal cookies, chaux au chocolate, English tea cakes, mandel kuchen, Sacher torte, Danish puff pastry, Swedish cookies — a mouth-watering collection of 223 recipes. 157pp.
22832-0 Pa. $2.25

ROSE RECIPES, Eleanour S. Rohde. How to make sauces, jellies, tarts, salads, potpourris, sweet bags, pomanders, perfumes from garden roses; all exact recipes. Century old favorites. 95pp.
22957-2 Pa. $1.75

"OSCAR" OF THE WALDORF'S COOKBOOK, Oscar Tschirky. Famous American chef reveals 3455 recipes that made Waldorf great; cream of French, German, American cooking, in all categories. Full instructions, easy home use. 1896 edition. 907pp. 6⅝ x 9⅜.
20790-0 Clothbd. $15.00

JAMS AND JELLIES, May Byron. Over 500 old-time recipes for delicious jams, jellies, marmalades, preserves, and many other items. Probably the largest jam and jelly book in print. Originally titled May Byron's Jam Book. 276pp.
USO 23130-5 Pa. $3.50

MUSHROOM RECIPES, André L. Simon. 110 recipes for everyday and special cooking. Champignons à la grecque, sole bonne femme, chicken liver croustades, more; 9 basic sauces, 13 ways of cooking mushrooms. 54pp.
USO 20913-X Pa. $1.25

THE BUCKEYE COOKBOOK, Buckeye Publishing Company. Over 1,000 easy-to-follow, traditional recipes from the American Midwest: bread (100 recipes alone), meat, game, jam, candy, cake, ice cream, and many other categories of cooking. 64 illustrations. From 1883 enlarged edition. 416pp.
23218-2 Pa. $4.00

TWENTY-TWO AUTHENTIC BANQUETS FROM INDIA, Robert H. Christie. Complete, easy-to-do recipes for almost 200 authentic Indian dishes assembled in 22 banquets. Arranged by region. Selected from Banquets of the Nations. 192pp.
23200-X Pa. $2.50

Prices subject to change without notice.
Available at your book dealer or write for free catalogue to Dept. GI, Dover Publications, Inc., 180 Varick St., N.Y., N.Y. 10014. Dover publishes more than 150 books each year on science, elementary and advanced mathematics. biology, music, art, literary history, social sciences and other areas.